Family Choice in Schooling

Family Choice in Schooling

Issues and Dilemmas

Edited by

Michael E. Manley-Casimir
Simon Fraser University

LexingtonBooks
D.C. Heath and Company
Lexington, Massachusetts
Toronto

Library of Congress Cataloging in Publication Data
Main entry under title:

Family choice in schooling.

  1. School, Choice of. I. Manley-Casimir, Michael E.
LB1027.9.F35   370.19   81–47024
ISBN 0–669–04546–2   AACR2

Copyright © 1982 by D.C. Heath and Company

Published simultaneously in Canada

Printed in the United States of America

International Standard Book Number: 0–669–04546–2

Library of Congress Catalog Card Number: 81–47024

The fundamental theory of liberty upon which all governments in this Union repose excludes any general power of the state to standardize its children by forcing them to accept instruction from public teachers only. The child is not the mere creature of the state; those who nurture him and direct his destiny have the right, coupled with the high duty, to recognize and prepare him for additional obligations.

—*Pierce* v. *Society of Sisters*
268 U.S. 535 (1925)

Contents

List of Tables

Introduction

Michael E. Manley-Casimir

In May 1980 the Faculty of Education at Simon Fraser University, in cooperation with the British Columbia Council for Leadership in Educational Administration, organized a major international symposium called Family Choice, Schooling, and the Public Interest. The impetus for the symposium came from a number of sources: the burgeoning interest in nonpublic schools in both the United States and Canada; the policy debate on increasing parental choice through vouchers and tax credits; the 1978 publication of Coons and Sugarman's monograph *Education by Choice* and their subsequent campaign in California to place their "Initiative for Family Choice in Education" on the state ballot; and the counterproposals, in California and elsewhere, for tax credits as an alternative fiscal mechanism.

British Columbia was a particularly suitable place for a symposium of this kind, for in 1977 the provincial government had introduced the Independent Schools Support Act, providing direct financial assistance to independent schools for the first time in the province's history. This development has attracted a great deal of attention from educational policymakers and analysts on both sides of the Canadian–U.S. border. In the United States, congressional interest in the effects of financing independent schools helped influence the National Institute of Education to finance a major longitudinal study of the consequences of British Columbia's decision to finance independent schools. This study—Consequences of Financing Independent Schools (COFIS) study—is under the direction of Dr. Donald A. Erickson, Director of the Center for Research on Private Education, University of San Francisco. Funding for the study comes largely from the National Institute of Education, but the British Columbia Ministry of Education also provides substantial support.

These developments in the United States and Canada provided the context for the symposium. Explicitly designed to be both interdisciplinary and comparative, the symposium brought together distinguished academics and policymakers from Canada, the United States, and the United Kingdom. The event attracted academics interested in educational policy issues, leading educational policymakers from provincial ministries of education and state departments of public instruction, representatives of professional associations—federal and provincial teacher and trustee associations, representatives of associations of independent schools, public school administrators—superintendents and principals, classroom teachers, high school students, and parents. The symposium provided a forum for exploring some of the issues in the debate on family choice and for sharing information about developments in British Columbia.

One of the primary objectives of the symposium was to produce a distinctive collection of original papers suitable for publication. This volume is the culmination of that objective. Most of the chapters are revised and edited versions of papers presented at the symposium. In addition, the volume contains several discussions not presented at the symposium but that nevertheless make important contributions to our understanding of the family choice debate. The latter include chapters by Elmer Thiessen and Cornel Hamm, both of whom attended the symposium and were interested in analyzing philosophical aspects of the debate; those by Richard Nault and Susan Uchitelle and by William Garner and Jane Hannaway were first presented at the symposium Empirical Perspectives on School Choice, at the 1979 American Educational Research Association Meeting in San Francisco; Donald Frey's contribution is based on a paper presented in 1979 at the National Urban Coalition's conference, Restoring Confidence in Public Education: An Agenda for the 1980s; finally, the chapter by Robert Kottkamp and Richard Nault was based on a paper presented at the 1981 meeting of the American Education Research Association in Los Angeles.

The sequence of chapters broadly follows the program of the symposium. Accordingly, the first four furnish a comparative perspective on the family choice issue—a perspective ably drawn for Canada by J. Donald Wilson and Marvin Lazerson and for the United States by Stephen Arons, Joel Spring, and William Ball. Immediately following, in chapters 5 and 6, Elmer Thiessen and Cornel Hamm examine central philosophical aspects of the debate. The next three chapters report studies of choice behavior: Richard Nault and Susan Uchitelle, a study of parental choice making; Robert Kottkamp and Richard Nault, a study of student choice making; and William Garner and Jane Hannaway, the client-school relationship in private schools. In chapters 10, 11, and 12 Donald Frey, William Burt, and John Coons and Stephen Sugarman examine the advantages and disadvantages of tax credits as opposed to vouchers as fiscal mechanisms for increasing family choice in schooling. Following this debate, E.G. West examines the self-destructive consequences of the public monopoly in schooling. Finally, Donald Fisher argues that the extension of family choice in education involves privatizing a public good. Thus, the chapters provide a coherent perspective on the salient issues of the family choice debate.

The introduction to this volume would not be complete, without recognition of the organizations and individuals whose cooperation, support, and assistance made possible the conduct of a major international symposium on family choice, and, subsequently, the production of this book. To these agencies and people I am deeply indebted and wish to record my thanks.

Simon Fraser University has made available a wide array of resources, including financial support from the Conference Fund and Programs of Excellence to support the symposium, the time and talents of the competent people in the Conference Division of Continuing Studies, and the manuscript typing resources of the Faculty of Education. The British Columbia Ministry of Education, the Federation of Independent School Associations, the Department of the Secretary of State in Ottawa, and the Koch Foundation provided financial support that made the symposium possible.

Many people help to shape and create a successful conference. Among those are a few whose contribution to the symposium's design and execution was outstanding. In this context, I acknowledge the important contributions of the Board of Directors of the British Columbia Council for Leadership in Educational Administration, who reacted to early drafts of the symposium program and who cosponsored the event. In addition, I wish to thank Lester Bullen, Inspector of Independent Schools in the British Columbia Ministry of Education, and Gerry Ensing, Executive Director of the Federation of Independent School Associations in British Columbia, who both served on the program advisory committee. The success of the symposium owes most, however, to the extraordinary administrative ability and energy of Margit Nance, Program Director for Conferences at Simon Fraser. Without her energy and commitment and that of her staff—notably Bev Ward, Bea Donald, Karen Kirkland, and Carolyn Tate—the symposium would not have achieved the success it did.

Finally, I wish to record my thanks to Eileen Mallory, whose manuscript typing ability is matched only by her unfailing good humor, her commitment to excellence, and her joy in completing another of "her" books.

1

Historical and Constitutional Perspectives on Family Choice in Schooling: The Canadian Case

J. Donald Wilson and
Marvin Lazerson

Who has the prior right to determine a child's education—the parent or the state? The Universal Declaration of Human Rights, article 26, says that parents do. In both the United States and Canada parents are free to choose whether to send their children to the state-run public system or to a variety of private fee-paying schools. In Canada, several provinces, through systems of public separate schools or public support of private schools, allow families greater choice, usually on the basis of denominationalism. A strict interpretation of the doctrine of the separation of church and state in the United States, however, restricts choice somewhat. For parents there, education ceases to be free if they decline to exercise their prior right to send their children to the public schools. How is it that the pattern of family choice in Canada differs so from that in the United States?

The answer lies in the evolution of public funding of separate and denominational schools in Canada. At the root of this pattern is a history of church-state relations at variance with the U.S. pattern. In contrast to U.S. constitutionalism, which denies state aid to separate schools (while extending religious freedom to all its citizens), Canadians have used constitutional provisions to guarantee state aid to such schools. The decision by the government of British Columbia in 1977 to provide funding at the rate of $500 per pupil per year to private denominational and nondenominational schools—called independent schools—was in marked contrast with U.S. tradition, which establishes an impermeable barrier between church and state. The passage of this bill in British Columbia, known as Bill 33, led many U.S. educators to make erroneous inferences about its meaning. Some talked of British Columbia's new "voucher system"; Bill 33, however, did not extend financial aid directly to the pupil or

The work reported here was financed as part of a major study of the Consequences of Funding Independent Schools, supported by grants from the National Institute of Education (Washington, D.C.) and the British Columbia Ministry of Education. Donald A. Erickson (University of San Francisco) is the principal investigator. The authors wish to thank Professor Cornelius Jaenen of the University of Ottawa and Professor George Tomkins of the University of British Columbia for their critical comments on an earlier draft of this paper.

the pupil's family, but rather to schools already established for a period of five years. Another common mistake was the failure to appreciate that passage of Bill 33 brought the province closer to a long-established Canadian practice of funding separate and denominational schools. Recently, on a late-evening telecast of "The 700 Club" from the United States, John E. Coons and Stephen D. Sugarman were interviewed about their proposal for family choice in California. After a discussion of state aid to Christian schools in the United States, the moderator excitedly announced, "My producer has just told me that Canada is now funding Catholic and other denominational schools and has been doing so since 1977. This is precisely what we want in our country." In fact, however, Catholic and other denominational schools had been receiving public funds in various Canadian provinces for almost 150 years before 1977.

The Canadian pattern of public funding of separate and denominational schools is markedly different from that of the United States. Canada's educational systems—ten provincial, two territorial, and one federal[1]—have evolved quite differently from those of the United States. Actually, the number of public systems is even larger, for Quebec has a dual confessional system providing for both Protestant and Catholic public schools, Newfoundland has a true denominational school system, and Ontario, Saskatchewan, and Alberta each have second public systems known as separate school systems.

As a result, educational comparisons between the two countries must be made with care. Such comparisons, however, may be highly instructive not only in an academic sense but also in terms of public policy.

Persistent Themes

Religion and Education

The basic framework for Canada's use of public monies for separate and denominational schools and, more generally, for the relation between the state and schooling was established in the nineteenth century. Fundamental to the creation of a system of free and universal education was the notion, then common, that education and religion were inseparable and that the state had a responsibility to foster, wherever possible, a harmonious relationship between the two. Religion in education was important, even essential, to both Protestants and Catholics. As John Strachan, Anglican bishop of Toronto and an early school promoter, stressed, "Knowledge if not founded on religion is a positive evil."[2] Thus it is not surprising that throughout North America churches and clergymen were almost invariably the initiators of schooling. In the United States, however, the impact of voluntarism and denominational competition, the lack of an established church, and the inability of any one denomination to exert overriding power in a state or region led to the consolidation of nondenominational, broadly Protestant common schools. The exact coloration of any given school reflected the religious and ethnic composition of its clientele, but in most schools a common Protestantism, complete with prayers, hymns, the King James Bible, and assertions of the Christian basis of U.S. society, was apparent.

As in the United States, the conviction soon appeared in the British North American colonies—that is, those that had not joined the American Revolution—that it was essential to organize truly public common schools for all children to attend. This conviction was spurred by the fear of both denominational factionalism and U.S. republican influence, but nondenominational public schools were also seen as an effective instrument in building a nation. In Nova Scotia and New Brunswick, for example, separate denominational schools were seen as socially divisive. In contrast, in Upper and Lower Canada (which became Ontario and Quebec after 1867) the trend was to accept dissentient and separate schools as a way to maintain some publicly controlled uniformity while also recognizing the validity of certain minority rights. This pattern was duplicated elsewhere later, for example in Saskatchewan and Alberta, with the result that the Canadian practice generally became one of subsidizing the education of some religious minorities in confessional, separate, and dissentient schools. The accommodation of these minorities was made for educational not religious reasons, reflecting a concession that the parent is an important agent of education and that schools should be responsive to parental demands in matters relating to moral and religious education.

The situation in early and midnineteenth-century Canada was strikingly different from that in the United States, primarily because of the great political power of those associated with the dominant Church of England in the early days of Upper Canada and because of the existence of a French Catholic majority in Lower Canada. These two conditions and the tensions they engendered, with nonanglican Protestants and Catholics fighting for their legitimate rights in Upper Canada and Anglo-Protestants seeking security against French Catholic domination in Lower Canada, impelled the state to avoid establishing a nondenominational common school system and moved it instead to assume legal protection and support for denominationally based schooling. (Of all Canadian provinces only British Columbia rejected this pattern—until 1977. The first school legislation enacted by the new province's legislature in 1872 established free nonsectarian public schools, thereby invoking the doctrine of the separation of church and state, which is probably unconstitutional in Canada.) These arrangements were enshrined in 1867 in the British North America (BNA) Act, and despite a growing secularization and increased homogenization among Protestant denominations in the twentieth century, the responsibility of the state to support denominational schools in some form has remained intact in most provinces. The concept that church and state are partners, not hostile and incompatible forces that must be kept at a distance, has made it possible for educational authorities in Canada to subsidize Jewish schools in Quebec and Hutterite schools on the prairies, to condone Amish schools in Ontario, and to permit the Salvation Army to develop its own public schools in Newfoundland. It is into this pattern that British Columbia is belatedly fitting itself.

By 1867, when four colonies of British North America were brought together to form the Dominion of Canada, each colony had its own system of common schools. The BNA Act, the British parliamentary statute that granted Canada a large measure of independence, established legal protection of the rights of those denominational schools then in existence. By the 1870s, the provinces that had joined Confederation [Canada consists of ten provinces and two territories. The provinces, with their date of entry into Confederation, are as follows: Ontario, Quebec, Nova Scotia, New Brunswick (1867); Manitoba (1870); British Columbia (1871); Prince Edward Island (1873); Alberta and Saskatchewan (1905); and Newfoundland (1949).]had established systems of free, universal, and compulsory education. The respective systems provided the bases on which modifications were made over the next century. To appreciate the current state of public funding of schools throughout Canada, then, it is necessary to understand each province's system in that crucial decade. The organizational structure, assumptions, and practices that emerged were contested, often bitterly, and occasionally modified, but on the whole there was little substantive administrative change between the end of the century and the 1960s. Not until then, a major period of educational reform marked by a tremendous expansion of schooling at the secondary and tertiary levels, was the relationship between the state, public money, and denominational schools modified, and even then the extent of change varied greatly by province. The events of the 1960s and 1970s, however, have not significantly altered the nineteeth-century shape of funding arrangements for separate and denominational schools, except in the case of British Columbia.

Federal-Provincial Relations

Before Confederation in 1867, each colony in British North America developed its own schooling system. After Confederation, by the provisions of section 93 of the BNA Act, each province maintained exclusive jurisdiction over its own educational structure. Provincial autonomy in educational matters therefore suggests the second persistent theme of Canadian schooling—the involvement of the federal government. Notwithstanding the fact that jurisdiction over education was accorded the provinces at Confederation, the federal government became involved over the years in several facets of education: land grants for schools in the West in the late nineteenth century, educational services for the population of the territories (Yukon and the Northwest Territories), the education of native peoples and of the children of members of the armed forces living on military bases at home and abroad. In this century the federal government has shown increasing interest in the relation between schooling and economic development. From 1919 and the passage of the Vocational and Technical Education Act through to the current concern about manpower training, the federal government has revealed a deep and continuing interest in vocational and technical education. Finally, since the passage of the Official Languages Act in 1969 federal authorities have taken steps to encourage throughout Canada both bilingual education and instruction in the other official language.[3]

To understand intergovernmental relations, we must start with the British North America Act of 1867, the formal document of Confederation.[4] Analyzing the complex politics and assumptions behind the BNA Act would take us too far afield, but a number of observations will be helpful. Changing economic and social factors over the past century have altered the thinking of Canadians about the role the federal government should play in education. In the 1860s education was very much a local concern, and each colony developed its own system of education. It would have been folly, therefore, to try to force on each new province substantive changes leading to some sort of nationwide uniformity. Moreover, the new nation was too diverse religiously, linguistically, and regionally for this to be practical. From the time of the British conquest of New France in 1760 the framework existed for a nation based on dualism. The United Empire Loyalists, Canada's first separatists, were not prepared to live in a French-speaking, Catholic, and Canadian (as opposed to British) civil-law state. Instead, they insisted upon a new province (Upper Canada) where they could regulate their own affairs based upon essentially British and Protestant traditions mixed with a large measure of anti-Americanism. In the French-speaking province (Lower Canada), educational guarantees were extended to the minority from the beginning. Similar guarantees were slow to come in what became Ontario, but nevertheless by 1867 the social reality of the new Dominion was clear. There were at least two ways, if not more, to be Canadian. Each society in the new nation had its own values, traditions, life styles, and language. Agreement on fundamentals was difficult. The creation of an ideal national type in which all Canadians could see something of themselves, and which they could all strive to emulate, was impossible. The national preoccupation became one concerned with differences, not with similarities, with creating a nation out of culturally disparate groups, not with establishing cultural uniformity.[5] There could never have been "a new Canadian man" in the sense in which de Crèvecoeur could speak of "a new American man." The basis for Canada's present-day pluralism is thus of long standing.

In terms of the BNA Act itself, two sections—93 and 133—are particularly pertinent (see appendix 1A). First, section 93 made all laws relating to education the exclusive responsibility of the provinces. Over the years, whatever the effects of federal decisions affecting education were to be, they occurred indirectly. Second, section 93, subsection 1 proclaimed it illegal to discriminate against any denominational school "which any Class of Persons have by law in the Province at Union." The implications of subsection 1 were profound and controversial, for its effect was to give all legally established existing denominational schools at the time of Confederation perpetual rights to public funds. What was left unsaid, however, was that denominational schools established by custom but not by law were not guaranteed the same right to existence. Moreover, as we explore more fully below, neither this subsection nor any other section protected language school rights as opposed to denominational school rights. Subsection 3 allowed the religious minority to appeal to the federal government against any provincial act or decision affecting the separate or dissentient schools that existed by law in 1867 or were afterward established. Subsection 4 provided for federal remedial legislation if a provincial legislature refused to do so at the request of the governor-general in council. In effect, section 93 made education the exclusive responsibility of the provinces but charged the federal government with ensuring that no provincial government would infringe on minority denominational rights. Finally, in what was to be a source of much confusion, section 133 of the BNA Act guaranteed the rights of both the English and French languages in the parliament, the Quebec legislature, and the courts of Canada. Section 133 did not, significantly, mention language rights in the schools.

In the wake of the BNA Act the provinces were free to forge their own educational statutes, subject to the guarantees for denominational schools already legally established. Five different administrative arrangements emerged. In Quebec there developed a *dual confessional* public school system composed of two separate and independent streams, Catholic and Protestant, representing the two confessions of Western Christianity. In each school district, the confessional schools of the minority are known as dissentient schools, but like the majority's public common schools control their own curriculum, teacher train-

Table 1–1
Legal Status of Separate, Confessional, and Denominational Schools

Nondenominational (public system only)	Informal Arrangements	Separate School Systems	Dual Confessional System	True Denominational System
British Columbia	Nova Scotia	Ontario	Quebec	Newfoundland
	New Brunswick	Saskatchewan	(Manitoba, until 1890)	
	Prince Edward Island	Alberta		
	Manitoba (since the late 1960s)	Northwest Territories		
		Yukon Territory		

ing, and inspection through their confessional section of the Council of Public Instruction. In fact, dissentient schools exist only outside Montreal and Quebec City. Thus, it follows that both the Protestant and Catholic schools of Montreal are public common schools by legal definition and are not covered by section 93 of the BNA Act in respect to minority or dissentient schools. After the establishment of a provincial ministry of education in 1964, however, confessional autonomy was considerably reduced to the point where the two branches essentially share a common curriculum.

Ontario, Saskatchewan, and Alberta established a *separate school* system, normally Protestant or Catholic segregated confessional systems in each province along with the common nonsectarian public schools. Both the separate schools and the nonsectarian public schools were administered by either a department or ministry of education with control over curriculum, teacher training and certification, special programs, and inspection. Four other provinces— Nova Scotia, New Brunswick, Prince Edward Island, and Manitoba—adopted informal arrangements for funding denominational schools. [Between 1871 and 1890 Manitoba had the dual confessional (Catholic and Protestant) system of Quebec. From then until the late 1960s it granted no aid to any religious group.] Officially there is a single nonsectarian public school system; alternatives to it are voluntarily funded by sponsors and parents. In practice, however, political compromises and administrative leeway allowed such schools to receive state funds with varying degrees of state supervision attached.

Newfoundland and British Columbia, until quite recently, have represented the poles of Canadian funding patterns. Before the late 1960s, Newfoundland provided support exclusively for denominational schools. Then, in March 1969 the Anglican Church, United Church, and Salvation Army signed a Document of Integration, which the Presbyterian Church later accepted. Each church thereby relinquished its right to operate its own schools, but retained an executive secretary to advise the provincial department of education on denominational questions. The other denominations—Roman Catholic, Pentecostal Assemblies, and Seventh Day Adventist—also appointed executive secretaries to the Denominational Education Commission operating outside the department but advisory to it. Until 1977 British Columbia alone did not fund any religiously based schools. With this variety of systems, both provincewide and regional analyses are necessary to understand separate and denominational school funding in Canada; neither on its own is sufficient.

The legal and practical power of the provinces in the area of education, the tendencies toward regional identity, and the awkward but real presence of the federal government greatly complicate educational analysis in Canada. Indeed, some have argued that education in Canada can only be understood through examining the individual provinces. We believe, however, that a blend of national interpretation and provincial interpretations is possible and necessary. Clearly, the form that separate school funding took depended on particular political alignments within each province—such as the power of Catholic votes, the relations between French-speaking, English-speaking, and other language Catholic groups, the extent of cooperation among Protestant groups, the influence of non-French and non-British immigrants. Many of the pressures, however, extended beyond provincial borders, and the outcome—the tendency to fund religiously oriented schools, albeit in different ways—was a national phenomenon.

Parental Choice and Taxation

One measure of the complexity that provincial, regional, and federal relations introduced into school funding in Canada is the conflicting legal basis of parental choice and taxation. Canadian courts have established that denominational rights are based on religion, and that the religion of the parents is the decisive factor. The question that naturally arose out of these decisions is: do the parents have a free choice as to which school, separate or public, their children may attend, and for which they shall be taxed? In other words, can a Catholic be a public school supporter even if there is a Catholic separate school in his or her district? Can a Protestant be a separate school supporter if such a separate school is a Catholic school? The court findings have been as follows:[6]

> In Ontario, a Catholic parent may elect the school system to which his or her taxes go. The children will then attend the system to which such taxes are paid. Although a Catholic may choose to be a public school supporter, however, a noncatholic may not elect to support a Catholic separate school.

> In Saskatchewan, if a separate school exists in a district, the taxpayer has no choice but to support the school operated by members of his or her denomination.

> In Alberta, once a Roman Catholic separate school district is established, all Catholic residents are separate school supporters and all noncatholic residents are public school supporters.

In Edmonton and Calgary, Alberta and Saskatoon, Saskatchewan the school boards have arranged that noncatholic children may attend Catholic separate schools and Catholic children may attend public schools at no cost. But it is not clear whether noncatholics can be separate school supporters even if they declare themselves Catholic for tax purposes. It is noteworthy that these differences regarding parental choice are found in provinces that all adhere to one administrative pattern—the separate school system. In the two western provinces there was equal provision of corporation taxes, larger units, and secondary schools to both streams. In Ontario, however, not only were noncatholic parents denied the right to choose Catholic schooling for their children but also equal public support for both systems soon disappeared and funding for separate schools was not extended beyond grade ten.

Despite these striking differences among the provinces, certain factors remain common: the property tax remains the basic source of all school revenue; public schools, whether separate or common, are on the whole tuitionless; a centralized administrative structure (though varying in power) is in place in each province and normally exercises a similar supervisory role over both public and separate schools; until the 1960s all provinces insisted upon religious instruction in all public schools and religious exercises (the Lord's Prayer, Bible reading from selected passages) to open the day; and funding arrangements are quite similar in a number of provinces. All of which is to say that in a country where the provinces retain enormous power and where regional identities often override national identity, discussion of education on a nationwide basis is necessarily complex.

Religious Rights versus Language Rights in Education

Before the midnineteenth century there was little controversy over separate schools in British North America, for education of children was considered the duty of parents and church rather than of the state. Only with the introduction of publicly supported, nonsectarian schools did a controversy develop over separate, publicly supported, denominational schools. The existence at that time of other types of "separate schools," in the sense of alternate schools, did not arouse bitter controversy. There were schools for special linguistic groups, such as French, German, Gaelic, Algonkian, and for special racial groups, such as blacks and native Indians. The contrast between nineteenth and twentieth-century attitudes about language is perhaps expressed best in the following incident from the files of the Ontario Department of Education. It occurred near Windsor in Upper Canada in the midnineteenth century.

> Some French-speaking parents in that community were concerned that their children were not learning English because the teacher in the local public school spoke only French. They complained to the equivalent of the Department of Education only to be told that English was not a requirement for a teaching certificate and there was nothing to prevent the local school board from hiring a unilingual French teacher. The department saw nothing wrong in this and had no intention of interfering.[7]

It would be difficult to imagine either Franco-Ontario parents or the Ontario Department of Education expressing similar attitudes today. It was religion and education that aroused people's sentiment then, not language and education.

Thus, the BNA Act in section 93 protected the schooling rights of denominational minorities and omitted reference to language rights; section 133, which prescribed the use of French and English, made no mention of schooling. Religion and language were and remain legally distinct. Such a distinction was common to the midnineteeth century, when groups contended about religion and the protection of denominational status but were little concerned with language issues until late in the century.

In practice, however, the legal distinction has been confounded by the interweaving of religion and language into cultural patterns and ethnic identity. Religiously, the educational question for Canadians has been whether Canada was a country primarily of two religious groups—Protestant and Catholic, with some acknowledgment of other religious groups—or whether it was essentially a Protestant country that protected nonprotestant, primarily Catholic, rights. Linguistically, a similar educational question persisted: whether Canada was an English-speaking country with a bilingual province (Quebec)—a widely held view at the turn of the century—or whether it was truly a bilingual country, as stipulated officially in 1969. Both the religious and linguistic questions emerged directly out of the BNA Act, but only the former was tied to school policy in the act itself.

Just how crucial was the mixing of the language question with the religious one became clear during the half century before World War I, when a succession of school questions arose in New Brunswick, Manitoba, the Northwest Territories (Saskatchewan and Alberta), and Ontario. These conflicts involved the practical identity of language and religion—French Catholics, English-speaking Catholics, English Protestants—in a legal context that treated the two as distinct in educational policy. Similar conflicts have emerged among non-British, non-French immigrants in the twentieth century, and most recently in the politics of language and school legislation in Quebec in the 1970s. Appeals to the federal government by the English-speaking minority in Quebec against the passage of Bill 101 in 1977, which undercut their language rights in schools, were rejected by the Liberal government in Ottawa. The legal (though not the political) basis for this was supplied by the BNA Act: whereas the protection of denominational rights in schooling lay with the federal government, language rights *in schools* were the exclusive jurisdiction of the provinces. Prime Minister Trudeau, however, declared the language law "inconsistent with the federal government's concept of Canada." In this instance as well as in the case of state protection of denominationally based schooling, it becomes clear how powerfully the nineteenth-century resolution of educational funding arrangements has affected contemporary policies and practices.

Nationwide Changes since 1960

Between World War I and 1960 the structural relationships between church and state in education and in the funding of separate schools changed little. Between

1913 and 1937, Ontario expanded support to separate schools through a system of apportioning corporation tax funds on a formula based on Catholic/noncatholic affiliation of shareholders; Alberta and Saskatchewan also adopted this policy. Administrative leeway to provide support for Catholic denominational schools expanded in provinces like New Brunswick and Nova Scotia. In Quebec, the power of the Catholic church in public education remained unchallenged until the 1960s and the Quiet Revolution. Perhaps most portentous for the structure of separate school funding were the efforts begun primarily during the Great Depression, leading to the consolidation of small school districts, the development of progressive pedagogical and curricular reforms, and the expansion of the importance of schooling at the secondary level. Before the late 1950s, however, these trends had only marginal effects on separate school funding, and church-state relationships remained much as they had been for half a century.

In the past two decades, however, a number of significant alterations have occurred and political controversy over separate school funding has intensified. These are the products of at least four developments. First, the public system experienced tremendous growth, public officials and educators alike emphasized the importance and value of schooling, and provincial efforts stressed modernization and school consolidation. Second, in varying ways and to different extents, these changes have been accentuated by political decisions promoting bilingualism and biculturalism initially, and multiculturalism more recently. Third, dramatic changes in Quebec's educational structures followed the creation of its ministry of education in 1964, accompanied by intensified emphasis on the preservation of French language and culture. Finally, denominational school funding has been affected by the rapid growth of the Catholic population in Ontario, of Protestant evangelical denominational schools in Alberta and British Columbia, and of private Catholic and Jewish schools in Quebec. In practice many of these developments overlap. Their significance varies by province, but altogether they are changing the relation between the state and separate and denominational schools.

The 1950s initiated dramatic changes in the nature and structure of Canadian education. Between 1951–1952 and 1967–1968 elementary school enrollment more than doubled, and secondary enrollment more than tripled. From 1951–1952 to 1965–1966 secondary school enrollment as a percentage of fourteen-to-seventeen-year-olds went from 46 percent to 80 percent (compared with 77 to 92 percent in the United States), and for the first time postsecondary enrollment became significant, rising from 5 to 11 percent (in the United States, from 12 to 19 percent). Educational expenditures increased, interprovincial differences declined. The consolidation of small school districts accelerated, and the provinces took on from the local level more and more of the responsibility for funding public schools. In 1954 the provinces bore 38 percent of educational expenditures on elementary and secondary education; in 1973 the figure was 65.5 percent. Since the mid 1950s the amount of federal funds applied to elementary and secondary education was minimal except for vocational and technical education. Most of the funding changes thus occurred through the transfer of local responsibility to the provincial level. Perhaps most powerfully, school became the most significant avenue of access to more and more occupations.[8]

These developments had a multitude of consequences for Canadian education and helped reshape the framework for separate school funding. The growing importance of education as a means of access to the occupational structure, manifest in the conversion of the secondary school into a mass institution and the rapid expansion of postsecondary schooling, increased the financial costs of providing separate schools and raised questions about the adequacy of the secular instruction occurring within them. In both cases, separate school advocates had a larger stake in gaining more public funds. The consolidation of small school districts into larger units often meant that ethnically or denominationally homogeneous schools were converted into more heterogeneous institutions, complicating or eliminating the former ethnically or religiously monolithic basis of the original schools. This was particularly true in Atlantic Canada. The centralization of funding at the provincial level replaced the previous dominance of locally based financing and usually coincided with larger funding. Simultaneously, however, centralization tended to increase state supervisory powers and led to a diminution of autonomy among schools accepting provincial funds. The expansion of provincial involvement in schools and the growing importance of schooling itself affected separate school funding and church-state relations in every province. The formulation of issues, however, varied in the Atlantic provinces, Ontario, Quebec, Alberta, and British Columbia.

Atlantic Provinces

Each of the four Atlantic provinces (New Brunswick, Nova Scotia, Prince Edward Island, and Newfoundland) undertook major school consolidation in the 1960s and 1970s. Regional school boards, introduced in New Brunswick in 1967, reduced the number of school districts from 433 to 33. Though not formally affecting denominational schools, in fact the trend toward consolidation meant that children and teachers of several denominations were inevitably grouped together, with significant consequences for the Catholic school population. Prince Edward Island underwent a similar process in 1972, establishing five regional school boards to replace 217 local ones. With larger schools replacing smaller ones, the mix of students and teachers again became more heterogeneous, and the "gentleman's agreements" that allowed Catholic denominational schools to function autonomously lapsed. The amalgamation of school districts in Nova Scotia had a similar effect.[9]

If the trend to decreased autonomy for denominational schools has been apparent in New Brunswick, Prince Edward Island, and Nova Scotia, it has been a conscious policy in Newfoundland, where the most dramatic changes have occurred. Under the Terms of Union with Canada, Newfoundland entered Confederation in 1949 with its public school system organized along strictly denominational lines, a fact of life since 1874.[10] In 1967 a royal commission on education proposed two changes of direct relevance to the denominational system. The first was to reorganize Newfoundland's department of education "on a functional rather than denominational basis." The denominations would be reduced to an advisory capacity outside the department. The second recommendation was to reduce the number of school districts from 230 to 35, trying to accommodate geographic and denominational homogeneity wherever possible, but crossing denominational lines whenever necessary in the interests of strong administration and improved provision of services.[11]

Both recommendations were controversial, but both were implemented. The Anglican church, United church, and Salvation Army in 1964 informally agreed to try to integrate educational services (in fact, the process of "amalgamating" Protestant schools had been occurring in a number of industrial towns since early in the century), a process formally ratified in 1969 and supported by the Presbyterian church shortly thereafter. Legislation in 1969 accelerated the process by requiring consolidated school districts; by 1975 the number of school districts had been reduced to 36. In 1968 the legislature reorganized Newfoundland's department of education, eliminating denominational authority and reducing the formal denominational role to an advisory one. Denominationalism in Newfoundland was retained, but in a more indirect form than before. The basic legislation providing for denominationalism was not changed, for the "right to denominational schools, common (amalgamated) schools, or denominational colleges" was written into the Terms of Union with Canada in 1949. Any alteration would have required the approval of three governments—Newfoundland, the United Kingdom, and Canada.

Atlantic Canada presents a typical picture of how efforts to modernize the public schools reduced both the informal and formal authority and autonomy previously held by the Catholic denominational schools. In Nova Scotia, New Brunswick, and Prince Edward Island informal agreements continue to link church and state in education, allowing, for example, teachers in public schools in Catholic areas to wear religious dress, but the effort by provincial governments to improve educational services through more efficient and economic organizational structures, through the centralization and consolidation of funding so as to distribute public money more equitably, and by increasing supervisory control over all schools seriously challenged the denominational basis of schooling. Likewise, although denominationalism remained in Newfoundland, its role changed from a policymaking to an advisory one.

Ontario

What occurred in the Atlantic provinces in the 1960s and 1970s reflected a nationwide commitment to the economic and social value of higher levels of educational achievement. That national ideology also affected separate school funding in Ontario, although the issues were phrased very differently there and involved demands that public funds be extended throughout all separate secondary school grades.

Initially, public funds for Ontario's separate schools had been available through grade eight; that is, the public separate school system was essentially an elementary education system. With the establishment in 1908 of continuation schools for two years beyond the elementary level, Catholics acquired the right under certain circumstances to receive publicly funded separate schooling to grade ten. This was a relatively simple procedure because in law the two extra grades in a continuation school were regarded as elementary grades. Even today, the Ontario Secondary Schools and Boards Education Act specifies that the continuation grades may be provided by a public or a separate school board and that they are to be supported by public and separate school taxpayers. Toward midcentury, as it became more common for students to remain in high school beyond grade ten, Catholic lay and ecclesiastical authorities mounted pressure for an extension of separate school status to grade twelve or thirteen. The appearance of the *Report of the Royal Commission on Education in Ontario* (the Hope Report) in 1950 focused attention for a time on this issue. The commission, among other things, recommended restructuring the entire thirteen-grade school system on a 6: 4: 3 ratio. If such a grade structure were adopted, however, separate school authority would be restricted to the first six elementary grades rather than through grade ten, where provincial grants to separate schools ended. Moreover, the opportunity to lobby for extension of the separate system to the end of grade thirteen would be effectively halted. So opposed were four members of the commission to this recommendation that they refused to sign the majority report; they adopted instead a sectarian position in support of the extension of separate schools.[12]

In October 1962 the Catholic bishops of Ontario escalated the controversy, submitting to the premier and the Ontario legislature a highly publicized brief dealing with issues relating to the separate school question. The bishops' brief argued that the Catholic separate schools were public schools "open to all who wish to support them" and ought to be treated as such. Although the brief stressed a variety of issues—the desire to provide Catholic settings for the education of Catholic youth, the consultation of Catholic experts in the choice of school textbooks, separate training facilities for Catholic teachers, the benefits of the federal Technical and Vocational Training Assistance Act—its main objective was to extend public funding through the entire secondary school. Sensitive to the political repercussions of their appeal, the bishops concluded, "We are not unaware of the delicacy of this problem and the concrete difficulties which it presents." But, they added, "We are wholly convinced that the present situation of the separate public schools in the Province of Ontario constitutes a situation of injustice and that it is within our strict rights to require the necessary adjustments."[13]

The bishops' brief did indeed produce controversy. With 30 percent of

Ontario elementary school pupils in separate schools and with even larger numbers of Catholic youth going on to secondary school, the struggle between supporters of separate schools and those unwilling to extend funding through grades twelve and thirteen quickly involved the province's three major political parties. By the early 1970s the opposition Liberal and New Democratic parties had accepted the Catholic position. The public schools, they held, were now organized according to ministry of education policy on a kindergarten-through-grade-thirteen continuum; it followed that the separate schools ought likewise to provide continuous schooling throughout grade thirteen. Separate school students should not be forced to interrupt their schooling at the now anachronistic grade ten barrier. The justification was articulately presented by the Ontario Separate School Trustees' Association in 1969:

> This request [for funding through grade thirteen] seeks the removal of the pedagogical and financial shackles which restrain the separate schools from offering a complete educational service from Kindergarten to grade 12 (13) at the present time. It advocates lifting those restrictions which prevent separate school pupils from sharing as abundantly in today's progress as pupils in the other sector of the publicly-supported educational system.[14]

Thus far, Catholic efforts to extend public funding in Ontario have been unsuccessful, as successive Conservative governments have refused to take on the additional tax burden. Indeed, so opposed has the Conservative government been to any form of public funding for private schools (all schools not receiving public funds are considered private, so that students in grades eleven through thirteen in Catholic high schools are considered to be in private schools) that it declined even to apply on behalf of such schools for federal subsidies that are available in support of particular programs. Only in 1977 did the Conservative government agree to apply on behalf of private schools for federal French-language grants (in 1977/78 worth about nine dollars per pupil). Even this much accommodation has been controversial; the Toronto *Globe and Mail* complained: "The money involved is paltry. The principle is not."[15]

The politics of separate school funding in Ontario is in many ways unique. The separate school system there is large. Thanks to recent large-scale immigration from Catholic Europe (countries such as Italy and Portugal), 37 percent of Ontario's population is Catholic, and about 30 percent of elementary school pupils are in separate schools. Of the 177 elementary school boards, 60 are Catholic, and only 1 is Protestant. Public funding for separate schools is 95 percent of that provided public schools on a per-pupil basis. For francophones in some regions of the province, there is now another way to receive public funds for Catholic students in grades eleven to thirteen: they attend public French secondary schools. Significantly, this requires a shift in emphasis from religion to ethnicity. The same practice was followed in Manitoba from 1916 until 1965, when legislative provisions allowed for "shared services" for private (Catholic) schools, essentially textbooks, bus transportation, and the use of public school facilities for courses in home economics and industrial arts.

Two years later the government amended the public school legislation to facilitate the teaching of French and the use of French as a language of instruction.
In 1964 Saskatchewan, with a much smaller proportion of youth in separate
schools—about 16 percent of the total enrollment—agreed to extend the separate school system from grade eight to grade twelve, entitling it to full grants
and tax revenues.

Quebec, Alberta, and British Columbia

Since the late 1960s three provinces have led the way in providing public
support for private denominational schooling. The most generous has been the
Province of Quebec which extends financial support from public funds to all
sorts of day, ethnic, private, parochial, and independent schools. Legislation
dating from 1968 establishes two categories for funding.[16] Once an institution
is declared to be of "public interest" (largely dependent on the extent to which
its curriculum coincides with the provincial one), it receives a grant equal to
80 percent of the average cost per pupil "for public establishments of the same
class." Even though it has not been declared of public interest, an institution
may be recognized for grants. In this case the grant basis is 60 percent. The
great majority of private schools in Quebec are Catholic.

In 1967 Alberta added private schools, not previously eligible for funding,
to the public schools and the separate Catholic schools qualifying for tax support. A decade later British Columbia agreed to provide public money for its
independent schools by the provisions of Bill 33. These western provinces were
following the broadminded principle adopted in the United Kingdom of funding
"public education." In neither province has the aid been limited to denominational schools, but in both cases religiously based schools have profited the
most. Alberta's 1967 legislation and pertinent regulations in 1972 required that
private schools have been in operation for at least three years, that they have at
least two teachers, that all teachers have Alberta teaching certificates and teach
the Alberta curriculum, that students write provincial examinations, that the
schools be open to regular inspection, that school buildings conform to provincial standards, and that parents of students be Alberta residents. British
Columbia's Bill 33, passed in 1977, is much less stringent. Although eligible
schools must have been in operation for at least five years, teachers do not
need provincial teaching certificates, and there are virtually no admissions or
curriculum restrictions, except for vague requirements that schools not promote
racial or ethnic superiority, religious intolerance or persecution, or "social
change through violent action." The implementation of the act may, however,
bring about a closer monitoring of curriculum offerings than its wording seems
to indicate.

With a larger number of private nondenominational schools than Alberta,

British Columbia's legislation cannot be characterized exclusively as aid to religious schools. Nonetheless, the largest proportion of funds has gone to the province's Catholic schools and to schools run by Protestant evangelical groups. The latter are especially likely to benefit from the legislation: of the 230 schools listed in the directory of the Federation of Independent School Associations in British Columbia, 65 Protestant evangelical schools were established between 1977 and 1980, no doubt spurred into existence in part by anticipated government assistance after five years of operation. In Alberta, schools affiliated with the Christian Reformed churches have proliferated; the Association of Independent Schools and Colleges of Alberta and the Edmonton Society for Christian Education are among the most active education lobbyists in the province, especially in gaining advantageous changes in department of education regulations. Indeed, so effective have they been that grants to Christian schools, which began in the late 1960s at 33 percent of the basic per-pupil grant to public and separate schools, by 1980–1981 had reached 70 percent of the Foundation Grant (the Foundation Grant amounts to 70 percent of the average public school cost). In British Columbia, in contrast, per-pupil grants amounted to approximately 30 percent of the basic per-pupil grant, but indications were that the province's Federation of Independent School Associations would press government and ministry officials for increased levels of funding.

Conclusion

Whatever their roots, the extraordinary growth of denominational schools in Canada and the increased political power of denominational groups attest that control of the school has important consequences for group culture and economic position.[17] The growth in the ranks of the advocates of family choice seems firmly established. Denominationalism has gained an educational prominence few would have predicted twenty years ago.

Notes

1. The territorial systems are in the Yukon Territory and the Northwest Territories; the federal system is for the native peoples.

2. John Strachan to J.S. Sinclair, 23 May 1840, Strachan Letter Book, 1839–1845, Public Archives of Ontario, Toronto.

3. For an account of the role of the federal government in Canadian education from 1867 to 1970, see J. Donald Wilson, Robert M. Stamp, and Louis-Philippe Audet, eds., *Canadian Education: A History* (Scarborough, Ont.: Prentice-Hall, 1970), pp. 451–465.

4. On the background to the act and its subsequent role as a legal, quasi-

constitutional document, see Edgar McInnis, *Canada: A Political and Social History,* 3d ed. (Toronto: Holt, Rinehart and Winston, 1969), pp. 342–371, 503–510, 624–632, 641–645. Manoly R. Lupul provides a brief summary of the background and provisions for education in the act in "Educational Crisis in the New Dominion to 1917," in Wilson, Stamp, and Audet, *Canadian Education,* pp. 266–271.

5. Allan Smith, "Metaphor and Nationality in North America," *Canadian Historical Review* 51 (September 1970): 247–275.

6. For three Canadian cases dealing with this question—one in Ontario and two in Saskatchewan—see P.F. Bargen, *The Legal Status of the Canadian Public School Pupil* (Toronto: Macmillan, 1961), pp. 18–21.

7. Blair Neatby, "A Tale of Two Languages," *Language and Society* 1 (Autumn 1979): 25. Reprinted with permission. *Language and Society* is a publication of the Commissioner of Official Languages, Canada.

8. The data through the 1960s are summarized in Hugh A. Stevenson, Robert M. Stamp, and J. Donald Wilson, eds., *The Best of Times/The Worst of Times: Issues in Contemporary Canadian Education* (Toronto: Holt, Rinehart and Winston, 1972), pp. 75–86. For an overview of the post-World War II period, see Robert S. Patterson, "Society and Education during the Wars and Their Interlude, 1914–1945," in Wilson, Stamp, and Audet, *Canadian Education,* pp. 360–384; and Hugh A. Stevenson, "Developing Public Education in Post-War Canada to 1960," ibid., pp. 386–413. On the 1960s see J. Donald Wilson, "From the Swinging Sixties to the Sobering Seventies," in Hugh A. Stevenson and J. Donald Wilson, eds., *Precepts, Policy and Process: Perspectives on Contemporary Canadian Education* (London: Alexander, Blake Associates, 1977), pp. 21–36. One measure of the intensified concern with education was the appointment of more than twenty major provinical commissions of inquiry into education between 1950 and 1973.

9. Carl J. Matthews, ed., *Catholic Schools in Canada* (Toronto: Canadian Catholic School Trustees' Association, 1977). This is a very brief but useful compendium on recent changes affecting Catholic schools.

10. William B. Hamilton, "Society and Schools in Newfoundland," in Wilson, Stamp, and Audet, *Canadian Education,* pp. 136–141.

11. On the commission report and developments in Newfoundland more generally, see Frederick W. Rose, *Education and Culture in Newfoundland* (Toronto: McGraw-Hill Ryerson, 1976), pp. 144–164. For background to Newfoundland's political, economic, and cultural history, see Patrick O'Flaherty, *The Rock Observed: Studies in the Literature of Newfoundland* (Toronto: University of Toronto Press, 1979).

12. For an account of the Hope Commission and other royal commissions on education in the 1950s, see Stevenson, "Public Education in Post-War

Canada," pp. 396–403. The best single review of the history and status of separate schools in Ontario to the early 1960s is J. Bascom St. John, *Separate Schools in Ontario* (Toronto: The Globe and Mail, 1963).

13. The text of the brief is in St. John, *Separate Schools in Ontario,* pp. 29–40.

14. Quoted in Stevenson, Stamp, and Wilson, *The Best of Times,* pp. 195–198.

15. Quoted in Matthews, *Catholic Schools in Canada,* p. 29.

16. See *Law and Regulations: Private Education* (Quebec City: Editeur officiel, 1978) for details.

17. On denominationalism and education, see Robert F. Cummings, "Religious Pluralism in Education: Pressures for Public Financing and Implementation," in Stevenson and Wilson, *Precepts, Policy and Process,* pp. 97–114; and J. Donald Wilson, "Religion and Education: The Other Side of Pluralism," in J. Donald Wilson, ed., *Canadian Education in the 1980s* (Calgary: Detselig, forthcoming).

Appendix IA
Extracts from the British
North America Act, 1867

Education

93. In and for each Province the Legislature may exclusively make Laws in relation to Education, subject and according to the following Provisions:

1. Nothing in any such Law shall prejudicially affect any Right or Privilege with respect to Denominational Schools which any Class of Persons have by Law in the Province at the Union:
2. All the Powers, Privileges, and Duties at the Union by Law conferred and imposed in Upper Canada on the Separate Schools and School Trustees of the Queen's Roman Catholic Subjects shall be and the same are hereby extended to the Dissentient Schools of the Queen's Protestant and Roman Catholic Subjects in Quebec:
3. Where in any Province a System of Separate or Dissentient Schools exists by Law at the Union or is thereafter established by the Legislature of the Province, an Appeal shall lie to the Governor General in Council from any Act or Decision of any Provincial Authority affecting any Right or Privilege of the Protestant or Roman Catholic Minority of the Queen's Subjects in relation to Education:
4. In case any such Provincial Law as from Time to Time seems to the Governor General in Council requisite for the due Execution of the Provisions of this Section is not made, or in case any Decision of the Governor General in Council on any Appeal under this Section is not duly executed by the proper Provincial Authority in that Behalf, then and in every such Case, and as far only as the Circumstances of each Case require, the Parliament of Canada may make remedial Laws for the due Execution of the Provisions of this Section and of any Decision of the Governor General in Council under this Section.

Use of French and English Languages

133. Either the English or the French Language may be used by any Person in the Debates of the Houses of the Parliament of Canada and of the Houses of the Legislature of Quebec; and both those Languages shall be used in the respective Records and Journals of those Houses; and either of those Languages may be used by any Person or in any Pleading or Process in or issuing from

any Court of Canada established under this Act, and in or from all or any of the Courts of Quebec.

The Acts of the Parliament of Canada and of the Legislature of Quebec shall be printed and published in both those Languages.

Educational Choice: Unanswered Question in the American Experience

Stephen Arons

My purpose is to explore a question of educational choice that has not been forthrightly addressed in the United States but seems to be taken more seriously in Canada: what are the social and political consequences of majority control of schooling—of depriving a portion of society of the right to influence significantly the education of their children?

Discussion of this issue has two prerequisites: the construction of a brief context of history and constitutional law regarding educational choice in the United States, and the assumption (which I consider obvious enough to be stated without exploring its pros and cons) that all education is value laden. It is neither sensible nor realistic to talk about value-neutral education as if it were attainable or desirable. Because there are various hidden curricula in every school, and because children learn much more in the school than what is taught in the formal curriculum, much of the modern history of conflict over schooling can legitimately be seen as struggle for control of the process of socialization of children.

Historical and Constitutional Context

In 1789, when the U.S. Constitution was adopted, education was neither compulsory nor universal, and in most places it was not tax supported. The presumption apparently was that each family would provide its children with the formal and informal education they needed.[1] The inequalities built into this policy were legion. Slaves could not by law be educated because it was a crime in many states to teach a black child how to read. Furthermore, glaring inequalities in gender, class, and economic resources operated to distort the presumption so that, although it was the family's responsibility to provide education, many were unable to meet their own expectations or need. There were some so-called charity schools set up at the time to provide education for those who could not or perhaps would not provide for their children, but nowhere was there an assumption that society as a whole had the power or the responsibility to provide for education. Education was an individual rather than a social activity.

The strength of the parental prerogative in education can be gauged by what is called the "right of excusal."[2] At common law in the United States prior to the early twentieth century, state courts generally upheld the right of parents to have their children excused from any particular course or program of study in a public school. The courts inquired into neither the work objected to nor the parental motivation for requesting excusal as a condition of granting this partial absence from public school. School was regarded, in other words, as an opportunity of which children were entitled but not required to take advantage. It was assumed that the parents were as competent as or perhaps more competent than school personnel to determine *what* their children were to learn, or in cases of pedagogy, *how* they ought to be taught. The only restriction was that these requests for excusal not disturb the efficiency and good order of the schools; a restriction that was rather narrowly interpreted at the time. So, even as they availed themselves of public schooling for their children, families remained in legally recognized control of the content of individual education.

Beginning in the last quarter of the nineteenth century and into the early twentieth, compulsory school attendance became a fact on a state-by-state basis in the United States, and the entire relationship of families to schools was reversed. The effect of compulsion was to remove the presumption of parental control in education and to shift the locus of responsibility from the family to an institutionalized school operated by the government and responsive to group rather than individual needs. As historian David Tyack put it, "Reformers used the powers of the state to intervene in families and create alternative institutions of socialization."[3] Consequently, the new political structure of schooling made it necessary for heterogeneous groups to contend with one another over whose values, pedagogy, or world view the local school would adopt.

This transformation created a view of education that prevails to this day in the United States—that it is appropriate for educational decisions to be controlled by the political majority. This new majoritarian presumption about education has encouraged citizens to be more concerned with the education of other children than with the education of their own; in consequence, it has had the effect of gradually reversing the traditional presumption of parental competence: parents increasingly came to be viewed as presumptively incompetent in the area of education. It has also fostered the increasing and artificial professionalization of educational administration. Finally, it has eventually reduced the status of teachers to that of bureaucratized employees of the state.

Struggle for Control

In this context, dissent—in the sense of minority views—became less and less legitimate in the theater of school policy, and dissension more and more inevitable. The majoritarian assumption transformed the public schools into a battleground for determining public orthodoxy. This is the common insight of such diverse revisionist historians as Spring, Tyack, Katz, Nasaw, Bowles and Gintis, and others who have attempted to assess the pattern of United States school history.[4] To them, that history seems to consist of battles to determine what the dominant socialization ethic should be in school policy. Even the selection of school history texts reflects such a struggle over orthodoxy.[5] Although these historians have different interpretations of whose values were ascendant at any given time, all share the perception that it was a war over how children were to be socialized.

The Role of the Supreme Court

The U.S. Supreme Court has dealt only indirectly with the issue of suppression of dissent and establishment of orthodoxy in the public schools. Since the 1920s the Court has ruled on cases involving the balance of power in schools between dissenting parents and political majorities; the results, however, are less than clear. The leading decisions fall into four areas. First, the Court has removed prayer or other religious ceremonies and teachings such as creationism, which are based upon religious concepts, from the area of orthodoxy that schools may establish.[6] Whenever it appears that the inclusion of such observances or curriculum has a nonsecular purpose or effect or tends to establish a religion with government approval, the Court has held that it violates the First Amendment's "wall of separation" of church and state.

Second, the Court has protected subcultures—at least when religiously based—from destruction by public school orthodoxy. In the *Yoder* case, children (above eighth grade) of an Amish community were exempted from Wisconsin's compulsory school attendance law because the effect of school socialization was to destroy their religious and community values.[7] The fact that the Amish are a cohesive, religiously based culture protected them under the First Amendment from the imposition of competing values by the political majority exercised through the school system; but the particular values protected—such as cooperativeness rather than competitiveness—might be held just as strongly by nonreligious families in noncohesive communities.

Third, in 1943 the Court dealt with secular orthodoxy in schools when it ruled that public school children could not be required to pledge allegiance to the flag. The Court viewed the flag salute as a confession of belief prohibited by the First Amendment and affirmed the existence of "a sphere of intellect and spirit" that may not be infringed by the government or the political majority.[8] The Court pointed out the dangers of conflicts over orthodoxy in public schools:

Probably no deeper division of our people could proceed from any provocation than from finding it necessary to choose what doctrine and whose program public educational officials shall compel youth to unite in embracing. Ultimate futility of such attempts to compel coherence is the lesson of every such effort. . . .[9]

Fourth, the Court affirmed the right of the family to escape public school orthodoxy and choose nongovernment school socialization by ruling unconstitutional an Oregon law requiring all students to attend public schools.[10] The Court stated that "the child is not the mere creature of the state" and that parents have the right to secure an education for children outside the mechanisms made available by the state. That case, decided in 1925, has been followed by several others that relieve private schools of the burdens of pervasive state regulation, although they remain vague about how much regulation is permissible.[11] There are, then, some limits to government imposition of values through compulsory schooling. The right to choose an alternative to government school is, however, thrown into severe doubt by the economics of schooling. By paying school taxes to support the public schools as well as tuition to the private school of their choice, those who choose nongovernment schools must pay for the schools they choose *against* as well as the one they choose for their children to attend.

Generally, then, the Court has removed some forms of orthodoxy from public schools, has protected some forms of subcultures of dissident value systems, and has left some choice to parents. It remains unclear, however, what is the balance of power. This is the consequence of the failure in the United States to confront the central question of whether majority control of educational decisions is compatible with or contrary to the requirements of the First Amendment.

Effect of Judicial Decisions

What is the current effect of the vagueness that the courts have allowed to persist? The answer can be seen in two battles over parental power and school policy. The first is the epidemic of censorship now taking place in the United States: several studies and my own travels attest that in all parts of the country books are being banned from public school classrooms and libraries; books are being burned; teachers are being fired; and curricula are being altered radically from one year to the next in response to political pressures.[12]

This epidemic is frightening, not only as a threat to free expression and the value of literature, but for the cultural insecurity it betokens. In 1979 and 1980 I talked to parents involved in attempting to remove books from the schools as well as those attempting to keep the books in school. I have talked to school superintendents, teachers, state school authorities, and lawyers in an effort to piece together some understanding of what this phenomenon signifies.

There appear to be two kinds of censorship taking place. The first is the result of organized efforts by ideologically articulate groups of parents. They may be concerned about the role of women in society, either from a traditional or liberated point of view; they may be concerned about the structure of authority in the society; they may be concerned about the differences between what is now called scientific creationism and evolution; they may be concerned about the presence of racist stereotypes or sexist stereotypes in teaching materials. But they all share an articulateness about what it is that they perceive as wrong; and they are all fighting tooth and nail, and with some sophistication, to coerce the schools to adopt their own world view in terms of what is taught to students.

The second group seems less rational. It includes people who usually voice their objections under the banner "Get the filth out of the school," or they may wish to ban Bernard Malamud's *The Fixer* because it is "anti-Semitic" or the works of Langston Hughes because they are "anti-Negro."[13] These are people who are not making a connection between their actions and their thoughts; their reasoning is pretextual; it cloaks their anger and frustration, but it is an arbitrary and ineffective disguise for hysteria.

Both of these groups, the ideologically articulate and the fearful, are suffering from a general collapse of cherished explanations about American culture. Values and beliefs traditionally presumed to be shared, explanations provided by upbringing and by the fabric of the culture are becoming dysfunctional. What is going to happen, what is predictable, why things happen, how to survive, all become confused and confusing. When these explanations are not working or when people perceive them not to be working, insecurity, fear, even panic and loss of identity result. It is a cultural crisis of some depth, for it destroys the foundation of the lives and behavior patterns of many people. Few are exempt from these feelings and most therefore ought to be sympathetic with the emotions and the desires of the parents who feel a loss of control over their own future and their children's upbringing. The painful and ultimately unacceptable contradiction in this situation is that at a time when the explanations are collapsing, people are seeking to use a coercive mechanism to impose an order at any cost. The process is often repressive and resembles scapegoating: people make themselves feel normal by describing someone else as abnormal. The externalization, labeling, and elimination of evil become the primary mechanisms of creating social cohesion, and success is irrelevant to whether or not the scapegoated idea or belief is harmful.

Some of these controversies have resulted in highly emotional, polarized communities. Neighbors do not talk to each other any more; people who thought they shared many perceptions about the world become isolated from one another; compromise positions advanced by teachers, many of whom were fired when books were banned, have been roundly rejected. Proposed mediation and compromise solutions are not meeting the real emotional and cultural needs of the people who promote censorship.

So far the legal solutions being advanced—claims for equal time, for the view that the school ought to be a marketplace of ideas rather than a vehicle of value inculcation, that children ought to be excused if their parents' values are offended—do not seem to satisfy the parties. There is very little sympathy for these points of view, and even if they were to be established, they leave so large a part of the value-laden curriculum and structure untouched that it remains necessary for parents to continue the struggle for control of school socialization.

Censorship and selection struggles can be interpreted as part of a battle over public orthodoxy in the schools. One of the results of these struggles is the destruction of the decision-making process within the school system. The conflicts are not resolvable. School boards are faced with situations in which they must choose between competing groups of parents, whose right to influence the upbringing of their children the board may wish to support but whose values are incompatible. In such a situation it is impossible for the most conscientious school board member to respect the First Amendment, and constant and destructive strife over irreconcilable issues of conscience is made inevitable by the majoritarian structure of schooling.

The second type of current struggle over parental power and school policy involves home education. In the United States there are literally millions of dropouts and pushouts—children who do not attend school, children whose condition public education officials lament but generally regard as unavoidable. In contrast, there is an extraordinarily small number of parents who approach the school superintendent or school board and request permission to educate their children at home according to their own devices and their own values. These individualistic families meet with personal antagonism and institutional hostility in the form of criminal charges, loss of custody of children, harassment, fines, jail sentences, and, in one case, death. Why do these generally healthy and loving families with eccentric but sane visions about education meet with such attacks?

These families are social mutations. The parents, perhaps inarticulately at the outset (though they become very articulate after a year or so of defending themselves in court), see something wrong with the value system prevailing in the public schools and often in the private schools as well. They are not sure exactly what it is, but they know they want to try to develop something different. They need some room. When they ask for that room they are perceived as a threat. One hundred years after the reversal of the presumption of parental control of schooling, it is understandably threatening to education professionals to hear parents say, "I can do this job as well as you can for my kids, even though I didn't have to go to an education school and get a doctorate." It is, moreover, a threat to the entire concept of majority control of education. In this context it is not considered legitimate for parents to be more concerned about their own children's upbringing than they are about the upbringing of other children.

School personnel are also in an unenviable position. Although the schools preach democratic tolerance, minority rights, and the right of dissent in class, school personnel themselves have found that their work is so mired in bureaucracy and so institutionalized that their daily lives are a contradiction to their ideology. Being confronted with people who are radically individualistic and who seem to be in a position to live by their beliefs highlights an ambivalence in their own lives that becomes intolerable and that may account for the extreme reactions home-schoolers encounter. These conflicts over home schooling are often protracted and rarely resolved to the parents' satisfaction. The law's vagueness on parental powers does not help. The struggles become, in effect, a repression of dissent at its most significant point, the formation of young minds.

These modern examples of struggles between parents and schools show, among other things, that the failure to enhance family choice of schools and to place clear limits on the power of the majority over education policy has destructive consequences for parents, children, schools, and culture.

The Consequences of Majoritarian Schooling

I am not suggesting that compulsory schooling ought to be eliminated. But the current and by no means immutable structure of education in the United States encourages and even necessitates continuing battles over public orthodoxy. By requiring that the majority decide how all children should be socialized we in effect require that people contest the most intractable issues of individual conscience in the most accessible form of politics. This is the kind of strife that the First Amendment was intended to eliminate by isolating religious issues from the political process. Two or three hundred years ago it was learned that if the government attempted to make religious decisions, the result would be a religious factionalization and eventual destruction of the political process. Today religion is not the primary expression of conscience and the church is not a significant institution for socializing children. In schools we have chosen to attempt to resolve issues of basic conscience and values through a majoritarian structure, and the result is that we are overloading the decision-making operation.

We are also suppressing dissent, which is clearly contrary to the First Amendment. Freedom of expression concerns not only expression of opinions and beliefs but also their formation. It is a denial of the reality of thought and language to contend that one has the freedom to express oneself if the ability to generate opinions, beliefs, or world views is subject to majority manipulation. More significant still is the fact that we are suppressing dissent among those to whom it is most important, the poor, the working class, ethnic minorities; and we are repressing it where it is most important, in the formation of belief in childrearing institutions. The present structure of schooling in the United States taxes dissent by providing free choice for the rich and compulsory government socialization for the poor. It is economic discrimination in the distribution of First Amendment rights to condition the provision of "free" education upon the acceptance of majority-approved value inculcation in government schools.

Majoritarian schools distort the political process in the United States. We are legitimizing some ideological positions in school while stigmatizing others. The effect is to weaken the balance in political debate, to restrict the ability of large numbers of people to participate effectively in political debate upon achieving adulthood, and to undermine the legitimacy of any national consensus.

The current structure of education in the United States is broadly inconsistent with the values advanced by the First Amendment and represented in the system of freedom of expression. This inconsistency between majoritarian control of schooling and the principles of the First Amendment becomes more crucial and more painful at a time when cultural explanations are collapsing and people are more in need of open communication and room to develop values than they are of repressive enforcement of orthodox views. And so the question of educational choice for families transforms itself into the question of what structure of education is most likely to survive in a diverse society undergoing a cultural crisis. This is not a question currently being taken seriously in the United States.

Notes

1. Bernard Bailyn, *Education in the Forming of American Society* (New York: Norton, 1960).

2. Joel S. Moskowitz, "Parental Rights and State Education," *Washington Law Review* 50 (1975):623–651.

3. See, generally, David Tyack, *The One Best System* (Cambridge, Mass.: Harvard University Press, 1974).

4. Tyack, *One Best System;* Michael Katz, *The Irony of Early School Reform* (Cambridge, Mass.: Harvard University Press, 1968); David Nasaw, *Schooled to Order* (New York: Oxford University Press, 1979); Samuel Bowles and Herbert Gintis, *Schooling in Capitalist America* (New York: Basic Books,

1976); Joel Spring, *Education and the Rise of the Corporate State* (Boston: Beacon Press, 1972).

5. Jean Anyon, "Ideology and United States History Textbooks," *Harvard Educational Review* 49 (August 1979):361–386.

6. Abington v. Schempp, 374 U.S. 203 (1963); Epperson v. Arkansas, 393 U.S. 97 (1968).

7. Wisconsin v. Yoder, 406 U.S. 205.

8. West Virginia v. Barnette, 319 U.S. 624 (1943).

9. Id. at 641.

10. Pierce v. Society of Sisters, 268 U.S. 510 (1925).

11. Farrington v. Tokushige, 273 U.S. 284 (1927); State of Ohio v. Whisner, 351 N.E. 2nd 750 (1976).

12. Surveys by the National Council of Teachers of English in 1977, by the Association of American Publishers in April 1981, and my own travels during 1979–1980.

13. Pico v. Board of Education, 474 F. Supp. 387 (E.D. N.Y. 1979), *rev'd*, 49 U.S. L.W. 2274 (2d Cir. 1980).

Dare Educators Build a New School System?

Joel Spring

Government-operated schools are destructive to the political culture of a democratic society and are one of the major obstacles to the free development and expression of ideas. The ideologists of the American Revolution feared that government-operated schools would become a means by which those who controlled the government would impose a particular political ideology. The dominant ideology pervading the public schools supports the political power of those who control the schools. Dare educators build a new school system? They do not dare to build a new system because their economic position depends on the continuation of the government school monopoly.

This essay explores these issues, first, by considering the concerns of the ideologists of the American Revolution and comparing those concerns with the research literature on the results of political socialization in U.S. public schools; second, by showing that the results of that research are directly related to the type of political structure controlling American education and the ideology that gives legitimacy to that control; and, finally, by considering the alternative and examining the claim by government educators that they are the true friend of the poor.

Ideologues and Researchers: Revolution and Socialization

The pamphlets and other writings of the American Revolution were clearly concerned to create a society where there was freedom of expression and thought.[1] These concerns were based not upon some abstract moral principle but on the belief that scientific, technological, and social progress depended on the free evolution of ideas. Government-operated schools, they feared, would impose a standardized ideology that would halt the free evolution of political, scientific, and social thought.

One of the earliest concerns was expressed by the Irish political leader Robert Molesworth in his study of tyranny, *An Account of Denmark as It Was in the Year 1692*. He identified as a key element in the perpetuation of existing power the gaining of absolute popular obedience through the operation of schools by state-supported religious groups. Molesworth wrote, " 'tis plain, the education of Youth, on which is laid the very Foundation Stones of the

Publick Liberty, has been of late years committed to the sole management of such as make it their business to undermine it. . . .''[2] The problem was that the schoolmasters or religious orders primarily served the interests of those in control of the government; or, as Molesworth put it, ''. . . enslaving the Spirits of the People, as preparative to that of their Bodies; . . . those Foreign Princes think it their Interest that Subjects should obey without reserve, and all Priests, who depend upon the Prince, are for their own sakes obliged to promote what he esteems his Interest.'' Molesworth believed that obedience to the state and authority were the primary things taught by schools in a tyranny. In his view the major service that religion, through the education of youth, performed for the state was ''to recommend frequently to them what they call the Queen of all virtues, Viz. Submission to Superiors, and an entire blind Obedience to Authority. . . .''

Two of Molesworth's friends, John Trenchard and Thomas Gordon, gave a broader defense of freedom of thought and expression in *Cato's Letters*, recognized as the most important writings influencing the revolutionary spirit.[3] Trenchard and Gordon argued that a country needed freedom because without freedom there would be no growth in human wisdom and invention and, consequently, no progress in economic development. They wrote, ''The least Cramp or Restraint upon Reasoning and Inquiry of any Kind, will prove soon a mighty Bar in the Way to Learning.''[4] A short passage in *Cato's Letters* forcefully summarizes what they considered the interrelationship between freedom, liberty, and prosperity and, considered in opposite terms, tyranny, slavery, and misery: ''Ignorance accompanies Slavery, and is introduced by it. People who live in Freedom will think with Freedom; but when the Mind is enslaved by fear, and the Body by Chains, Inquiry and Study will be at an End.'' In this condition, ''Men will not pursue dangerous knowledge, nor venture their Heads, to improve their Understandings. Besides, their Spirits, dejected with Servitude and Poverty, will want vigor . . . to . . . propagate Truth; which is ever High-Treason against Tyranny.''[5]

As this libertarian tradition evolved in the eighteenth century, concern about freedom of thought and expression became specifically linked with opposition to government-operated schools. The most famous of this libertarian tradition were Joseph Priestley, William Godwin, Matthew Boulton, James Watt, Erasmus Darwin, Samuel Galton, and Josiah Wedgwood.[6] Their ideas, inventions, and technological developments sparked the industrial revolution and increased interest in the application of science to the improvement of the human condition.

One of the clear and often-stated concerns of this group was government systems of education. English historian Brian Simon has written with regard to Priestley and this group of intellectuals, ''In common with Godwin, however, and indeed all other dissenters, Priestley was adamantly opposed to education becoming a function of the state. Should it do so, it would not achieve the object he desired; on the contrary, it would be used to promote uniformity of thought and belief. . . ."[7] Historian Caroline Robbins summarized Joseph Priestley's views about state-provided education thus: "The chief glory of human nature, the operation of reason in a variety of ways and with diversified results would be lost. Every man should educate his children in his own manner to preserve the balance which existed among the several religious and political parties in Great Britain."[8]

Priestley's friend William Godwin gave the fullest expression to fear of the consequences of government schooling on the political life of a nation. Godwin argued that the two main objects of human power were government and education. Of these two, education was the more powerful because "government must always depend upon the opinion of the governed. Let the most oppressed people under heaven once change their mode of thinking and they are free."[9] If individuals can control the opinion of the people through education, they can control government. If education is made a function of government, those who control government can use education to maintain and strengthen their control. Godwin gave warning regarding government-operated schools to his own and future generations in his study of government; *Enquiry Concerning Political Justice:* "Before we put so powerful a machine under the direction of so ambiguous an agent, it behooves us to consider well what it is that we do. Government will not fail to employ it, to strengthen its hands, and perpetuate its institutions."

The immediate reaction to these concerns in the context of government schooling in the United States today is to dismiss them because apparently no ideology is taught in the schools. This seeming lack is part of a general political education designed to produce citizens who are apolitical and willing to submit their lives to management by professional experts holding power in government bureaucracies. What this means in the specific context of education is that the professional power of educators depends upon a system of schooling that produces apolitical citizens.

Political Socialization and Political Structure

The findings regarding political socialization in the schools have been fairly consistent over the last two decades. Although there is some debate about how much influence the schools have on political knowledge and attitudes, there is general agreement that the schools emphasize a concept of citizenship that includes obedience to the law and voting as the major form of political action. There is little stress on rights and their protection, active citizenship, and a realistic appraisal of the exercise of political power.

Robert Hess and Judith Torney have written that "Teachers' ratings of the importance of various topics clearly indicate that the strongest emphasis is placed upon compliance to law, authority, and school regulations." They warned, "The school focuses on the obligation and right to vote but does not offer the child sufficient understanding of the procedures open to individuals for legitimately influencing the government." Hess and Torney concluded, "Indeed, it seems likely that much of what is called citizenship training in the public schools does not teach the child about the city, state, or national government, but is an attempt to teach regard for the rules and standards of conduct of the schools."[10]

One of the most interesting conclusions of political socialization studies is the apparent lack of effect of the schools on political attitudes and knowledge. This does not mean that these attitudes and knowledge are developed in a separate context but that they are never developed. This is an important point, for it supports the idea that the present system of government control depends for its perpetuation upon a lack of political sophistication in the general population. In this context, the schools become servants of power by not raising the level of political awareness and knowledge. Kenneth Langton and M. Kent Jennings, for example, investigated the effects of a high school civics curriculum on political knowledge and sophistication and found that the changes were "so miniscule as to raise serious questions about the utility of investing in government courses in the senior high school, at least as these courses are presently constituted." The results were the same in their investigation of a high school history curriculum.[11]

The findings of Langton and Kent are directly related to the lack of meaningful content in high school history and civics courses. One of the most noted features of these curricula is their blandness and lack of controversy. When controversy and studies of conflict are removed from the study of government, that study is reduced to the dull mechanics of government operations. How can one raise political interest and discourse without the excitement of the real world of political power? Langton and Jennings express a certain skepticism that the civics curriculum even attempts to achieve political sophistication and interest.

Political scientist Dean Jaros also blames the blandness of the content of courses for their ineffectiveness. In addition, he argues that teachers contribute to this result. "Probably in response to pressure—real or imagined—from influential groups in society, teachers may avoid discussion of all but the most consensual community- and regime-level values." Because of these real or imagined pressures, "Most teachers, often abetted by the tests that they use, strike poses of explicit political neutrality." As a result, "Teachers fail to communicate the fact that public policy involves social conflict and the resolution of different value positions."[12]

With an argument similar to that of William Godwin, Richard Dawson and Kenneth Prewitt, in their comparative study of political socialization, write, "A polity cannot afford to have its school system rent by partisan debates; but neither can it afford a public education system negligent in transmitting the basic norms of the society. This is the general pattern for public school systems.'' In the United States, they argue, the only permissible subjects are ones like the two-party system, free enterprise, and the basic freedoms. On the other hand, Dawson and Prewitt write, "Liberal or conservative positions, foreign policy views, party allegiances . . . are seen as partisan values; and the teacher generally is expected to avoid particular interpretations of such issues.''[13]

The results of political socialization studies demonstrate that the school is contributing to the development of an apolitical citizenry. In fact, the latest review of research literature on political socialization in the *Review of Educational Research* notes a significant decline in the political knowledge, attitude, and participation rates of students in the United States.[14]

The development of an apolitical citizenry has accompanied an increasing transfer of governmental decision-making power from elected representatives to professional bureaucrats. This transfer of power has occurred most clearly in government schools and is reflected throughout the U.S. political structure.

The rise of professional control of the schools and the development of the structure of schooling are fairly well documented. The history of education presents the following pattern of development in the political structure of education in the United States. First, in the latter nineteenth and early twentieth centuries, complaints that the schools were being used by political groups or parties to dispense favors through the appointment of teachers, school administrators, and the awarding of school contracts resulted in a reform cry "Get the schools out of politics!''[15] Getting the schools out of politics usually meant making school board elections nonpartisan and school boards small. By making school boards small, and in urban areas elected on a citywide basis instead of by district, representation tended to be drawn from elite members of the community. In addition, nonpartisan elections usually meant elections controlled by civic organizations reflecting the interests of elite groups. Every study of the social composition of school boards from the beginning of the century finds their membership to be drawn from professional and business occupations out of proportion to the general population.[16]

But the rise of elite school boards is only part of the story. The other part is the steady transfer of power from school boards to professional educators. Again the change was justified in terms of getting the schools out of politics. It was argued that elected school board members represented political concerns, whereas educators represented the children or students. School administrators and teachers were portrayed as disinterested professionals whose sole goal in life was to serve students. For educators, getting education out of politics meant putting it in the hands of the professional.[17]

The findings of Zeigler and Jennings in *Governing American Schools* suggests that this goal was achieved. Their close observation of the workings of school boards found that school administrators used specific methods to control educational politics at the local level.[18]

Other changes in U.S. education in the twentieth century have resulted in the transfer of power from elected representatives to professional experts. The involvement of the federal government in shaping curriculum in the 1950s removed control even further from the average citizen.[19] In fact, one of the most important areas of educational policy is very seldom even discussed outside the circles of professional educators—the control and financing of educational research. The control of the production of new ideas has a tremendous influence over a system that is committed to continued change.

In recent years federal policies and money have dominated the production of new knowledge. By 1965 the federal government was providing more than 71 percent of the money for educational research in the United States. Richard Dershimer, former executive officer of the American Educational Research Association, writes, "Every research and development project initiated by the federal government was initiated by a small handful of persons, in other words, by a professional-bureaucratic complex." He goes on to claim of government-sponsored research programs in education that "many of these remain in existence today not because of any widespread public demand but because elements in the complex still support them."[20]

The rise of professional control was legitimized by the ideology of equality of opportunity. In the context of schooling in the United States, however, equality of opportunity does not mean an equal chance to compete in the marketplace for occupations. In fact, the U.S. school system, through tracking, vocational education, and vocational guidance, has been designed to provide unequal opportunities to compete outside the schoolhouse. Equality of opportunity, rather than being a function of the marketplace, has been internalized in the school under the management of experts.[21]

The trend began in the early part of the twentieth century, when the schools were called upon to increase industrial efficiency by identifying abilities and interests of students through vocational guidance and matching those traits with an educational program and future occupational destination.[22] This process represented a significant break with the nineteenth-century argument that people should receive equal educations and that equality of opportunity would occur after schooling, in competition for jobs.

Making equality of opportunity an internal function of schooling has also been justified in terms of being fairer than the marketplace. Professional testers armed with I.Q., interest, and aptitude tests have claimed to do a fairer job than the marketplace. Professional curriculum experts and administrators claim to have created educational programs that will provide a fairer matching of individual traits with occupational needs.

The Professional Educator as Friend of the Poor

Making equality of opportunity part of the internal operation of schooling has had another important function in justifying the control of the professional. It has allowed the professional educator to claim to be the true friend of the poor. In the early twentieth century professionals claimed power by portraying themselves as friends of the children. Now they justify it as friends of the poor.

The ideology of equality of opportunity and the political power of professionals are directly related to the results of political socialization studies. The production of an apolitical citizen is ideal for a political system in which power is to reside in the hands of expert managers. The rise of the administrative state has been accompanied by the decline of the political person.

To achieve a rebirth of the political person we must get government completely out of the business of education and research. We need competitive educational institutions that reflect a wide variety of ideologies. We must recognize that the evolution and progress of U.S. culture and society depends on the free interplay and development of ideas.

Whenever it is suggested that government schooling be abolished, there is always an educator who waves the flag of the poor. It is important to understand that as professional educators have built their careers on the backs of the poor, there is no evidence that schooling has done anything significant to eliminate poverty in U.S. society. In fact, some have argued that schools have reduced equality of opportunity and made the class structure of the United States even more rigid.[23]

One thing we do know is that even with the expansion of government education and welfare and the rise to power of professionals since World War II, the actual conditions of the poor have worsened. The evidence is most clear for black citizens who struggled for both civil rights and economic advancement during the past three decades. The results have been an advancement of the black middle class with the aid of education and an increase in the number and deprivation of poor blacks. The irony is that the advancement of many middle-class blacks has been in government and educational programs designed to serve the poor. In other words, part of the black middle-class population is building its careers on the backs of a poor black underclass and depends on the continued existence of that class.[24]

Schooling is not the answer to eliminating poverty; a dynamic and growing economy is. In the past two decades the experts who have come to manage the U.S. economy have created or contributed to chronic inflation, unemployment, and declining productivity. There is no proof that continued expert management of the economy will produce any better results.

The hope of the poor is not in education nor in the continuation of the power of professional experts. Their hope is in eliminating the present stagnation of our political culture and in breaking the grip of bureaucratic domination of our society. An important step in that direction would be to destroy the ideological domination of government schools and thus to help revitalize U.S. political life.

Conclusion

Dare educators build a new school system? The answer is obviously no, for their power and economic positions depend on the continuation of the current system. Where will or could a movement begin to make significant changes in the system if government schools train apolitical students to accept a managed society? The only possibility is to educate a citizenry by means of the very problems produced by the system. Increased poverty, unemploymeent, inflation, and declining productivity have accompanied an expanding government bureaucracy and increased spending in welfare and education programs. This is the basic contradiction of our times. It could be the contradiction that produces the next wave of change in U.S. society. If the schools were transformed in the nineteenth and early twentieth centuries, they can be transformed in the future. This time it might not be by educators but by citizens angered by current conditions.

Notes

1. For a detailed study of these pamphlets see Bernard Bailyn, *The Ideological Origins of the American Revolution* (Cambridge, Mass.: Harvard University Press, 1967).

2. Robert Molesworth, *An Account of Denmark as It Was in the Year 1692* (Copenhagen: Rosenkilde and Bagger, 1976). All quotations are taken from the preface, whose pages are unnumbered.

3. Bernard Bailyn writes, "So popular and influential had *Cato's Letters* become in the colonies within a decade and a half of their appearance, so packed with ideological meaning, that . . . it gave rise to what might be called a 'Catonic' image, central to the political theory of the time. . . . " *Ideological Origins,* p. 44.

4. *Cato's Letters,* ed. Leonard Levy (1755: reprint ed., New York: Da Capo Press, 1971), 2:33.

5. Ibid., p. 32.

6. For a study of the intellectual background of this group see Caroline Robbins, *The Eighteenth-Century Commonwealthman* (Cambridge, Mass.: Harvard University Press, 1959), pp. 32–378.

7. Brian Simon, *Studies in the History of Education, 1780–1870* (London: Lawrence & Wishart, 1960), pp. 34–35.

8. Robbins, *Commonwealthman,* p. 350.

9. A more detailed discussion of Godwin's educational ideas can be found in Joel Spring, *Primer of Libertarian Education* (New York: Free Life Editions, 1975). The quotations from Godwin are from pages 13–33.

10. Robert Hess and Judith Torney, "The Development of Political Attitudes in Children," in *Political Socialization,* ed. Edward Greenberg (New York: Atherton Press, 1970), pp. 72–74.

11. "Effects of the High School Curriculum," in M. Kent Jennings and Richard G. Niemi, *The Political Character of Adolescence: The Influence of*

Families and Schools (Princeton: Princeton University Press, 1974), pp. 187–191.

12. Dean Jaros, *Socialization to Politics* (New York: Praeger, 1973), p. 105.

13. Richard Dawson and Kenneth Prewitt, *Political Socialization* (Boston: Little, Brown and Co., 1969), pp. 157–164.

14. Lee H. Ehman, "The American School in the Political Socialization Process," *Review of Educational Research* 50 (Spring 1980):99–119.

15. The following are in general agreement about the changes in the political structure of American education: Joel Spring, *Education and the Rise of the Corporate State* (Boston: Beacon Press, 1972); Joseph Cronin, *The Control of Urban Schools* (New York: The Free Press, 1973); and David Tyack, *The One Best System* (Cambridge, Mass.: Harvard University Press, 1974).

16. The following are the major studies of the social composition of school boards from the early part of the century to 1980: Scott Nearing, "Who's Who in Our Boards of Education?," *School and Society* 5 (20 January 1917):89–90; George Counts, *The Social Composition of Boards of Education* (Chicago: University of Chicago Press, 1927); Harmon Zeigler and Kent Jennings, *Governing American Schools: Political Interaction in Local School Districts* (North Scituate, Mass.: Duxbury Press, 1974); and Kenneth E. Underwood, Wayne P. Thomas, Tony Cooke, and Shirley Underwood, "Portrait of the American School Board Member," *The American School Board Journal* 167 (January 1980):23–25.

17. For a history of the development of professional control in education see Cronin, *Control of Urban Schools;* Tyack, *The One Best System;* Raymond Callahan, *Education and the Cult of Efficiency* (Chicago: University of Chicago Press, 1962); and Joel Spring, *Educating the Worker-Citizen* (New York: Longman, 1980), pp. 80–135.

18. Zeigler and Jennings, *Governing American Schools.*

19. I have discussed the evolution of federal involvement in curriculum development in *The Sorting Machine: National Educational Policy since 1945* (New York: David McKay, 1976), pp. 93–140.

20. I have provided a more detailed analysis of research policy in *Educating the Worker-Citizen,* pp. 135–160. The quote by Richard Dershimer is taken from his book, *The Federal Government and Education R & D* (Lexington, Mass.: Lexington Books, D. C. Heath and Company, 1976), p. 2.

21. This meaning and process of equality of opportunity is explored in more detail in Spring, *Educating the Worker-Citizen,* pp. 45–80.

22. See Paul Violas, *The Training of the Urban Working Class* (Chicago: Rand McNally, 1978); Marvin Lazerson and W. Norton Grubb, eds., *American Education and Vocationalism* (New York: Teachers College, 1974), pp. 1–57; and Spring, *Education and the Corporate State.*

23. For a summary of the major studies regarding education and life out-

comes see Caroline Hodges Persell, *Education and Inequality* (New York: The Free Press, 1977), pp. 153–171.

24. See William J. Wilson, *The Declining Significance of Race: Blacks and Changing American Institutions* (Chicago: University of Chicago Press, 1978), pp. 122–144.

4 Parents in Court

William Bentley Ball

Parents in Canada appear to have been less litigious than those in the United States in educational matters. Both *Regina* v. *Wiebe* and the Independent Schools Support Act, however, indicate that the problems are much the same for parents in both countries.[1] Whether the U.S. constitutional system and popular attitudes toward the courts cause parents in the United States to be more prone (or more subject) to litigation, I cannot say. Whatever the cause, litigation has increased tremendously in the United States in the past two decades. This litigation has produced an impressive body of precedents in three areas of law relating to parents and education:

1. Parents are in court to secure some form of governmental aid for the education of their children.
2. Parents are in court because the state contests their decision to opt for a form of nonstate education.
3. Parents are in court to contest particular aspects of state education.

In each class of these cases parental rights—indeed, the very definition of these rights—surface as important issues.

The Governmental Aid Cases

Some U.S. groups have described the governmental aid cases as attempts by the Catholic church to obtain public monies. As the attorney for parents who entered these cases, I can testify that their view of the matter is somewhat different. What they see are household budgets, grocery bills, tax burdens (including taxes to support the schools of the state), and the minds and souls of their children. Typically, the sequence of events is as follows:

1. A state legislature enacts a bill providing some sort of aid, through the use of public funds, for a child's education in a nonstate school.
2. Citizens who know that a majority of such schools are church related bring suit to have the act declared violative of the Establishment Clause of the U.S. Constitution; that is, violative of church-state separation.

43

3. Attorneys for the state defend the act against this charge.
4. *Parents* enter the case saying, in effect, *"We* (or our children) are what this case is all about." They raise constitutional points in favor of the act (especially in terms of freedom of religion).
5. The court tries the case. The losers eventually appeal it to the U.S. Supreme Court, which up to now has overridden the parents' constitutional claims and has held the enactment to violate church-state separation.

The basic claim of most parents is essentially a religious liberty claim and usually takes this form:

1. The state may never condition participation in a general public welfare benefit upon surrender of a fundamental constitutional right.
2. The particular "aid" enactment is a public welfare benefit because it supports education.
3. The right to educate one's child in a private (including religious) school is a fundamental constitutional right.

I have represented parental interests in some of the principal cases that have reached the Supreme Court,[2] and in most of these I have presented this three-point argument—with notable lack of success. The Court has focused on one question alone: does the act violate the Establishment Clause? It has ignored the question: does denial of the benefit violate a parental liberty, such as the free exercise of religion? The Court's decisions so far amount to the following: If an enacted program is to avoid contravening the Establishment Clause, it must have a secular legislative purpose and a primary effect that neither advances nor inhibits religion; and it must be one that does not excessively entangle state and church.

The application of this test makes fascinating reading. In *Board of Education* v. *Allen,* the Court held that secular textbooks could be loaned by the state directly to nonpublic school children. In 1975, in *Meek* v. *Pittenger,* the Court reaffirmed this. The Court's reasoning in these cases is interesting.

First, the benefit is a public welfare benefit, *not* because it benefits the education of children, but because it is a benefit already extended to public school children. This concept of *public,* it may be argued, displaces the earlier sense of the common good with "public institution," and the ultimate meaning is that the public may be aided (that is, the common good advanced) only on a basis of parity with governmental institutions.

Second, within the terms allowed by that parity, children in nonstate schools may be governmentally aided (and therefore parental choice aided) through benefits that have a secular purpose, that do not have a primary effect of ''advancing'' religion, and that do not get the state too involved in the administrative, financial, or (especially) religious affairs of the church. The loan of secular textbooks meets these criteria, said the Court. The Court has also upheld safety and health programs paid for (or even administered) by the government—still, however, within the ''parity'' limitation.[3] The latter programs are justified on the basis that the child (within ''parity'') is a proper object of benefits of a physical nature. In *Meek* the Court, in affirming the provision of one kind of educational aid (textbook loans), denied other forms, such as instructional equipment, on the ground that loan of the latter ''has the unconstitutional effect of advancing religion because of the predominantly religious character of the *schools* benefiting from the Act.''[4] That is to say, the religious character of the schools did not affect the constitutionality of the loan of textbooks, and the secular interest in the education of children did not affect the constitutionality of the loan of equipment. Furthermore, *Meek* conditionally upheld Pennsylvania's program of providing so-called auxiliary services to non-public school children—counseling, testing, psychological services, speech and hearing therapy—by personnel from the public school system. The condition was that these services be provided, not on the religious school's premises (which would violate church-state separation) but on public school premises, a neutral *cordon sanitaire*.

The Supreme Court has also dealt with other endeavors to obtain governmental help for parents: it has struck down state acts that would provide maintenance and repair to private school buildings;[5] it has voided legislation that would give a tax break to parents[6] (this was not a tuition tax credit measure); it has held unconstitutional a parent tuition reimbursement act;[7] and it has declared null and void an act that provided state reimbursement to religious schools for performing state-mandated teacher-prepared tests.[8]

The belief of many American parents that they have a right, founded on principles of social justice and related, as they see it, both to a policy of pluralism and to fundamental liberties, persists today despite this lack of success in obtaining meaningful tax benefits; its main focus now is on the tuition tax credit.

A link exists between these and the second class of cases. The link resides in the Court's deeper focusing on church-state separation through its development of doctrine respecting ''excessive entanglements'' between the two.[9] In *Lemon* v. *Kurtzman* the Court applied the ''entanglement'' rulings developed in 1970 in *Walz* v. *Tax Commission* specifically to a governmental aid program involving church schools.[10] It held those schools to be pervasively religious and said that government could not involve itself in the affairs of such schools.[11] The relation of this principle to parental rights has become enormously important in that group of cases in which parents have found themselves in court because the state has contested their right to choose private religious education for their children. These I regard as the most significant parental rights cases.

The Governmental Control Cases

In the governmental aid cases parents are in court seeking financial assistance; in the governmental control cases parents are in court seeking protection of rights to educate and, quite often, protection from jail and other criminal penalties.

Over the past six decades constitutional law in the United States has moved toward explicit recognition of parental rights (as against state control) in education. Prior to 1972, however, the Supreme Court dealt with only a handful of cases involving these parental rights. Despite the fact that in many of these cases no parents appear to have been in court and that in two of them education was not involved, each case contained rulings that later became important.

Meyer v. *Nebraska*[12] was a 1923 case involving the State of Nebraska's prohibition of the teaching of an elementary school child in a language other than English. In the course of vindicating the constitutional right of a teacher in a Lutheran parochial school to teach Bible stories in German, the Supreme Court explored the implications of total state control of education. The Nebraska supreme court, upholding the criminal conviction of the teacher, stressed the dangers of allowing the children of foreigners to be taught the language of their parents from early childhood. This would "naturally inculcate in them the ideas and sentiments foreign to the best interests of this country."[13] The Court rejected this position utterly and spoke, instead, of the right to teach and the right of parents to engage a teacher to instruct their children. It said, in particular, that the statute materially interfered with "the power of parents to control the education of their own [children]."[14] These rights, said the Court, were "within the liberty" of the Fourteenth Amendment. But the Court went beyond this. It recognized, even in Nebraska's seemingly narrow limitation of rights of parents and teachers, the more profound danger of the state's role as a sort of *primary parent*. Noting the training of citizens practiced in Sparta, the Court said: "In order to submerge the individual and develop ideal citizens, Sparta assembled the males at seven into barracks and intrusted their subsequent education and training to official guardians."[15] In comment, the Court went on to observe: "The desire of the legislature to foster a homogeneous people with American ideals prepared readily to understand current discussions of civic matters is easy to appreciate."[16] Adopting any scheme even remotely approaching such control of children, however, would be "doing violence to both letter and spirit of the Constitution." The Court acknowledged the "power of the state to compel attendance at some school and to make reasonable regulations

for all schools,''[17] but it did not specify what it meant by "reasonable regulations.'' Whatever it meant by that phrase must clearly be read in light of the
Court's dominant statement concerning parental (and teaching vocational)
rights.

Again, in *Pierce* v. *Society of Sisters*[18] no parents were in court but it was
largely in the name of parents that the Surpreme Court held void an Oregon
statute that said with refreshing candor what some statists in education today
say with depressing indirection—namely, that all children must be educated by
the state.[19] Behind that claim looms the proposition that all children belong to
the state. We are all familiar with the Court's ringing answer to that proposition,
summarized in its famous statement, "The child is not the mere creature of the
state,'' that it is parents who "have the right, coupled with the high duty,'' to
prepare the child for his future. Our "fundamental theory of liberty,'' said the
Court, "excludes any general power of the State to standardize its children by
forcing them to accept instruction from public teachers only.''[20] *Pierce* by no
means held that the state is powerless in the sphere of education or that parents'
rights are without limits. The Court spoke of the power of the State

> reasonably to regulate all schools, to inspect, supervise and examine them,
> their teachers and pupils; to require that all children of proper age attend some
> school, that teachers be of good moral character and patriotic disposition, that
> certain studies plainly essential to good citizenship must be taught, and that
> nothing be taught which is manifestly inimical to the public welfare.[21]

These general statements concerning inspection and supervision, teacher qualification, and "good'' and "inimical'' studies proved to be subject to the exi-
gencies of future constitutional development. Doctrine concerning teaching
rights, the "right to know,'' church-state entanglement, and religious liberty,
for example, might, when the generalities came to be tested in concrete factual
situations, seriously narrow or even vitiate those generalities. In fact, even
before those subsequent developments the Court in 1927, in the *Farrington*
case, struck down the Territory of Hawaii's Foreign Language Schools Act.[22]
The act, motivated by fear of the Japanese, was actually a comprehensive
scheme to regulate private schools. The scheme had been challenged on
grounds, inter alia, that is unreasonably interfered with "the fundamental right
of parents and guardians to direct the upbringing and education of children
under their control.''[23] The Supreme Court had this to say:

> The foregoing statement is enough to show that the school Act and the meas-
> ures adopted thereunder go far beyond mere regulation of privately-supported
> schools where children obtain instruction deemed valuable by their parents and
> which is not obviously in conflict with any public interest. *They give affirm-*
> *ative direction concerning the intimate and essential details of such schools,*
> *intrust their control to public officers, and deny both owners and patrons*
> *reasonable choice and discretion in respect of teachers, curriculum and text-*

books. Enforcement of the Act probably would destroy most, if not all, of them; and, certainly, it would deprive parents of fair opportunity to procure for their children instruction which they think important and we cannot say is harmful. The Japanese parent has the right to direct the education of his own child without unreasonable restrictions; the Constitution protects him as well as those who speak another tongue.[24]

Thus matters long stood. Further positive development in U.S. law followed a criminal prosecution brought in 1968 by the State of Wisconsin against Amish farmers for refusing to enroll their children in any high school.[25] General familiarity with the facts of that case makes it unnecessary to repeat them here. Some comments, however, are useful as we reflect on *Wisconsin* v. *Yoder* more than a decade from the day on which my Amish friends were handed a paper informing these most peaceable of all Americans that they had offended "the Peace and Order of the State."

First, *Yoder* is not just an "Amish" case. Its effect is not confined to the peculiar situation of a sixteenth-century peasant people in our midst—special law dealing with an antique curio. The Supreme Court in *Yoder* states very broad principles that now must control future litigations:

> . . . only those interests of the highest order and those not otherwise served can overbalance legitimate claims to the free exercise of religion. We can accept it as settled, therefore, that, however strong the State's interest in universal compulsory education, it is by no means absolute to the exclusion or subordination of all other interests.[26]

Second, in *Yoder* the state based its case on the supposed need of all children for what the state defined as education. But the Court noted that the value of all education "must be assessed in terms of its capacity to prepare a child for life" (and it believed that the Amish way of life for its teenagers was one that fitted the children for the life they were about to enter). In this matter the Court gave strong recognition to parental judgment.

Finally, as in all the contemporary compulsory attendance cases, the state cited the 1944 Supreme Court decision in *Prince* v. *Massachusetts*.[27] *Prince* is the classic decision on *parens patriae*, or the power of the state to protect children when their parents do not. In *Prince* a religious society had used a child to hawk religious tracts on city streets at night, and the Court held that, notwithstanding any religious interest, state laws protecting child labor must be applied. In *Yoder* the Supreme Court refused to extend application of the *Prince* case to the Wisconsin Amish. In responding to the state attorney general's urging of *Prince*, the Court said:

> Indeed it seems clear that if the State is empowered, as *parens patriae*, to "save" a child from himself or his Amish parents by requiring an additional two years of compulsory formal high school education, the State will in large

measure influence, if not determine, the religious future of the child. Even more markedly than in *Prince,* therefore, this case involves the *fundamental interest of parents, as contrasted with that of the State, to guide the religious future and education of their children.* . . . This *primary role of parents* in the upbringing of their children is now established beyond debate as an enduring American institution.[28]

This ruling is central to the current widespread controversy sparked by new efforts of states to regulate private schools. The quartet of cases from Vermont, Ohio, North Carolina, and Kentucky illustrates this very well.[29] For purposes of illustration, I shall combine the facts of these four cases.

State A's board of education becomes alarmed at the rapid growth of fundamentalist Christian schools within the state. State A takes a new look at its statutes or regulations relating to private education and concludes that it has power to require that all private schools be state approved or state licensed or state certified, these terms being roughly equivalent. State A believes it has two legal weapons for enforcing the approval requirement: compulsory attendance proceedings against parents who enroll their children in nonapproved schools, and injunctions against nonapproved schools. It notifies the parents or the schools of impending enforcement. The parents and/or schools elect either to defend themselves in the action that State A eventually brings, or to launch a preemptive strike by suing the state first in an attempt to secure an injunction against the state's threatened action. In any event, the matter goes to trial. At trial the following facts emerge:

The state's witnesses contend that the state has ultimate responsibility for all education within it, that it requires in all schools compliance with very minimal educational standards, that there is a great danger to children and to the public in permitting the existence of schools that do not meet these minimum standards, and that these standards properly provide regulation in six basic areas: teacher certification, curriculum, physical facilities and equipment, safety and sanitation, textbooks, and teaching methods.

Witnesses for the defense consist of five interest groups: parents, children, school administrators, staff members, and educational experts. The parents prove to be capable and intelligent individuals, deeply devoted to their children, who display complete awareness of, and satisfaction with, the education their children are receiving at the nonstate school. The children express satisfaction with, and often enthusiasm for, their school environment and the teaching. They express themselves in good English and with conviction. They stand up well under cross-examination. The school administrators are sometimes not college graduates and are frequently ministers; they testify in detail about the educational program and the results they feel they are achieving. They are able to produce statistics showing good achievement test results. The staff members exhibit a strong sense of dedication to the children and a keen interest in teaching. All the witnesses in the Christian school cases advance primary religious claims. They contend that they have no conscientious choice except to pursue the Christian education in which they are engaged, and the school administrators, parents, and staff members express a fundamental conscientious objection to state licensing of the religious ministry that is the Christian school. They reject the view that theirs is a bifurcated education, partially religious and partially secular. Experts in the field of religion and the field of education present their evidence. The religious experts buttress the claim that Christian education, in biblical context, is essentially religious and does not admit the possibility of bifurcation. The educational experts devote themselves mainly to discussion of available educational research; they conclude that teacher certification provides no real guarantee of good teaching and that proof of good teaching can be found only in good results. They say that those good results can, to a substantial extent, be identified by results shown on nationally standardized achievement tests. They also express the belief that the "parent market" affords a very important index to good education. They deride the educational propriety of the state's prescription of textbooks to be used by private school pupils. They agree that states may require a basic curriculum, but they point out that once the state moves into areas outside an extremely narrow core of subject matter, it is moving into areas upon which there is universal disagreement. These experts agree that the state may prescribe a curriculum consisting of mathematics, English grammar, English spelling, English reading, English writing, geography, history, science, government, arts, and physical education, but that it must leave the private school to determine the content of these subjects. The witnesses note that there is no consensus about subjects such as "private enterprise system" or "environment." These witnesses also cite much research showing values related to innovation and experimentation in education and freedom to "do things differently." They therefore challenge state prescriptions (such as those advanced in some jurisdictions) that "teaching in private schools shall be equivalent to that offered in public schools." Finally, the experts reject any state role in imposing competency testing on private schools. They cite many examples of competency tests administered to public school pupils and assert they are of low quality and yield meaningless results.

With these facts on record, the court must then decide whether there are First Amendment values involved in the case; that is, values related to freedom of expression and learning as well as to basic parental rights; and, if so, whether State A's regulatory action truly represents not merely a public interest but a "compelling state interest." In the Vermont, Ohio, and Kentucky cases, the state supreme courts found that genuine fundamental constitutional claims exist for parents and school administrators and that the imposition of state regulation served no "compelling state interest."[30]

The decisions in these cases undoubtedly represent a healthy trend toward liberty in education, in terms not only of religious liberty but also of parental liberty and general educational freedom. The courts, when presented with facts, have not been overwhelmed by the sometimes frenetic claims of state educational officials that if education is not state controlled, public education faces doom, lives of countless children will be ruined, and the nation will be set on a course to disaster. Sensibly, the courts have asked for more than mere assertions; they have asked for facts, and the facts have not been forthcoming. In contrast, parents and private school people who have resisted the state have provided abundant testimony giving strong indications that the totally publicly controlled and publicly funded education system has not, in some states, managed to achieve the excellence in education that public educators have said is the state's goal in seeking to regulate private schools. In addition, there has been much testimony about disorder, drug use, and violence in particular public schools.

In all the cases involving religious schools, the courts have emphasized a new element, which does not appear in the pre-1972 cases: the "entanglement" issue. One of the very strong reasons advanced by the courts for prohibiting state supervision of private religious schools has been an apparent resolve to keep church and state separate. In most of the contemporary cases where government has sought to impose itself upon religious schools, the "entanglement" ruling of the Supreme Court has proved fatal to the effort.[31]

I hope that we are at the end of litigation over these issues in the United States. I fear, however, that we are not, that we may be in for much more of it. One of the root causes of these litigations is undeniably the fact that some state legislators have misconceived the roles of government, of parents, and the role of nontax-supported schools under the U.S. Constitution.

The Public Education Protest Cases

The third and last set of cases involves parents of children enrolled in the public schools who find unacceptable certain programs in those schools and go to court to have them terminated. These litigations fall into two general periods: the wave of cases between 1948 and 1963, in which parents protested theistic religious practices or observances in the public schools, and those in which parents have protested, on grounds of religion or conscience, nontheistic religious practices in the public schools or programs deemed offensive to morality.

In its 1948 decision in *McCollum* v. *Board of Education,* the Supreme Court held that public school "released time" programs violate the Establishment Clause.[32] Under such programs priests, ministers, and rabbis could come into the public school and be available in isolated teaching situations for religious instruction of public school enrollees. The Court, in a suit brought by the parent of a public school child, held that this tax-supported program, taking place on the public school premises, violated the Establishment Clause. The school district, in efforts to uphold that statute, showed that there were provisions in the law allowing the child to be excused from any requirement to participate in any such instruction. The Court, however, said:

> That a child is offered an alternative [excusal] may reduce the constraint; it does not eliminate the operation of influence by the school in matters sacred to conscience and outside the school's domain. The law of imitation operates, and non-conformity is not an outstanding characteristic of children. The result is an obvious pressure upon children to attend.[33]

In 1962 the Supreme Court, in another action brought by parents (*Engel* v. *Vitale*), voided use by New York public schools of a twenty-two-word nondenominational prayer.[34] The prayer was optional for any school and, within any school, no child was required to participate. The Supreme Court nevertheless said: "When the power, prestige, and financial support of government [are] placed behind a particular religious belief, the indirect coercive pressure upon religious minorities to conform to the prevailing officially approved religion is plain."[35]

This decision caused great controversy and was followed the next year by the famous "Bible-reading" and "Lord's Prayer" Supreme Court cases from Pennsylvania and Maryland, respectively. The Court, in this consolidated case (*School District of Abington Township* v. *Schempp*) held unconstitutional state requirements of Bible-reading and prayer programs in the public schools.[36] In each case parents were the plaintiffs. The Court, in a very extensive opinion, said that it was neither attacking religion nor establishing secular humanism. It went on to say that schools could indeed teach religious literature as literature and could offer courses in comparative religion. But although the Court's opinion in *Schempp* settled one controversy, it latently fueled another. The public schools have, by and large, now observed the Court's ban on any form of theistic religious teaching, observance, or exercise in the public school. But the tide that ebbed in the 1960s appears likely to rise again in the 1980s. In a number of communities prayer is now being reintroduced in schools at the insistence of parents and with the consent of school boards. As the evangelical but nonfundamentalist revival in the United States continues, breaches of the Court's ruling in *Schempp* are likely. So long as the Court considers the *Schempp* decision to be a valid and subsisting interpretation of the Constitution, these breaches are not likely to be upheld in the courts. But what sanctions could be applied, or how effectively, is difficult to say. It is growing increasingly clear that there is widespread, though not universal, dissatisfaction with the exclusion of religion from the public schools.

An even more significant development concerns parents who, like the plaintiff parents in the *McCollum, Engel,* and *Schempp* cases, believe their tax funds are being used for the promotion of religion, namely, secular humanism. These parents question how tax funds may be denied to support reading a few verses from the Bible in a public school but may be employed to finance fully a womb-to-tomb program under the name, say, of "health," which deals with the nature of man and the basic problems of human beings in relation to values, virtue, work, sexuality, family, illness, and death, all in terms of secular norms and values. Similarly, other parents are protesting specific public school programs that promote secular values, notably sex education programs, which they feel deeply offend their moral beliefs and which they believe involve matters of familial privacy and the sexual privacy of the child. Little litigation has yet appeared in connection with these protests, but it is safe to predict that the 1980s will witness an intensive struggle by parents in the nation's courts to reverse governmental efforts to foster a secular humanist value regime in public education.[37]

Notes

1. Regina v. Wiebe, (1978) 3 W.W.R. 36. Independent Schools Support Act, 1977, 9 Eliz. 2, ch. 319.

2. Board of Education v. Allen, 392 U.S. 236 (1968); Sanders v. Johnson, 403 U.S. 955 (1971); Lemon v. Kurtzman, 403 U.S. 602 (1971); Sloan v. Lemon, 413 U.S. 825 (1973); Meek v. Pittenger, 421 U.S. 349 (1975); and School District of Pittsburgh v. Pennsylvania State Department of Education, 483 Pa. 539 (1979), *appeal dismissed,* 443 U.S. 901 (1979).

3. In School District of Pittsburgh v. Pennsylvania Department of Education, opponents of Pennsylvania's Nonpublic School Busing Act argued that the fact that the act permitted school districts to transport nonpublic school children beyond the boundaries of their district of residence violated "parity." The courts did not agree.

4. Meek, *supra* at 363.

5. Committee for Public Education v. Nyquist, 413 U.S. 756 (1973).

6. Id.

7. Sloan v. Lemon, *supra.*

8. New York v. Cathedral Academy, 429 U.S. 1089 (1977).

9. Hints of that doctrine are seen at least as early as 1947 in Everson v. Board of Education, 330 U.S. 1 (1947); a further perception of it appears in Allen, *supra.* It remained for the court in Walz v. Tax Commission, 397 U.S. 664 (1970) to state the doctrine extensively.

10. 397 U.S. 664 (1970).

11. *Walz, Lemon,* and *Meek* specify the forbidden entanglements as including "continuing day-to-day relationships," situations that lend themselves to "confrontations and conflicts," relationships "whose very nature is apt to entangle the state in details of administration" of church schools, "negotiations," the need for "government analysis of secular as distinguished from

religious activities,'' ''audits,'' ''sustained and detailed administrative relationships for enforcement of statutory or administrative standards,'' or ''programs
whose very nature is to entangle the state in details of administration.''

12. 262 U.S. 390 (1923).

13. Id. at 398.

14. Id. at 401.

15. Id. at 402.

16. Id.

17. Id.

18. Pierce v. Society of Sisters, 268 U.S. 510 (1925).

19. I have discussed the origins of that statute and its implications in my
chapter ''Pierce: The *Dramatis Personae* Live On,'' in *Freedom and Education:* Pierce *v.* Society of Sisters *Reconsidered,* ed. Donald P. Kommers and
Michael J. Wahoske (Notre Dame, Ind.: Center for Civil Rights, University of
Notre Dame Law School, 1978), pp. 1–10.

20. 268 U.S. 510, 535.

21. Id. at 534.

22. Farrington v. Tokushige, 273 U.S. 284 (1927).

23. Id. at 288.

24. Id. at 298 (italics added).

25. Wisconsin v. Yoder, 406 U.S. 205.

26. Id. at 215.

27. 321 U.S. 158 (1944).

28. Id. at 232 (italics added).

29. State of Vermont v. LaBarge, 134 Vt. 276 (1976); State of Ohio v.
Whisner, 47 Ohio St. 2d 181 (1976); North Carolina v. Columbus Christian
Academy (No. 88314, Franklin Cy., Ct., 1978); and Rudasill v. Kentucky State
Board of Education, 589 S.W. 2d 877 (1980).

30. In *North Carolina* the trial court did not consider those issues but
believed that the state had to an extent exceeded its statutory powers in imposing certain of the regulations. Both sides appealed the case to the North Carolina supreme court, but while the case pended there, the state statutes were
amended in order to protect the religious liberties of parents and religious
schools, and the case became moot.

31. See Caulfield v. Hirsch, 95 L.R.R.M. 3164 (1977), (E.D., Pa. 1977);
McCormick v. Hirsch, 460 F. Supp. 1337 (M.D., Pa. 1978); Grace Brethren
Church v. California, (No. CV 79-93 MRP, C.D. Cal. 1979).

32. McCollum v. Board of Education, 333 U.S. 203 (1948).

33. Id. at 227.

34. 370 U.S. 421 (1962).

35. Id. at 431.

36. 374 U.S. 203 (1963).

37. Of interest in this connection are Torcaso v. Watkins, 367 U.S. 488

(1961); Fellowship of Humanity v. County of Alameda, 153 Cal. App. 2d 673 (1965); and the recent decision of the U.S. Court of Appeals for the Third Circuit, wherein that court banned transcendental meditation programs in New Jersey's public schools, Malnak v. Yogi, 592 F.2d 197 (3rd Cir. 1979).

5 Religious Freedom and Educational Pluralism

Elmer J. Thiessen

A recent case, *Regina* v. *Wiebe,* in the Alberta provincial court made Canadian legal history.[1] It marked the first time that a provincial bill of rights, and specifically the principle of religious freedom, was used to override part of another provincial statute, namely, the compulsory attendance regulations of the School Act.

In the fall of 1977 a group of conservative Mennonites in central Alberta removed their children from the local public school and placed them in a school of their own, even though the Alberta department of education had rejected their earlier application for private school status. This led to the prosecution of one of the parents, Elmer Wiebe, along with forty-four other Mennonite parents, who were similarly charged with contravening the compulsory attendance regulations of the School Act. One of the central issues in the case was that of human rights, which attracted William Pidruchney, an Edmonton lawyer, to enter the case as an *amicus curiae,* or friend of the court, on behalf of the Mennonites. Three issues came to the fore in the position of the Mennonites and the arguments used by Mr. Pidruchney on their behalf.

1. The Mennonites were concerned about the liberal progressive philosophy prevailing in the public school system. They rejected the claim that public schools are religiously neutral, because for them a liberal progressive philosophy is itself a religious position.
2. A central conviction of the Mennonites was that their children should be educated in accordance with their own religious beliefs. This gave rise to Mr. Pidruchney's argument: "The threads of their religious beliefs are tied to education and the exercise of religious freedom in relation thereto."[2] To separate religious education from secular education, as was necessary if they sent their children to the public school, was offensive to the Mennonites. They wanted their own school, where the entire curriculum would reflect their religious faith.
3. Finally, the Mennonites felt that as parents they had the right to educate their children in accordance with their own religious beliefs.[3] Their response to the charge that this was indoctrination was that all approaches to

education involve indoctrination. The choice for the Mennonites, therefore, was not between a neutral public school and an indoctrinating parent or private school but between one form of indoctrination and another.

Each of these issues raises the problem of religious freedom. Their combined force led Judge Oliver to conclude that Elmer Wiebe, and by implication the other forty-four Mennonites, were not guilty because the School Act involved an infringement on their religious freedom.[4] In effect, Judge Oliver was saying that religious freedom entails educational pluralism.

The *Wiebe* case is significant not only from a legal perspective, but also from an educational one. Unfortunately, educators and those legislating education have generally failed to see that there is a problem of religious freedom in the monolithic state system of education prevailing in North America. The *Wiebe* case highlights three aspects of education related to the problem of religious freedom. I wish to deal here with each of these issues in turn from a general, philosophical perspective. First, I examine the argument underlying the claim of the Mennonites that the curriculum of the public school is not religiously neutral. Second, I explore the possibility that interrelations exist between religion and the other forms of knowledge. Third, I consider the argument that religious education necessarily entails indoctrination. Finally, I argue that the affirmation of religious freedom necessarily requires commitment to a policy of educational pluralism.

The Religious Character of Secular Humanism

The generally maintained position with regard to the nature of the public school curriculum is that it should be secular and religiously neutral.[5] The defense of the secular curriculum's religious neutrality is quite simple. It is generally assumed that religion must be defined in terms of a belief in God or in the supernatural.[6] If, therefore, the curriculum is designed in such a way that children are nowhere initiated or indoctrinated into a religious frame of mind, that is, if they are nowhere told to believe in God, then the curriculum is religiously neutral. Of course, this does not preclude teaching *about* religion from a historical, anthropological, or philosophical perspective.[7] What is scrupulously to be avoided, however, is the teaching *of* religion, or inculcating a belief in God.

The fundamental problem with this defense of religious neutrality is that it rests on an inadequate concept of religion.[8] Many of the great world religions, such as early Buddhism, Zen Buddhism, and the Hinayana Buddhism, assume an atheistic stance. Many versions of pantheism tend to identify God with nature and thus make no reference to the supernatural. It is not even adequate for some forms of Christian belief, such as the position defined by the "God is dead'' theologians. It follows, therefore, that we cannot conclude that a curriculum is religiously neutral simply because it does not inculcate belief in God or the supernatural.

What, then, is an adequate definition of religion? I shall consider this question first from a philosophical and then from a legal perspective. R.B. Edwards considers two important proposals for a broader, more adequate definition of religion.[9] He deals first with Paul Tillich, whose definition has gained wide acceptance among both philosophers and theologians. Tillich defines religion as ''the state of being grasped by an ultimate concern.''[10] For Tillich, man defines his existence in terms of a variety of concerns, some of which are more important than others. Careful probing will reveal an underlying concern of an ultimate value, which forms the focal point of a person's existence and which gives meaning and unity to a person's whole life.

Edwards next considers Wittgenstein's suggestion that a word need not have a common meaning. Instead, the objects called by a common name are related to one another by a variety of characteristics that are shared in varying degrees, like family resemblances. Edwards considers the possible family traits of religion, including a belief in a supernatural intelligent being or beings, a complex world view interpreting the significance of human life, belief in experience after death, a moral code, the use of prayer and ritual, the claim that some truths are revealed, a deep and intense concern, and the institutionalized sharing of some of these traits. Some religions may possess all these family traits. Others may possess only some features but would still be called religions. Edwards finds that one or two of these traits, namely, ultimate concern and an answer to the significance of human life, are nearly universal in religion. This seems to reinforce Tillich's definition of religion. Thus, Edwards suggests that the two approaches to defining religion need not be seen as at odds with each other, but rather as complementary.

Is secular humanism a religion? It seems appropriate to describe secular humanists as possessed by an ultimate concern, for they are generally very committed to the promotion of scientific and democratic values. Secular humanism also is characterized by many of the other family traits of religion listed by Edwards: it clearly involves a complex world view that interprets the significance of human life, and it has a moral code. Humanists object to the notion of revealed truth, but some of the presuppositions or first-order principles of science and democracy are in some ways similar to revealed truths, as conceived by the humanist. Presuppositions of science and democracy are also rationally unprovable, unfalsifiable, authoritative, and unquestioned.[11] Secular humanism also involves institutionalized sharing of these traits. In fact, for Dewey and others, the public school is the central vehicle of sharing and transmitting humanistic values and concerns.[12] Within this context we may not find a worship ritual, but there surely is something akin to ritualistic celebrations of the values of democracy and science. Thus, if we adopt a family resemblance approach, it follows that secular humanism must be called a religion.

This conclusion is further confirmed by examination of the legal definition of religion. A recent essay in the *Harvard Law Review,* entitled "Toward a Constitutional Definition of Religion," reviews the definitions of religion presupposed by the U.S. Supreme Court pronouncements concerning the two religion clauses of the First Amendment.[13] Initially religion was clearly understood as entailing a relationship of man to some supreme being. Beginning in the 1940s this traditional understanding of religion came under increasing challenge. In 1961 the Supreme Court interpreted the Establishment Clause as applying also to nontheistic faiths and explicitly identified Buddhism, Taoism, ethical culture, and secular humanism as religions. Since then the Court has consistently adopted an expansive definition of religion, closely parallel to Paul Tillich's analysis of the essence of religion as involving "ultimate concern." The *Review* concludes that the free exercise clause of the First Amendment is in fact best interpreted in terms of this broader definition of religion.[14]

It seems, therefore, that there is considerable agreement that religion should be defined in a broader sense to include nontheistic faiths.[15] Given this more comprehensive definition of religion, it is difficult to avoid concluding that secular humanism is a religion. Many would agree with the Alberta Mennonites in viewing secularism or humanism as a religion. If so, we need to confront some of the educational implications of this view. The fundamental question, dealt with in a later section, is: If secular humanism is a religion, is there not a violation of religious freedom in our public schools?

Religion and Other Forms of Knowledge

Another assumption concerning religion underlies the argument that a curriculum can be secular and religiously neutral. It is generally assumed that religious knowledge is not related to the rest of knowledge, and that religion can therefore be isolated from the remainder of the curriculum. It is then argued that religious neutrality can be achieved in the public school in one of two ways. Religion can be taught as a separate course, within carefully defined parameters so as to ensure neutrality; so students are taught only "about" religion. The second way to achieve neutrality is to avoid all religious instruction in the public school, leaving this aspect of education to the home or the church, for those who so desire. This argument presupposes a certain view of the structure of knowledge. I wish to evaluate this argument and its view of the structure of knowledge within the context of the now classic curriculum theory of R.S. Peters and Paul H. Hirst.[16]

Hirst and other curriculum theorists have analyzed the rationale behind the traditional division of knowledge into subjects, disciplines, or areas of research.

Hirst argues that there is a definite structure to knowledge that provides the basis for the subject divisions common in school curricula. He identifies several "forms of knowledge," each distinguishable in terms of certain concepts peculiar to that form, a distinctive logical structure, and unique criteria of truth.[17] Hirst usually treats religion as one of the forms of knowledge, although he sometimes expresses doubts about this.[18] Here, I assume that religion is a form of knowledge, although, as I point out later, I do not believe my argument is entirely invalid if this assumption is not granted.

For the argument under consideration, the important feature of Hirst's curriculum theory is his claim that human knowledge can be divided into a number of irreducible forms that are "logically distinct, autonomous, independent, unique, fundamental."[19] While admitting the possibility of some elements, concepts, and logical laws common to all the forms, Hirst contends that something unique to each form still remains. This aspect of Hirst's theory seems to suggest that religion can be isolated from the other forms of knowledge.

Another feature of Hirst's analysis, however, undermines the possibility of isolating religion from the other forms of knowledge. Though stressing that each form is ultimately unique and irreducible, Hirst points out that this does not mean that the forms of knowledge are entirely independent of one another. Instead, he repeatedly insists that the forms are interrelated.[20] This explains why "one discipline often makes extensive use of the achievements of another."[21] Thus, scientific knowledge, for example, is found to be relevant to the problems considered in other forms. Hirst even expresses sympathy with the notion of an "overall hierarchical pattern" of logical relations between the forms.[22] He feels, however, that we have not mapped the structure of knowledge in enough detail to be able to specify the exact nature of the interrelations of the forms of knowledge. Nevertheless, he remains firm in his claim that these logical interrelations exist.

We can now apply Hirst's analysis to the argument that religious neutrality can be achieved in the public school by isolating religion from the rest of the curriculum. I agree with Hirst that a school curriculum must do justice to both the independence of each form of knowledge and the interrelations among them. I argue, however, that Hirst and other defenders of a religiously neutral curriculum are slighting those interrelations. If the forms of knowledge are logically interrelated, as Hirst maintains, then it is impossible to divorce religion completely from the other forms.

P.J. Sheehan, after acknowledging Peters's and Hirst's analysis of education and the structure of knowledge, stresses, as I have, the logical interrelations among the forms of knowledge. This leads him to certain conclusions concerning religious education. He argues that "religious education cannot be regarded as simply the study of an independent and sharply defined area of knowledge." Instead, all our experience needs "to be re-interpreted in the light of a religious vision." Sheehan further maintains that the interrelation between religious education and the initiation into the other forms of knowledge is a two-way process. Not only does religious education involve the attempt "to understand apparently non-religious experience in religious terms," but it also "draws continually on the resources of other disciplines in the clarification and justification of its central religious concepts."[23]

There is an important objection to such an argument, namely, that I have not shown exactly *how* religious knowledge is related to the other forms. In fact, it seems difficult to show how beliefs in physics, mathematics, or history are interrelated with beliefs in religion. After all, what difference could religion make to such claims as $2 + 2 = 4$, Caesar crossed the Rubicon and $E = mc^2$? Even some Christian scholars deny the relevance of religion to the other forms of knowledge: Aelred Graham, for example, argues against the idea of a Catholic or noncatholic mathematics of physics.[24]

In reply to this objection, one might first want to agree with Hirst that "we have not as yet begun to understand the complex inter-relations of the different forms of knowledge."[25] To conclude from our current inability to show precisely how the forms are interrelated, that there are no interrelations, however, is simply fallacious. Further, we must be careful not to demand of the religious person that he must first show the *logical relation* between "God exists" and "$2 + 2 = 4$" before any kind of connection is admitted. Unfortunately, Hirst lends some support to this sort of demand by talking about "logical inter-relations," or a "logical hierarchy." Elsewhere, however, he indicates other types of connections that need to be explored.[26] Others have proposed various models to explain the relation between religion and the other forms of knowledge.[27] It should be noted that some of these proposals do not require that religion itself be a form of knowledge. It is for this reason that I suggested earlier that the argument of this section is not entirely invalid even if religion is not a form of knowledge.

My primary concern has been to argue that there is an interrelation between religion and the other forms of knowledge. Because it is beyond the scope of this discussion to describe the precise nature of this connection, my conclusions in this section must remain somewhat tentative. It should further be noted that so far we have dealt only with the general relation of religion to the forms of knowledge. A complete analysis of this relation would have to take into account the specific content of religion and the forms of knowledge. Justice would also have to be done to the fact that there are different claims and theories competing for acceptance within each of the forms of knowledge, including religion. Here I merely wish to suggest that if there are interrelations among the different forms of knowledge generally, then it is plausible to conclude that the content accepted in one form of knowledge will be somehow interrelated with the content in another form.

Taking into account various strands of the argument so far, we can make an even stronger case against the idea that a curriculum can be secular and religiously neutral. Given that secular humanism is a religion, and thus one of the theories competing for acceptance within the religious form of knowledge, and given that the content of the religious form of knowledge is necessarily interrelated with the content of all the other forms, then the entire curriculum will be influenced by the religious vision of secular humanism. The notion of a secular, religiously neutral curriculum is therefore self-contradictory.

These considerations help us to understand why some Christian parents are so concerned to establish schools whose curriculum reflect their Christian beliefs. If the content of the religious form of knowledge is somehow interrelated with the content of the other forms of knowledge, then all courses should reflect a Christian orientation. For the Christian, all truth is God's truth. The presupposition of God's existence cannot be divorced from the rest of a school curriculum; this constitutes the strength of Pidruchney's argument in the defense of the Mennonites of Alberta that *the threads of their religious beliefs are tied to education.*

Assuming that the argument so far is sound, it follows that the question is not "whether" but "which" religion is being implicitly and explicitly taught in the various courses offered in a school. Is the curriculum being interpreted in the light of the religion of secular humanism or Christianity or some other religion? This is the question of central concern in dealing with the protection of religious freedom.

The Curriculum and Indoctrination

Another argument frequently used to support the idea that a curriculum can be religiously neutral involves an appeal to the danger of religious indoctrination. For many, the teaching of religion is a paradigm of indoctrination.[28] This problem is thought to be especially acute within church-related schools.[29] It is generally assumed that public schools are largely exempt from indoctrination, either because no religion is taught or, if it is, because it is taught so as to avoid indoctrination, for example, by teaching about religion.[30] Thus, again religious neutrality is maintained and the public school is seen as the key to avoiding the evils so prevalent in the church, in the church-related school, and in the home.

Although the concept of indoctrination has attracted much attention from contemporary analytic philosophers, there is still far from general agreement as to the meaning of indoctrination. This lack of consensus in itself suggests that the argument of the previous paragraph is already problematic. If we do not know what indoctrination means, can we be sure that there is a problem of indoctrination in church-related schools, or that public schools entirely avoid it?

R.S. Peters and Paul Hirst describe education in terms of the initiation of an individual into the forms of knowledge. The term *initiation* figures significantly in descriptions of liberal educations.[31] Peters even suggests there is some similarity between initiation and socialization.[32] But exactly what is involved in this process of initiation, especially in its early stages? I suggest that this process must be described in terms of indoctrination, on the basis of the criteria generally accepted by Peters, Hirst, and others who have advocated the notion of liberal education discussed above. I will focus on only one aspect of the initiation process in order to support this conclusion. The process of initiation is necessarily authoritarian. The parent, the teacher, or society determines what public traditions the child is initiated into. The child does not have a choice here. Teaching that is constrictive or authoritarian and that violates the principles of liberty and respect for persons, however, is generally associated with indoctrination.[33] It therefore seems that initiation necessarily involves indoctrination.

Peters and White argue that the child's lack of choice over the content of initiation does not involve indoctrination because this need not involve a misuse of authority, and will eventually lead to an autonomous state.[34] But surely this is to beg the question. To point to future results of an authoritative situation is to sidestep the real issue, which involves the initial stages of the initiation process, when the child is not given a choice. Further, Peters's distinction between a proper and an improper use of authority is not at all clear. Peters himself in some recent essays has admitted that there is still a need to clarify this and other ambiguities or dilemmas inherent in liberal education.[35]

Indeed, many philosophers conclude that indoctrination is unavoidable.[36] The unavoidability of indoctrinatory teaching methods is one of the fundamental obstacles to a consensus about the characteristics of indoctrination. This problem has also led to confusion as to whether or not indoctrination is a pejorative term. In my view, a feature generally associated with the pejorative sense of indoctrination is unavoidable in the initiation of children into the forms of knowledge. One of the basic reasons for the frequent charge of religious indoctrination has to do with the fact that the religious instruction of children has an involuntary component. Children do not choose which religion they are initiated into; either the parents or the church must make this choice. Yet, the problem of a child's inability to choose the traditions into which he is initiated is a problem that applies to the teaching of all the forms of knowledge, not just the religious tradition. If, therefore, we do not wish to label this as indoctrination, we should not accuse religious parents or teachers of indoctrinating on the grounds that they do not respect the freedom of the child. The child is simply not autonomous; someone has to make a choice for the child, and it is inconsistent to view this as acceptable in the teaching of certain forms of knowledge but unacceptable in the teaching of religion.

The problem of compulsory initiation (or indoctrination) into the forms of knowledge is further complicated by the fact that the forms of knowledge are not religiously neutral. The public school is initiating children into the religion of secular humanism, and compulsory attendance and a compulsory curriculum leave children with no choice about their initiation. Surely, as the Mennonites argued, this should be just as objectionable as initiating children into the Christian religion in a Christian school.[37]

The Educational Consequences of Religious Freedom

We say we believe in religious freedom. This fundamental principle is reaffirmed in the Canadian Bill of Rights, the U.S. Constitution, and the Universal Declaration of Human Rights. I contend, however, that in the area of education we do not practice what we preach. I believe the public school system—the predominant pattern of education in North America—necessarily involves a violation of religious freedom.

Secular humanism is at the heart of the curriculum of the public schools of North America, and secular humanism is a religion; therefore, the public schools are not religiously neutral. Furthermore, the religion of secular humanism pervades the entire curriculum of the public school because religious presuppositions are in some way related to the other forms of knowledge. The child attending the public school is not given a choice of which religious tradition he is being initiated into. Surely it is a violation of religious freedom to impose this single religion on all students, some of whom are from different religious backgrounds?

The fact that in North America the government generally supports and controls public education is especially critical for the problem of religious freedom. This can best be illustrated by referring to the two religion clauses of the First Amendment of the U.S. Constitution: "Congress shall make no law respecting an establishment of religion, or prohibiting the free exercise thereof. . . ." But if public education is supported and controlled by the state, and the curriculum of the public school is imbued with a secular humanistic orientation, and if, as I have argued, secular humanism is a religion, then surely the public school system is invalidated by the Establishment Clause of the First Amendment. Hence, I agree with David J. Vold, who, after arguing for a broader definition of religion, bluntly concludes that secular public education is unconstitutional.[38]

Although these arguments lend support to Christian parents who want a Christian education for their children, it does not provide support to those calling for a return to a more Christian-oriented education in the public schools. If it is objectionable to impose a humanistically oriented curriculum on Christians, then it is equally objectionable to impose a Christian curriculum on students of other religious backgrounds. Any attempt to retain certain Christian practices in the public schools, or even to "Christianize" the public schools, is incompatible with the principle of religious freedom.

If a system of public education with a common curriculum, of either a Christian or a secular nature, is acknowledged to be objectionable because it violates religious freedom, what is the alternative? I suggest that the only way to achieve religious freedom is to allow for a greater degree of pluralism in education. This pluralism could be achieved in a number of ways. It might be possible to leave the structure of the present system intact and design a pluralistic curriculum that recognizes Christian and other interpretations of reality. Or, we might arrange for a variety of schools within a city or school district, each with its own distinctive approach and curriculum, but all operating under the umbrella of the public system of education. Or, finally, we might want to dispense entirely with a state-supported and controlled system of education and thus provide for a more comprehensive pluralism that deals with both the content and structure of education. These suggestions are in no way new. John Stuart Mill, for example, in an eloquent defense of freedom of thought, warned against the dangers of a state system of education and suggested that the proper role of government in education be limited to ensuring that every child get a good education. The choice of where and how the child should be educated is best left to the parents.[39]

Notes

1. Regina v. Wiebe, 3 W.W.R. 36 (1978). My brief summary of this case draws upon both the provincial court decision and Joanne Levy, "In Search of Isolation: The Holdeman Mennonites of Linden, Alberta, and Their School," *Canadian Ethnic Studies* 11, no. 1 (1979), pp. 115–130; and *St. John's Edmonton Report*, 30 January 1978, pp. 27–30; and 13 February 1978, pp. 30–34.

2. Regina v. Wiebe at 48.

3. Id. at 62.

4. Ibid.

5. D.J. Vold, "A Case for Religion in the Public Schools," *Educational Theory* 24 (Winter 1974):102; School District of Abington v. Schempp, 374 U.S. 222, 299 (1963); Paul H. Hirst, *Knowledge and the Curriculum* (London: Routledge and Kegan Paul, 1974), p. 182; William Frankena, "Public Education and the Good Life," *Harvard Educational Review* 31 (Fall 1961):414; M.R. Lupul, "Religion and Education in Canada: A Call for an End to Hypocrisy," *Journal of Educational Thought* 3 (December 1969):144, 148.

6. Frankena, "Public Education," p. 419; Lupul, "Religion and Education in Canada," p. 141; Hirst, *Knowledge and the Curriculum*, p. 44.

7. Hirst, *Knowledge and the Curriculum*, pp. 182, 187; Frankena, "Public Education," p. 414; Lupul, "Religion and Education in Canada," p. 146.

8. This point is made by Vold, "Religion in the Public Schools," p. 103.

9. R.B. Edwards, *Reason and Religion: An Introduction to the Philosophy of Religion* (New York: Harcourt Brace Jovanovich, 1972), p. 6.

10. Quoted ibid., p. 7; see also "Toward a Constitutional Definition of Religion," *Harvard Law Review* 91 (March 1978):1066.

11. I have argued this point at length in my dissertation, "Indoctrination, Education and Religion: A Philosophical Analysis" (Ph.D. diss., University of Waterloo, 1980), pp. 151–264.

12. John Dewey, *Education Today*, ed. Joseph Ratner (New York: Greenwood Press, 1969), pp. 74–86, 144–149, 348–370.

13. "Toward a Constitutional Definition of Religion," pp. 1056–1089.

14. Ibid., pp. 1072–83.

15. Frankena acknowledges that religion can be defined as "any kind of ultimate creed," in which case "even atheism and naturalism are religions," but he limits himself to a narrower definition without giving any reason for doing so, "Public Education," p. 419. John Dewey, in *Education Today*, clearly identifies secular humanism as a religion, pp. 17, 74–86, 144–149.

16. R.S. Peters, *Ethics and Education* (London: Allen and Unwin, 1966); Hirst, *Knowledge and the Curriculum;* P.H. Hirst and R.S. Peters, *The Logic of Education* (London: Routledge and Kegan Paul, 1970).

17. Hirst, *Knowledge and the Curriculum*, p. 44.

18. Both Hirst and Peters frequently list religion as one of the seven or eight forms of knowledge. Hirst, *Knowledge and the Curriculum*, pp. 44, 88, 137, 144; Peters, *Ethics and Education*, p. 50; Hirst and Peters, *The Logic of Education*, p. 64. At times, however, Hirst expresses doubts about this, pp. 65, 180. Moreover, in one essay he suggests that some recent work in the philosophy of religion seems to offer hope for including religion as a form of knowledge, p. 185. I have argued elsewhere that on Hirst's own criteria, religion must be a form of knowledge; E.J. Thiessen and L.J. Roy Wilson, "Curriculum in the Church-State Controversy: Are the Mennonites Justified in Rejecting the Public School Curriculum?" *Salt: Journal of the Religious Studies and Moral Education Council*, 1 (Spring 1979):16–20.

19. Hirst, *Knowledge and the Curriculum*, pp. 84, 137.

20. Ibid., pp. 89, 138, 145, 150.

21. Ibid., p. 52.

22. Ibid., p. 91.

23. P.J. Sheehan, "Religious Education," in *Concepts in Education: Philosophical Studies*, ed. J. V. D'Cruz and P.J. Sheehan. (Melbourne, Australia: A Mercy Teachers' College Twentieth Century Publication, 1973), p. 72.

24. Aelred Graham, "Towards a Catholic Concept of Education in a Democracy," *Harvard Educational Review* 31 (Fall 1961):403.

25. Hirst, *Knowledge and the Curriculum*, pp. 26, 52.

26. Hirst entertains a nonlogical relation in another context when he defends the relevance of philosophic beliefs to educational theory and practice. Here he argues that the part that philosophic beliefs play in educational theory is "not that of axioms in a deductive system." Instead he calls for a "much looser" type of connection between the two, "Philosophy and Educational Theory," *British Journal of Educational Studies* 12 (November 1963):51–64.

27. See, for example, the writings of Wittgenstein, Herman Dooyeweerd, and Michael Polanyi. P.J. Sheehan probably has a nonlogical relation in mind when he describes our experience as being "reinterpreted in the light of a religious vision"; "Religious Education," p. 72.

28. See, for example, John Wilson and Antony Flew in *Concepts of Indoctrination*, ed. I.A. Snook (London: Routledge and Kegan Paul, 1972), pp. 103, 114.

29. See, for example, T.F. Green, Antony Flew, and J.P. White, ibid., pp. 40, 75–77, 120, respectively. See also R.G. Woods and R. St. C. Barrow, *An Introduction to Philosophy of Education* (London: Methuen, 1975), p. 65.

30. Tom Malcom and Harry Fernhout, *Education and the Public Purpose: Moral and Religious Education in Ontario* (Toronto: Curriculum Development Centre, 1979), pp. 20, 22, 24, 27.

31. Peters, *Ethics and Education*, p. 46; Crittenden, "Indoctrination as Mis-education," in Snook, *Concepts of Indoctrination*, p. 138; cf. Hirst, *Knowledge and the Curriculum*, pp. 38, 69.

32. Peters, "Education and Initiation," in *Philosophical Analysis and Education*, ed. R.D. Archambault (London: Routledge and Kegan Paul, 1965), p. 89.

33. Willis Moore, "Indoctrination and Democratic Method," in *Concepts of Indoctrination*, ed. I.A. Snook, p. 93; cf. Flew, "Indoctrination and Doctrines," ibid., p. 86; Crittenden, "Indoctrination as Mis-education," ibid., p. 142; Peters, *Ethics and Education*, pp. 35, 42.

34. Peters tries to distinguish between a proper and an improper use of authority when he describes the teacher-pupil relationship as one in which "the teacher has to learn to be in authority and to be an authority without being authoritarian"; *Authority, Responsibility, and Education*, 3d ed. (London: Allen and Unwin, 1973), pp. 47, 54. J.P. White argues, "We are right to make him unfree now so as to give him as much autonomy as possible later on"; *Towards a Compulsory Curriculum* (London: Routledge and Kegan Paul, 1973), p. 22.

35. R.S. Peters, "Ambiguities in Liberal Education and the Problem of its Content"; "Dilemmas in Liberal Education," in his *Education and the Education of Teachers* (London: Routledge and Kegan Paul, 1977) pp. 47, 68.

36. Richard H. Gatchel, "The Evolution of the Concept," in *Concepts of Indoctrination*, ed. I.A. Snook, p. 15; cf. Thomas F. Green, "Indoctrination

and Beliefs," ibid., p. 45; William H. Kilpatrick, "Indoctrination and Respect for Persons," ibid., pp. 49–51; R.F. Atkinson, "Indoctrination and Moral Education," ibid., p. 57; Moore, "Democratic Method," ibid., p. 96.

37. Robin Barrow has argued this same point, but with regard to the narrower problem of initiating children into either a religious or a nonreligious tradition. Barrow argues that we cannot avoid the issue by suggesting that children's beliefs should not be formed by parents, or by society at all, because they are initially formed in response to their immediate environment. If, therefore, we cannot avoid influencing belief in some way, then surely it is just as objectionable to promote disbelief in God as it is to promote belief in God: "Religion in the Schools," *Educational Philosophy and Theory* 6 (1974): 49–57.

38. Vold, "Religion in the Public Schools," p. 103. A recent editorial in *Christianity Today* makes the same point concerning universities: "But government support of the monopolistic religion of secular humanism in our public universities violates not only the first half of the religion clause of our constitution, it also destroys the second . . . by economically penalizing those who choose to attend Protestant, Catholic, or Jewish colleges or universities, *Christianity Today* 24 (7 November 1980):10.

39. J.S. Mill, *Utilitarianism, Liberty and Representative Government* (London: J.M. Dent & Sons, 1968), p. 160.

6

Constraints on Parents' Rights Concerning the Education of Their Children

Cornel Hamm

Do parents have the right to decide what educational experiences their children should receive? This appears to be the central question in the debate over family choice in schooling. Those who join the debate advance arguments ranging from financial, administrative, and legal considerations to psychological, sociological, and historical ones.[1] All too little attention has been paid to moral and educational considerations, which lie at the core of the issue and upon which this discussion focuses.

The initial question is ambiguous. On the one hand, it can be read as a factual legal question; on the other, it can be viewed as a moral question about the status of parents' rights, whether or not they are institutionalized in a legal system. The legal aspects can be ascertained relatively easily by consulting statutes and/or common law (or perhaps the constitution). The moral aspects require assessment of reasoned arguments to ascertain whether there are grounds for claiming such rights for parents independently of legal considerations. It raises the question: *Should* parents have the right to decide in the legal sense because they *do* have the right in the moral sense? Such arguments require careful examination of the nature and justification of parents' rights over their children and of paternalism in general and how these are related to children's rights. It is with these issues that the first part of this chapter is concerned.

The second part of the chapter is concerned with the nature and importance of education. It attempts to outline an answer to the question: What precisely is it that children (or parents on their behalf) have a right to when it is said they have a right to education? Parental rights of control in education, it will be argued, are significantly different from rights of control in matters other than education. If it is indeed education, rather than some other social concern or childrearing practice, that is at issue, then many of the "family choice" arguments should be viewed in a different light. Accordingly, the final section reconsiders some "pro-choice" arguments from the perspective of education.

In general, what I wish to explore, explain, and elaborate is the following proposition: if children have the right to education, it is *children* who have the right and it is the right to *education*.

Children's Rights

Although my concern here is with the rights of parents, it is necessary to consider first the rights of children, for I shall argue that the rights of parents with respect to their children's education derive from the rights of children; that is, children's rights are the primary consideration in any discussion of parents' rights over them.

Do children have rights? And if so, what is the status of those rights? It is clear that adolescents have moral (and often legal) rights to a considerable degree; and they have them in the same sense and for the same reasons that adults have them, for they share features of personhood characteristic of adults. It can be assumed that rational adults have rights (in the non- or extralegal sense) that are dependent on consensus, contract, special relations, merit, and moral considerations (such as the right to fair treatment), all of which arise as a result of relations between rational autonomous agents. To the degree that children acquire the characteristics of rational agency—the possession of language, beliefs, goals, interests, attitudes, abilities, and so on—they also incrementally acquire moral rights.[2] The gradual acquisition of rights by children and young people complicates the question of parental rights because whatever parents' rights are initially, they must be continuously modified in light of a child's development toward full rational agency. But that is a separate issue. Arguments for paternalism in general and parents' rights in particular must establish that infants and small children in their prerational stage have a right to knowledge and understanding sufficient to enable them to become rational agents even though initially they have no rationality, and the right progressively to acquire more knowledge and understanding to reach a norm considered sufficient for autonomous agency; and that is the central issue with respect to children's rights to education. There seems to be a nearly universal tendency to assert that prerational children have a right to such an education. It seems equally clear that such a right is radically different from what are referred to as "social contract" rights and interpersonal "moral rights."[3] That they are not social contract rights seems obvious from the fact that prerational children are *ex hypothesi* not in a position to make promises, enter into special relationships, make deals, and the like. That they are not of moral rights follows from the fact that they have not yet acquired the fundamental capacities of rational moral agents, "the capacity to experience and enjoy value in all its forms and the capacity to choose among competing alternatives which values to pursue."[4]

With what justification, then, can we assert that prerational children have rights to well-being in general and to education in particular? A number of arguments, only a few of which are here briefly examined, have been advanced, and none is entirely satisfactory. One is the argument from potentiality, which suggests that any being with the potential to become a rational agent, as a normal infant does, ought to become one and, more to the point, has the right to become one, presumably because it is required by rationality that rationality be maximized. This is unsatisfactory because it is both counterintuitive (it leads to the unacceptable view that fetuses, sperm and ova, the chemistry for sperm and ova, and so on are all to be assigned rights) and may very well be counterproductive (because a disproportionate amount of effort and resources devoted to the production of candidates for rational agency may well result in a reduction overall in the achievement of rationality through education).

Another approach is to suggest that although prerational children do not have rights in the normal sense of the word, adults nevertheless have duties toward them, including the duty to educate them. But this is hardly sufficient to establish children's rights, for whatever force the term *rights* possesses by way of the notion of entitlement is vitiated. The success of the argument rests on the questionable supposition that duties and rights can be disentangled, that they are not correlatives. The correlative thesis—that "rights and duties are different names for the same normative relationship"—would have to be shown to be false for this argument to be valid.[5] Arguments to dismantle the correlative thesis are not very convincing. One such argument holds that because prerational children have rights but cannot have duties, rights and duties are noncorrelative. This argument clearly begs the question; for to ask whether adults have duties toward their children *is* to ask whether the children have the corresponding rights.

Nor can we rationally accept a simple unexamined assertion that adults have the duty (and children a corresponding right) without making a case for it. Yet such is the approach taken by those who assert that we know intuitively that prerational children have such rights or that they are God-given. This stand will hardly persuade those who do not have such an intuition or share such a faith and does not constitute a justification.

Still another argument is the claim that adults have duties to children (and the latter corresponding rights) because of a tacit agreement between adults to bring up their children in a socially acceptable manner to ensure continuance of a rationally ordered society. There seems to be considerable force in such an argument; but rather than establishing rights for children it merely shows that we have duties to other adults and that other adults can claim a right against us.

How, then, are we to establish that prerational children have rights, particularly the right to education? It may be appropriate to discuss the rights of prerational children as long as it is recognized that we are doing so in an entirely different sense—the sense in which some functions of language concerning rights proper are appropriated to support and strengthen our fundamental commitments to children. These we can refer to, not surprisingly, as natural human rights. To call rights *natural* is to stress the fact that they are not subject to confirmation by moral argument but are rather expressions of deep-seated natural human urges, in this case the urge to perpetuate the species in its most advanced form. This, shall we say, naturalistic imperative, is of course not a justification of rights and duties proper, but it is why we attach to our bedrock commitment the compelling force usually reserved for expressions of rights proper. Lacking any reasoned argument adequate to justify granting rights proper to prerational children, we can frame the naturalistic imperative hypothetically thus: If we want our children to be *X*, then it follows that we must do certain things. If we want them to be anything at all, it follows that we must provide for their welfare (food, care, shelter, and so on); and if we want them also to be rational autonomous agents, we must provide for a certain kind of education. Depending on the strength of our commitment we can, and some do, adopt the linguistic convention of referring to this commitment as a duty and ascribing to children the benefit of doing our "duty" as though it is their "right." Peffer argues that the advantage of referring to these adult concerns as children's "rights to well-being" is that it adds the pressure of coercion because there is a "conceptual link between rights and coercion."[6] Adopting the language of rights with respect to children, then, reinforces the immeasurable value and sense of kinship we accord to infants, who will become fellow human beings.

To pose the issue of prerational children's rights in the form of a hypothetical imperative also forces us to articulate the conditionals, to state precisely what our fundamental commitments are in terms of our vision of human advancement and fulfillment. Those who view human fulfillment in terms of material success within a rigidly cohesive and controlled society may view the child as a resource for industry and/or the state and will lean toward paternalistic interventions to ensure that the child is properly trained and socialized, the right to such interventions resting primarily with the state. Those who view human achievement in terms of subservience to God (or the church, or Allah) will likely be committed to the indoctrination of children, the right to do so resting with the parents, who acquire the duty as surrogates of the divinity. Those who view the achievement of rational autonomous agency as the human ideal will be committed to the provision of an education commensurate with the achievement of autonomy, including (and primarily) the provision of knowledge and understanding in whatever manner best brings that about. These few options are not, of course, mutually exclusive or exhaustive. They may merely illustrate some trends. Nor are they meant to illustrate that the pursuit of rationality is optional for human beings. We are not, as William Bartley III has persuasively argued in *The Retreat to Commitment*,[7] all doomed to an equally irrational ultimate commitment such that no rational arguments can be advanced in support of rational pursuits. R.S. Peters may well be right when he says that man is "a creature who lives under the demands of reason."[8] These considerations cannot be discussed in detail here. The point is that we articulate rights of prerational children in terms of what it is we want them to become, in terms of our vision of humanity. The issue of parents' rights in education, based, as

I shall argue, on children's rights, must be debated in terms of our conception of what our duty to children is, and thus, of what they have a right to. Assuming the position that man's highest form of achievement is rational autonomous agency, it follows, as Kant clearly articulated,[9] that children cannot be regarded as chattels of parents and as belonging to them simply by virtue of their biological tie. Parents' rights are limited by both logical and empirical considerations that enhance the child's becoming a rational autonomous agent, for this is what the child, from the liberal rational perspective, has a right to.

If we assume that children have a right (even if only in this revised sense of the word) to an education conducive to rational autonomy, we can then argue that parents' rights over them are derived from this right.

Parents' Rights over Their Children

One class of rights proper that is all too often overlooked is the right that arises as a consequence of duties. It is a fundamental, if commonplace, observation in moral discourse that "the ought implies the can." It could not be the case that anyone ought to do something or other that he cannot do. Provided, however, that a person can and ought to do something, it follows that he must have the right (say, to freedom) to do so. If I have a duty to provide you with a meal and am able to do so, I must be given the right to do so; that is, I must be given the freedom to do so, and perhaps even the resources to do so, and so on. I submit that adults' rights, including parents' rights, over children are primarily of this sort. In the first instance children have rights and adults corresponding duties. But because adults have the duty, they in turn acquire rights, the rights to freedom and access to perform their duty. It is because of the duties parents have to their children that certain rights over their children accrue to them. This is quite a different concept from the view that children are the property of parents or the state or someone else and that the parent or the state or someone else has some self-evident right to do with them as he pleases. No one has an a priori right over children. Nevertheless, given that small children are incapable of acquiring on their own what is their right, paternalism in some form is inevitable. The question now becomes: who, the parent or the state or someone else, has the right to paternalistic agency? On this question the argument of Amy Guttman is very persuasive.[10] She argues that from a liberal perspective the answer will depend on who can best satisfy the interests of children, leaving open the possibility that it may not be the parent, even though it is usually conceded that parents are in the best position to do so. There may indeed be good pragmatic reasons for according to parents the duty (and the corresponding paternalistic right) to provide children with *some* basic welfare needs—affection, food, shelter. These reasons are connected with natural parental affection, intimate knowledge of the child, parental sense of duty stemming from the fact that parents (at least sometimes, and perhaps increasingly so) deliberately bring the child into being, and so on. We can then agree that parents have the presumption of right in certain areas concerned with children's well-being. But there may be equally good grounds for suggesting that this may not extend to another primary need—education. Indeed, that is the position I shall defend below. In any case, the question is now theoretically open to empirical assessment. The question "Who has the right?" becomes relatively unimportant, and "Who has the competence?" of preeminent importance. To assess competence requires clear understanding of the criteria. The debate then must shift to the conceptual and epistemological issues concerning education.

What Is the Right to Education?

Assuming, then, that prerational children have a right to education by virtue of our commitment to perpetuate the species according to our vision of the human being as a rational autonomous agent, what more precisely are we committed to when we assume the duty to provide education? More particularly, what would be the content of children's right to education? And who is competent to decide this? Guttman argues that content will "depend upon what is adequate for living a full life within their [a particular child's] society—for being capable of choosing among available conceptions of the good and of participating intelligently in democratic politics. . . ."[11] In this she agrees with Haydon, whose notion of right to education is equivalent to "a right to socialization."[12] But this is surely an impoverished notion of education. It may be that a particular socialization in a sophisticated society may simultaneously result in education. That will depend upon whether or not the society is an educated one. There are shared characteristics between socialization and education. But surely the right to education is much more specific and more demanding than the right to socialization. Injunctions to provide children with education, as in the United Nations Charter, are certainly not synonymous with socialization. Indeed, such an injunction needs to be invoked sometimes precisely because children have been merely socialized. I am not contending that children should not be socialized, but rather that in some contexts socialization alone is insufficient. Melden asks, "Do children have the right to an education designed to provide them with an understanding of their cultural and political heritage along with those skills necessary for their effective participation in the society into which they are born? Surely they ought to receive such education."[13] Yes, surely, in some cases. At least that much may be necessary as a precondition for acquiring rational autonomous agency; but it does not guarantee it. Only if such an education can guarantee rationality as well as autonomy has the right to education been realized. In some societies a child may acquire the minimum competency to participate effectively and still lack rationality. One can imagine a social group in which children participate in social practices based on myths, lies, and blinding dogma. It is doubtful in such cases that we could speak of autonomy, let alone rational autonomy.

If it is rational autonomous agency we deem children have a right to, then both much more and much less is being implied by the right to education. What is implied is an introduction to and at least elementary mastery of a full complement of categories of rationality, enabling free and intelligent choice. Despite the fact that unreflective people sometimes still fail to distinguish between education and career training, between education and general childrearing, between education and socialization, between education and indoctrination; it is becoming quite apparent to those whose business it is to reflect on the nature of education that something more specific and more important is represented by the term *education*. It does indeed represent initiation of newborn members of a society into those elements of the society's culture that are deemed most valuable. Education, that is to say, is a normative concept. But it represents also a great deal of knowledge; not merely isolated bits of free-floating inert knowledge, but knowledge in breadth and depth, with understanding, corresponding attitudes and sensitivities, and a sense of the distinctiveness and interrelatedness of various kinds of knowledge. As such, it represents a mastery of extant conceptual schemes around which experience and knowledge are structured as well as mastery of various ways of testing for knowledge and of organizing facts. These modes of knowledge and experience—logic and mathematics, physical sciences, history and the social sciences, aesthetics, rational morality—are the fundamentals of man's achievement as a rational being. They are embedded in our language, our traditions, our institutions; they are public in character, and they represent the basic ingredients for the development of the rational mind.[14] There is, in other words, a conceptual link between knowledge and rationality and between both of these and education.

In general, then, the right to education is not explicable in terms of the right to participate in the particular social order into which a child happens to be born. There is, however, a sense in which the right to education is contingent upon a particular society. In any given society education will compete with other goods, and an individual's right to it will be limited by availability and fair distribution. But assuming there are no severe restrictions on the means to provide education, the right to it is not restricted in its nature and quality to a particular society. Genuine education can be claimed by every child against the whole world. The quantity of education is locally limited; but the nature and quality of education, by reason of its conceptual link with knowledge and truth, is independent of a particular society.

If that is so, the grounds are clear for claiming that on the question of who (the parent or state) has the right to decide on the content of education, the presumption must be that that right rests with the state, or the state and professionals, or at least within the wider society. The reason for this is that knowledge and truth are public in character. And, relying on Mill's argument[15] that truth will flourish better in a free marketplace of ideas, it seems reasonable to suggest that competency to decide on content rests in the wider community.

Because Mill's principle is an empirical one, however, all that it entitles us to claim is that there is a presumption that the society at large—and in a democratic society, the state—is more competent than an individual parent or a small group of parents to fulfill the paternalistic duty of providing education. It is, however, only a presumption. In any particular society at any given time the facts may dictate otherwise. The state, with the majority of citizens behind it, might very well be bent on a program of indoctrination or politicization or narrow functional training that could reduce the level of rationality acquired by the child in school. In such cases, the parent or a group of parents may well be more competent to carry out paternalistic responsibility with respect to choice of content. The strongest case that can be made for parents' rights, and possibly for private schools, is the contention that the public school has ceased to function as an educational institution. Once the conceptual criteria for education, based on an analysis of rationality, knowledge, and truth, are laid bare, the question of competence can be empirically adjudicated. There is, then, to repeat a point, no a priori reason why the right to decide on content should rest with the parent or the teacher or anyone else. Whoever claims the right may do so only if he can demonstrate superior competence in choosing for the child those experiences that will enhance the child's rationality, for that is what the child has a right to and what we have a duty to provide.

The child, then, has a right to paternalistic action enabling him to become a rational autonomous agent. Because there is a conceptual connection between rationality and education, it follows that the child's educational right is limited to those experiences that will enhance his rationality. These experiences must be distinguished from other experiences a child may also have a right to—the right to be socially competent and adept, the right to be skilled enough to make a living, the right to care and protection, and so on. Failure to maintain or acknowledge this distinction has resulted in muddled thinking by those who argue that parents should have the right to decide what kinds of schools their children should attend. Let us briefly examine some of these "pro-choice" arguments.

Some Pro-Choice Arguments Considered

In *Education by Choice: The Case for Family Control,* Coons and Sugarman argue that the family is in the best position to decide what is in the best educational interest of the child.[16] Agreeing with the principle of subsidiarity (responsibility for dependents should rest with the smallest and most intimate social groups with whom the dependent is involved), they suggest that the family is most likely to satisfy a child's best interest, including his schooling, because the parent cares for, listens to, and has the most intimate knowledge of the child. The presumption that the parents have the right to provide for a child's general welfare (food, shelter, and so on) because their judgment is superior regarding an individual child's needs, is extended to include the right over a child's educational welfare. "By shifting to family choice in education we mean to bring that field more in line with society's treatment of child-rearing generally."[17] "Education would be chosen by the family in the way that a food stamp family decides what it eats."[18] And there is the problem. By incorporating education with childrearing, Coons and Sugarman clearly indicate that their concept of education is not commensurate with rational autonomous agency, for there is little similarity between a child's (or family's) private preference for food and the public principles that govern knowledge and understanding required for rationality. Indeed there is very little one can discover about the content of an education or about a child's educational needs by studying individual children. These are largely problems in epistemology and ethics. Given that intimate knowledge of a child's interests and wishes is unnecessary for selecting educational content (teaching methods and instructional sequencing might be more relevant concerns), it is pointless to decry, as they do, that in public schools "students and teachers are assigned to one another in an impersonal process," an alleged defect that the exercise of family choice is intended to correct.[19] What is even more problematic in the Coons and Sugarman argument is the subtle shift to combine children's needs with parents' interests under the rubric of family interests, and it is family which has the presumption of the right to choose. Thus the "family" (parents?) should have the right to impose "preferr[ed] religious education or a political indoctrination different from that presently imposed in public school."[20] Again there is evidence that Coons and Sugarman do not or cannot distinguish between education and indoctrination. I by no means want to defend public schools that indoctrinate students, but it is unacceptable to argue that there is no alternative to indoctrination. There are numerous arguments that competently distinguish between education and indoctrination, and it is now clear not only that indoctrination is not education, but also that it is antithetical to education. And not only do children not have the right to be indoctrinated; they have a right *not* to be indoctrinated, for indoctrination can severely inhibit the development of autonomous rational agency. So the Coons and Sugarman argument to establish parental right on the basis of parents' superior knowledge of the needs and wants of children cannot be sustained. It just is not, educationally speaking, necessary for schools to serve the wants of families or children (or the state or teacher, for that matter) pure and simple, unless the wants coincide with the child's right to become a rational autonomous agent through genuine education. Just because "many children and their families might prefer programs emphasizing science, the classics, McGuffy's reader, music, the Baltimore Catechism, or the sayings of Chairman Mao''[21] but do not find them served in the local public schools, it does not follow that anything is amiss in the school and that somehow the child's right to an education (or the parent's right on the child's behalf) has been in the least abrogated. Parents in theory (and often in practice) might well oppose genuine education precisely because education toward rational agency is antithetical to their doctrinal interests and private preferences. Parental frustration (and equally the child's, the teacher's or the state's) overt failure to achieve their preferred results in schools may at times be the surest indication that the child's right to education is satisfied.

Another type of argument advanced in favor of family choice concerns the allegedly advantageous position of family to influence the child's moral development.[22] The argument goes like this:

1. Neutrality in values is not conducive to moral development.
2. The public school, with some exceptions, attempts to be value neutral.
3. Parents' choice of schools ensures that the school, by taking on parental values, or at least the values of the local group, will not be neutral.
4. Under these conditions children will more readily develop morally.

This argument is seriously flawed and demands fuller criticism than can briefly be given here. It seems correct to suggest that moral neutrality is not conducive to the development of morality. It is improbable that a child will learn to be moral if he is taught nothing and has no model to follow. Only if the values taught and exemplified are moral ones will the desired moral development occur. Not just any values will do. It might well be the case that the imposition of nonmoral, private, idiosyncratic preferences undermines moral development. With respect to private, subjective values it may be entirely appropriate for the school (and perhaps parents as well) to remain neutral. Has a parent, or anyone, a right to impose on a child arbitrary matters of taste? On nonarbitrary values, such as aesthetics and academic disciplines, the public school has not been nor attempted to be neutral. The whole point of operating a school at all is to transmit knowledge and understanding deemed to be of value; so it is false to suggest that public schools are neutral. It is also false to suggest that public schools are neutral with respect to moral values. If the public school is a genuine educational institution, inculcating breadth as well as depth of knowledge and understanding, then it attempts to introduce children to all logical forms of rationality, including rational morality. This possibility, of course, rests on the view that there is a form of rule-governed ethical discourse with intersubjective, universal rational principles. These fundamental principles—fairness and equality, freedom, consideration of interests, truthfulness, and respect for persons—and derivative principles—such as nondiscrimination, specific freedoms, being kind, keeping promises, and so on—are and have long been justifiably incorporated within the tradition of the public school.

Imagine a school attempting to operate without the principle of telling the truth! Is not the process of any education, including the learning of language, premised on telling the truth? The public school does not operate in a moral vacuum. This is not to say that it is doing an adequate job of moral education; nor is it to deny that the public school is often extremely confused on this issue. But it does mean that it can and should be doing an adequate job. And if it does, the pro-choice argument crumbles. It crumbles because of false assumptions about the public school, because of failure to distinguish between various sorts of values, and because it leaves undefended the suggestion that parents in the alternative model will indeed be teaching moral values rather than religious or other nonmoral idiosyncratic values.

The pro-choice argument based on the failure of professionals to agree on teaching method and content also cannot be sustained. Why, because teachers cannot agree on content and method, does it follow that parents should have the right to decide? If there is no "best way," then surely it is foolish for parents to claim the right to decide what that best way is.

This list of pro-choice arguments is not exhaustive. But even a brief examination of the pro-choice position suggests that one major purpose of the arguments advanced is to camouflage an intent other than improved education. This intent is to make room for religious indoctrination. A recent joint study by the Educational Research Institute of British Columbia and the University of San Francisco's Center for Research on Private Education found that over half of the parents questioned cited religious influence as their main reason for sending their children to independent schools.[23] A growing number of parents are seeking the right so to influence their children. But if what I have argued here is correct, then the question must be decided in terms of the child's right to become a rational autonomous agent. The question of parents' rights in this connection is relatively trivial compared to the difficult epistemological issues of whether religion constitutes a form of knowledge (as distinct from mere belief or dogma); of whether religious education proper is possible (as distinct from religious indoctrination or from learning about religion); of whether or not we are hampering children from developing into autonomous rational agents when we teach them that matters of faith are indistinguishable from matters of knowledge and truth and that as a result there is as much evidence for the Pope's infallibility as for the second law of thermodynamics or for the principle of telling the truth.

Conclusion

We set out to explore the proposition: *if* children have a right to education, then it is *children* who have this right and it is the right to *education*. The hesitation to ascribe rights to prerational children stems from the assessment that there is still lacking a convincing argument to establish that they have rights in the normal sense of that term. Nevertheless, we can proceed to talk as if they do and thereby bind ourselves to the fundamental commitment to perpetuate the species in the most advanced form. Those whose commitment is to a vision of man as a rational autonomous agent are committed to an education conceived of as initiating children into all extant forms of rationality—forms constituting autonomous conceptual schemes around which the mind is formed and knowledge becomes possible. This freedom of knowledge is central to autonomous agency. Because of the conceptual link between rationality and knowledge and between knowledge and education, and further because knowledge is essentially public in character, it follows that there is a presumption in favor of a wider public (in a democratic society, probably the state) having the right to make decisions on the content of education. If public schools are devoted to education proper, then much of the debate of who has the right to decide recedes into oblivion. The debate then centers around epistemological issues and about specific facts regarding conpetency. Parents' rights in education are thus limited by their specific duties to provide an education leading to rational autonomy. This will consist largely of the right to decide on the child's general welfare needs and the preconditions for education. On the central educational question, the content of education, the right is the parents' only when the wider public demonstrably fails in its task. This is not because the public has an a priori right either, but because the child, on the way to becoming a rational autonomous agent, has a right to public forms of knowledge and to public truth.

There are, of course, those who take a more cynical and skeptical view of the possibility of attaining knowledge. For them, all education is merely a matter of conditioning and/or indoctrination into a favored point of view. Even the notion of rationality is only another dogma, another doctrine. Coons and Sugarman concur with Chesterton's remarks that "Dogma is actually the only thing that cannot be separated from education. It is education."[24] Their implied conclusion is that because children have to be indoctrinated in schools in any circumstance, it might as well be the favored doctrine of the parent. But surely this is fundamentally mistaken. Just because children need to be taught something if they are to receive an education, it does not follow that it must be dogma or doctrine. Paternalism does not imply indoctrination. It is a contradiction in terms to suggest that education, when it means initiation into forms of rational understanding, is nothing but indoctrinating people with rationality. That is simply a definitional point. The substantive point, that rationality is of limited value, is incoherent. For to be in a position to arrive at such a viewpoint is to subscribe to the value that is being denied. There are no rational grounds to refute rationality. To claim that there is no such thing as rationality, no such thing as knowledge, is virtually to claim that there is no such thing as education. And if education thus becomes impossible, it seems curiously contradictory for those who hold such a view to claim that parents should have the right to decide what it should be.

Notes

1. See, for example, J.E. Coons and S.D. Sugarman, *Education by Choice: The Case for Family Control* (Berkeley: University of California Press, 1978).

2. For a good argument in support of gradualism with respect to children's rights see D.G. Brown, "The Rights of Children," *Journal of Education, University of British Columbia* 17 (1971):8–20.

3. Rodney Peffer, "A Defense of Rights to Well-Being," *Philosophy and Public Affairs* 8, no. 1 (1978), pp. 82–83.

4. Ibid., p. 78 (ascribed to Gregory Vlastos).

5. S.J. Benn, and R.S. Peters, *Social Principles and the Democratic State* (London: Allen and Unwin, 1959), p. 89.

6. Peffer, "A Defense of Rights," p. 77.

7. William Warren Bartley, III, *The Retreat to Commitment* (New York: Alfred A. Knopf, 1962).

8. R.S. Peters, "The Justification of Education," in *The Philosophy of Education,* ed. R.S. Peters (London: Oxford University Press, 1973), p. 254.

9. Immanuel Kant, *The Science of Right,* Britannica Great Books, vol. 42, trans. W. Hastie (Chicago: University of Chicago Press, 1952), p. 420.

10. Amy Guttman, "Children, Paternalism, and Education: A Liberal Argument," *Philosophy and Public Affairs* 9, no. 4 (1980):340. Anyone seriously interested in the family choice debate would do well to study this excellent article.

11. Ibid., p. 349.

12. Graham Haydon, "The 'Right to Education' and Compulsory Schooling," *Educational Philosophy and Theory* 9 (1977):5.

13. A.I. Melden, "Olafson on the Right to Education," in *Educational Judgments,* ed. J.F. Doyle (London: Routledge and Kegan Paul, 1973), p. 214.

14. R.S. Peters, *Ethics and Education* (London: Allen and Unwin, 1966), pp. 23–62. See also P.H. Hirst and R.S. Peters, *The Logic of Education* (London: Routledge and Kegan Paul, 1970), pp. 17–41.

15. See J.S. Mill, "On Liberty," in *Essential Works of John Stuart Mill* ed. Max Lerner (New York: Bantam, 1961), pp. 268–304.

16. Pp. 49–70 passim.

17. Ibid., p. 65.

18. Ibid., p. 67.
19. Ibid., p. 54.
20. Ibid., p. 59.
21. Ibid., p. 10.
22. Ibid., p. 75–87.
23. *The Vancouver Sun*, 29 March 1981.
24. Coons and Sugarman, *Education by Choice*, p. 81.

7

School Choice in the Public Sector: A Case Study of Parental Decision Making

Richard L. Nault and
Susan Uchitelle

On two occasions we have had the opportunity to examine the school choice behavior of a group of public school parents who were given clear choices about where they could send their elementary-school-aged children.[1] The parents live in three optional attendance zones in a large suburban school district and are given a choice of placing their children in one of two designated district schools. We decided to focus on the choice behavior of these parents to learn how they made their decisions, what factors influenced their choices, and whether as a result of their choicemaking they became more knowledgeable about the schools they selected.

Our interest in the choice behavior of parents currently given school options was prompted by our reading of the school reform literature, in which authors press for greater parent sovereignty in schooling. These arguments take two related approaches. Some authors argue that parents have diverse views about how and what their children should be taught. They propose that public schools develop distinctive identities (one school might stress the basics, another might offer expanded training in the performing arts) and that parents be allowed to select the school that most closely fits their conception of how schooling should proceed. From such matches, they predict, greater parent satisfaction will result.[2] Others argue that if parents could select schools, schools would become more responsive to parent aspirations and be more likely to offer quality instruction. Parents could leave schools with which they were dissatisfied. Ineffective schools would either reform or close.[3] Voucher schemes and public-school-of-choice plans are among the most common mechanisms proposed to afford parents choices.[4] Tuition tax credits, which would allow more parents to use private schools, similarly would expand choice. Proponents of these plans imply that if given options, parents would survey the schools available to them, attend to differences in the schools, and select the school most suited to their children. Their choice making would for the most part be deliberative. Parents would not automatically choose the closest or most convenient school, particularly if the instruction offered there was at cross purposes with the ways the parents chose to raise their children or was seriously deficient compared with instruction offered at other schools.

We examined the choice behavior of the parents living in the community we call Collegeville, because their choices were in many ways similar to the choices that would be afforded parents if public schools were to give them more systematic options. We felt scrutiny of their behavior would usefully inform the now largely speculative arguments about what would happen were school options to become more commonplace. The Collegeville optional attendance zones seemed for several reasons an ideal setting for such an investigation. Collegeville parents living in the optional zones were not assigned to a neighborhood school; they were given instead a choice of two schools. The program was not experimental. For reasons that even district officials are now uncertain about (they suspect the plan may have been introduced to relieve overcrowding), parents in these zones have made similar choices for over ten years. And the schools from which the parents chose represented different views about how schooling should proceed. The schools involved (four of the nine elementary schools in the Collegeville system) were not intended to be instructionally different. Over time, however, they had developed distinctive identities. The major differences in the schools are summarized in Table 7–1. Besides differences in instructional organization, the schools differed in the racial and socioeconomic composition of their student populations. Parents could make decisions about the instructional approaches they preferred and the student population to which their child would be exposed.

We conducted two investigations of the choice-making behavior of the parents living in these zones. In the first, largely exploratory investigation, we probed whether parents living in these zones were more likely to research their alternatives actively or to make generally unreflective choices based on such

Table 7–1
Summary Characteristics of Families and Schools in Collegeville Optional Attendance Zones

	School Choice	
Zone 1	*Rock Hill*	*Avery*
White middle- and upper-middle-class families	92% white, 8% black; conventional, graded classroom structure	52% white, 48% black; variety of classroom options, including open and multi-age classrooms
Zone 2	*Clear Ridge*	*Avery*
Parents from racially integrated neighborhood; middle- and upper-middle-class backgrounds	59% black, 41% white; conventional, graded classroom structure	52% white, 48% black; variety of classroom options, including open and multi-age classrooms
Zone 3	*Clear Ridge*	*Avery*
Largely black middle- and working-class families	59% black, 41% white; conventional, graded classroom structure	93% black, 7% white; nongraded, individualized program

narrow criteria as racial composition or distance to the schools. We wanted to discover the extent to which the parents could be described as deliberative choosers, and to the extent we were able to detect major deliberation, the factors that most influenced their choices. In the second study we continued to focus on these issues, but expanded our investigation to learn if parents who were given choices became more knowledgeable about their schools than parents living in other areas who were assigned to a neighborhood school. In our first survey we discovered that many of the parents living in the optional zones had actively researched the schools available to them. We introduced this comparative analysis into our second investigation to learn if this behavior was simply typical of the school familiarization behavior in which most middle-class parents engage or if the extended search patterns we found could be linked with the opportunity for choice.

In the first investigation we gathered from system officials the names of all parents living in the optional attendance zones who the previous fall had used the Collegeville schools for the first time: parents new to the district or who had enrolled their oldest child in kindergarten. All but two of the fifty parents identified agreed to be interviewed. Sixty-four percent of the families were white, 36 percent black. Thirty-seven percent were in the highest of the Hollingshead categorizations of social position. The remaining families were more or less evenly distributed among the next three quintiles.

In our second investigation, conducted two years later, we again asked for the names of parents living in the zones who that fall were new to the district (as before, parents who had moved to Collegeville over the summer and those whose oldest child was a kindergartner). The Collegeville administration identified for us thirty-eight families they believed fit our description. We were able to conduct systematic interviews with twenty-eight families. Three of the twenty-eight familes were black. Fathers in all but two had completed some post-high school education. Three of the remaining ten families could not be contacted, one family chose not to be interviewed, three families were new to this country and generally unfamiliar with U.S. schooling, one family moved during the study, and two families were not new to the system.

To compare the school knowledge of parents given a choice with that of parents not given a choice, we identified and interviewed twenty-five parents living in neighborhoods in areas adjacent to the optional attendance zones. We spoke with two district officials and asked them to identify the residential areas closest to the optional attendance zones that were most like the residential areas within the optional zones. We then randomly selected from these areas twenty-five families using the Collegeville schools for the first time. The optional attendance zones and selected comparison areas generally were part of discernible residential neighborhoods in Collegeville. There was no reason to anticipate that parents living in areas adjacent to the optional zones would be systematically different from those living within the zones. Comparisons of the parents on several major dimensions (race, schools used, type of dwelling, mother's education) revealed only one difference. The fathers in the families afforded choice tended to be somewhat better educated than those in families using a neighborhood school. In our analyses we adjusted for this difference when appropriate.

Collegeville is large (slightly over 47,000 persons in 1970) and diverse. The populations selected for study to some extent reflect this diversity. Two of the three attendance zones, however, are located in the most affluent areas in the city. The families selected for study therefore, tended to be disproportionately well educated (only four of the fathers in the second sample, for example, had not gone on to some postsecondary education) and well off. The distinctiveness of the populations, of course, limits the generalizability of the findings.

The data for these investigations were gathered during half-hour to forty-five-minute semistructured interviews, most often with the mothers in the target families. In some instances the father participated in the interview; in a very few cases he was the primary source of the data. During the interview the respondents also completed checklists probing the reasons why they moved to Collegeville, the major reasons why they chose the school they did, and the search activities in which they engaged before the schools opened in the fall.

Major Findings

Educational Background and Awareness of Choice

The Collegeville school system makes little effort to inform parents living in the three optional attendance zones that they have a choice of schools. District officials include maps illustrating the zones only in some system literature. In some instances parents, unaware of their option, enroll their child in what they believe to be the neighborhood school. Office staff at that time may inform the parents that they have a choice or, believing the parents already are aware and have made a decision, may proceed with registration.

In both investigations we found parents who were unaware that they had a choice and a relationship between awareness and educational levels. Twelve of the forty-eight parents in the first investigation said they did not know they had a choice. These parents tended to be less well educated than the parents who knew they had a choice. (See, for example, the comparisons of fathers' educational backgrounds reported in Table 7–2.) In the second investigation we identified five families in which the parents were unaware of the choice opportunity. In four of these cases the father had accumulated among the least years of schooling of parents in the population. On the whole our data indicate that the less well-educated parents tended to be less aware of their option.

As part of our first interviews we asked the parents to describe how they

Table 7–2
Educational Backgrounds of Fathers in Families Aware and Unaware of School-Choice Opportunities

Father's Educational Level	Families Aware of Choice (N = 36)	Families Unaware of Choice (N = 12)
High School	5.5% (N = 2)	50.0% (N = 6)
College graduate or some college	25.0% (N = 9)	25.0% (N = 3)
Some postgraduate	27.8% (N = 10)	16.7% (N = 2)
Professional degree or Ph.D.	41.7% (N = 15)	8.3% (N = 1)

gathered information on the schools available to them. Analyzing their responses, we found that the less affluent parents also were less likely to have spent time visiting the schools before making a decision. Eighty-three percent of the twenty-three parents in the highest two social-class categories reported that they had visited at least one of the schools. Only 46 percent of the thirteen parents in the lowest two categories had made a similar visit. The numbers are small and the pattern only suggestive. These data indicate, however, that just as the less well-educated and well-off parents in the populations were less likely to have been aware that they had a choice, parents of lower socioeconomic status who were aware they had a choice also were less likely to have investigated the schools directly before making a decision.

Factors Influencing Choice

In both investigations we asked the parents to select from a list of fifteen items the factors that most influenced their choice. Although we worded the items somewhat differently in the second investigation, we probed in both the extent to which factors such as the principal's approach to education, the school's curriculum, distance to the school, the racial and socioeconomic composition of the student population, and facilities were important to the parents as they made their decision. Table 7–3 lists from the first and second investigations the three items the parents cited most frequently as "very important" to them and the three items they cited least frequently.

The parents seemed most concerned about the general atmosphere in the school and they seemed to appraise the atmosphere largely on the basis of the instructional and managerial styles of the two persons in the school—the principal and their child's prospective teacher—who were most likely to influence their child's early school experiences. The parents who visited the school re-

Table 7–3
Three Items Selected as Most Important and Least Important to Parents in Selecting Elementary Schools

Most Important	Least Important
First Investigation	
General atmosphere of school	Overall achievement levels
Principal's philosophy of education and attitude toward children	Convenience of transportation
	Physical facilities
Child's teacher's personal teaching style and classroom skills	
Second Investigation	
Overall curriculum and academic programs	Physical facilities
General atmosphere of school	Similarity of children's background
Principal's philosophy of education and attitude toward children	Convenience of transportation

ported they most often tried to meet the principal and, if school was in session, to observe the kindergarten teacher to whom their child would be assigned. They never mentioned or seemed concerned about the teachers in the upper grades. The Collegeville system allowed parents to request teachers. Parents could transfer their childen to other schools if that did not contribute to racial isolation in the system. The parents we interviewed might have tended to take one year at a time and to worry about upper-grade teachers in the future. Whatever their reasons, their reports indicated that the principal's and kinder-garten teacher's behavior largely defined the school atmosphere and that school atmosphere was among the most important factors in their choice.

It was unimportant to the parents whether transportation was provided or could be arranged (most of the schools were within reasonable walking dis-tance); so were the school's facilities. Though not unconcerned about achieve-ment levels, most parents ranked this measure of school output as comparatively unimportant. The parents may have felt that achievement levels were of little concern in selecting a school for a young child, or that, being well educated, they could supplement their child's schooling if necessary, or that if the school's atmosphere and their own child-rearing approaches were congruent, achievement would follow. Whatever their reasons, the parents evi-denced less concern with achievement levels than with the overall atmosphere in the school.

As evidenced both in their expressed attitudes and by their actual choices, the parents we interviewed also seemed to seek out rather than avoid racial and socioeconomic diversity. Most parents (86 percent) in the first group we studied said they ''wanted a school where the children would be exposed to children of different ethnic and racial backgrounds''; 11 percent said they ''wanted a school where the children's backgrounds were similar to their own.'' Far more parents in the second group said it was important to them to select a school that was "racially integrated" (95 percent) and "would provide exposure to children of diverse ethnic and racial backgrounds" (89 percent) than said they wanted to find a school where "the children's backgrounds were similar to our own" (32 percent). We looked also at the parents' placement decisions and noted whether they selected the school where their children would encounter a higher percentage of children of their own race. Our data indicate that for the majority of the parents this was not the case. Table 7–4 reports, for example, the percentage of parents in the first investigation who selected the school with the higher proportion of children of their own race. The table reveals that the bulk of the black parents and two-thirds of the white parents chose the school in which their children would encounter fewer schoolmates of their own race. Far more parents opted for than avoided racial diversity.

These data, of course, reflect the choice behavior of parents who were in many ways atypical. They were on the whole highly educated. They placed a premium on integrated life experiences. Forty-four percent of the parents indicated that one of the reasons they moved to Collegeville was that they wanted to live in an integrated community. For other clusters of parents the reasons for choice may well differ. Among these, however, factors related to school atmosphere seemed heavily to outweigh more narrow criteria (distance, attempts to avoid integration, school facilities, transportation) in determining final choices.

Parental Search Behavior

In both phases of our research we sought information on how systematically parents investigated the school available to them (whether, for example, they visited the schools while they were in session) and how much information they had gathered about the schools. Our findings suggest that systematic search was more common than cursory investigation and that the parents afforded choice became more knowledgeable about the school to which they sent their children than did similar parents assigned to a neighborhood school.

Table 7–4
Percentages of White and Black Parents Choosing Schools with Higher and Lower Proportions of Students of Their Own Race

	Percentage Choosing School with Higher Proportion of Students of Their Own Race (N = 10)	Percentage Choosing School with Lower Proportion of Students of Their Own Race (N = 26)
White Parents	33 (N = 9)	67 (N = 19)
Black Parents	13 (N = 1)	88 (N = 7)

The parents who had a choice tended to rely on two sources of information in making their decision: the advice of parents who already had children enrolled in the schools and information gathered during school visits. One parent describes a search that integrated information from both sources.

> We just kept our ears open. We didn't hear anyone say anything about Clear Ridge. Everyone was talking Avery. We didn't just hear good things, we also heard bad things. In any case we kept hearing things. (What did people say about the schools?) At Avery they said there are lots of rowdies and there are lots of fights in the johns. And then they said that all the new ideas in education are tried out at Avery. The school is very much alive. They are aware of what is going on. They don't mind trying things out and then dropping them if they don't like them. From all that I got the ideas the school was very much alive. (What did you want to know about the school?) I wanted to avoid going along with old ways just because they were used to them. Not that I am against going along with old ways but not for the reason that you are used to them. That was what I was afraid of. That may be the prejudice I had against Clear Ridge. No one discussed it so I took from that that they were conservative and going on in the way they had been going on for some time. (Did anything else concern you?) No, I think the main thing is the activity, because that was a sign for me of seriousness and more or less of independence of thought on the side of the principal and teachers. You know, people are not afraid to try out new ways. People have to decide to think for themselves. (Did you visit the schools?) Only Avery. I thought I had made up my mind by then. I walked through the school to get a feel for the atmosphere and then visited the kindergartens. (What were you looking for?) The atmosphere had to strike me as pleasant. In other words, had I on that first walk through the school seen many children frowning, for instance, or sulking, or running away from teacher, I would have given it a closer look. (Case 24)

Of the thirty-six parents in the first investigation who knew they had a choice, 72 percent talked with neighbors or friends who had prior experience with the schools, and 69 percent visited one or both of the schools. In our first investigation we developed a broad definition of "searchers" (parents who investigated one or both schools and appeared to have deliberated the options available) and "nonsearchers" (persons who by their description appeared to have given little time and thought to the decision) and asked independent judges to read the interview transcripts and assign the parents to one of the categories. Over 70 percent of the parents were judged to be "searchers"—to have been somewhat or highly active in appraising the schools available to them. Fewer than a third made a generally unreflective decision.

The nineteen parents in our second investigation who both were aware they had a choice and had lived in Collegeville longer than ten days before the schools opened in the fall were similarly active. Seventy-nine percent visited at least one school before registration (42 percent visited both schools), 74 percent spoke about the school with neighbors and friends, and 63 percent spoke with at least one teacher in the schools.

Parental Search Behavior and School Knowledge

A major question that prompted our second investigation was whether this activity was merely the extent of school familiarization undertaken by parents (particularly well-educated parents) who encounter schools for the first time or if these seemingly complete levels of investigation were more likely characteristic of parents afforded choice. To address this question we compared the search behavior of the parents given choices with the search behavior of parents living in nearby neighborhoods who were not given choices. Our analysis suggests that the parents with options engaged in more search activities and in the process seemed to have become more knowledgeable about the schools than did the parents assigned to neighborhood schools.

Table 7–5 displays the percentage of the parents afford choice and the parents living in nearby neighborhoods who were not given choices who engaged in various types of search activities.[5] More of the parents living in the neighborhoods where no choice was available spoke with acquaintances about the schools (82 percent versus 74 percent). In all other categories of investigation, however, the parents who had a choice were more likely to have engaged in active search. From this pattern one might reason that if parents have only a neighborhood school available, they are likely to find out from friends what sort of environment the school provides and probe further only if they hear the school is deficient. Afforded alternatives, parents may feel more impelled to undertake direct appraisals of the choices available.

The parents afforded choice also were more knowledgeable about the

Table 7–5
Extent of Search Activity of Chooser and Nonchooser Mothers

Nature of Contact	Choosers (N = 19)		Nonchoosers (N = 22)	
	N	%	N	%
Visited the school before registration or invitation to a school event	15	79	12	55
Spoke with neighbors and friends about the school	14	74	18	82
Spoke with teachers in the school	12	68	5	23
Visited classrooms while school was in session	10	53	7	32
Had contact with the principal before registration	9	47	6	27
Visited more than one school	8	42	—	—
Made more than one visit to the same school	7	37	4	18
Attended a planned school function before registration	4	21	2	9

school in which they enrolled their child than were the parents assigned to a neighborhood school. We asked the parents who had a choice and those who were assigned to a neighborhood school several questions about how much they knew about the school their child attended before the start of the school year. The results appear in table 7–6. The trend again was for the parents with options to be more knowledgeable.

In an effort to amplify this analysis we constructed a search activity score and a school knowledge score for parents in the comparison groups. The search activity score contained the total of the following activities by the mother: visiting the school before registration, making more than one visit to the school, attending a school function before registration, contacting the principal before registration, speaking with any teachers in the school, visiting any classrooms in the school, and speaking with acquaintances about the school. The school knowledge score reflected the sum of each item in table 7–6 that the mother reported knowing. The mean search activity scores of those afforded choice was 3.73; of those not given a choice, 2.4. The mean school knowledge score of those given a choice was 6.63; of those having no choice, 4.54. Using analysis of variance procedures, these differences were found to be statistically significant at the .05 level.

Table 7–6
Extent of Knowledge about Schools Possessed by Chooser and Nonchooser Mothers

Type of School Knowledge	Choosers (N = 19)		Nonchoosers (N = 22)	
	N	%	N	%
Knew the name of one teacher in the building	16	84	10	45
Knew what the general home backgrounds of the children were	16	8	14	64
Aware of general percentage of black and white children in building	16	84	12	55
Knew the name of the principal of the school	14	74	13	59
Knew how strictly their child's teacher ran the classroom	14	74	9	41
Were aware of the general grade level structure in the school	13	68	10	45
Knew what sort of teacher their child was getting	13	68	8	36
Knew the general degree of discipline in the building	13	68	12	55
Knew what sort of administrator the principal was	9	47	10	45
Knew what student reporting system was followed in the school	3	16	2	9

Table 7–7
Analysis of Variance in Search Activity and School Knowledge Scores of Chooser and Nonchooser Mothers

	Source of Variance	DF	SS	MS	F	P
Search activity scores	Among groups	1	17.97	17.97	5.19	.05
	Within groups	39	135.00	3.462		
School knowledge scores	Among groups	1	44.36	44.36	7.04	.05
	Between groups	39	245.88	6.30		

These analyses are, of course, at best suggestive: the procedures were exploratory, the sample size modest, the populations atypical. Bearing in mind these reservations, however, we can note that those who had school options did engage in a wider pattern of school investigation and began the school year more knowledgeable about the schools their children were to enter than did a group of similar parents assigned to a neighborhood school. Thus, a tentative argument could be made that the opportunity for choice engendered this behavior.

Summary

If we were to describe a model pattern of school choice among the parents we studied, it would be more accurately characterized as one of deliberative and reflective choice rather than as one based on cursory attention to only one or two school characteristics. The parents we interviewed in large numbers assembled information on the two schools available to them, were attentive to qualitative differences in the instructional and interpersonal environments established in the schools, and selected the school that seemed to offer their child greater opportunity for progress. The parents did not appear to believe that most schools offered the same sort of instruction and that their task was to find the school that offered the highest quality schooling, but rather that schools are qualitatively different and that their task was to select the school in which the adults held views most compatible with their own on how children should be treated and which seemed to offer their child the most educational potency. For the majority of the parents, information on distance to the school, racial composition of the student population, or reported achievement levels alone were not sufficient criteria on which to base a decision. Reflective appraisal of the total school press was more often the norm. If any subgroup departed systematically from this pattern it was the small number of parents interviewed who were comparatively less well off and less well educated. These parents were less likely to have been aware of their right to choose and, when aware, to have engaged in as complete an investigation of the alternatives available to them.

A comparison of the school knowledge of the parents given choices with the knowledge accumulated by parents with similar backgrounds who were not afforded choices revealed that the parents with choice were more informed at the beginning of the school year about the school their children attended. The need to become informed about the options available to them, it might be plausibly argued, contributed to the school awareness of these parents.

Implications

Those who advocate school assignment based on client sovereignty rather than on place of residence, in the belief that the resulting school diversity will yield more productive or satisfying school-family matches, should draw comfort from this investigation. Many parents we spoke with said they were glad they had been given a choice; no parent expressed dissatisfaction with the arrangement. Data from the more systematic phases of the interviews indicate that among this group of parents reflective choice was more common than cursory selection. We stress again the atypical characteristics of the parent populations and note that all of the Collegeville schools offer generally commendable education. Parents who are less well educated or parents in settings where the quality of instruction differs visibly from school to school may be less systematic. The majority of the parents we studied, however, seemed most intent on forging an optimal match between their childrearing agendas, their children's needs, and the instructional and social press of the school.

A by-product of the search process seemed to be that the parents afforded choice became more knowledgeable about the schools to which they sent their children. We can only speculate on the benefits of such familiarity. The questionnaire items we used tapped only the most cursory knowledge of the school (the name of the principal, the type of pupil reporting system used) and we have no way of knowing if increased familiarity is associated with enhanced parent-school relations. One can speculate that parents who are more knowledgeable about a school are more likely to find the school approachable, to possess perspective on actions taken by the staff, and to communicate to their children (particularly if such knowledge is associated with positive sentiment toward the school) a greater sense of membership in the school commnity. Obviously, additional studies of choice and attendant knowledge are needed before much can be made of this finding. A starting point for such efforts, however, may well be the pattern documented in this study—that the parents afforded choice were more knowledgeable about the schools to which they sent their children than were similar parents living within conventional school attendance boundaries.

It came as no surprise to us that the parents who took the trouble to investigate the schools available to them relied heavily upon appraisals of the principal's behavior in judging the overall press of the school. Popular wisdom states that principals "set the tone" for a school; we anticipated that parents would be attentive to their behavior or reputation. We were surprised, however, by the number of parents who investigated the kindergarten teachers to which their children would be assigned and made their final choices after comparing the teachers' approaches. Our experience with elementary schools suggests that kindergartens often are considered an adjunct to the program of instruction in the upper grades, a preparatory experience for "regular" schooling. We suspect that on some staffs the status of kindergarten teacher reflects this appraisal. There is, then, a certain irony in our observation that the instructional reputation of the kindergarten teacher may be second only to the reputation of the principal in influencing the school choice decision of parents.

We document in our work a relationship between social class, parental awareness of choice opportunity, and parental contact with the school in researching options; the less well-educated parents we interviewed were less likely to have been fully informed about their opportunity for choice. This finding replicates earlier work by Bridge and others that established in other choice settings a relationship between socioeconomic class and school knowledge.[6] Lower-income parents may remain less informed about the choices available to them for several reasons, including general feelings of alienation and their limited participation in social networks likely to provide useful school information. Whatever the reasons, however, our findings reinforce the arguments of others who contend that, if parents are able to transmit educational advantages to their children by careful school selection, designers of choice programs who seek to attenuate the educational advantages of socioeconomic class will need to include mechanisms that will compensate for the advantages of income and education.

Finally, we note that the majority of the parents we interviewed, when confronted with the choice of a school that was largely segregated and one that was desegregated, chose the school that provided the greater likelihood of integrated school experiences. Some critics of choice plans contend that if parents were allowed to choose schools, racial isolation in schools would increase. We do not discount this possibility. Our research provides at least one instance, however, of a group of parents who seemed far more intent upon providing for rather then precluding integrated school experiences for their children.

Notes

1. For lengthier discussions of these research efforts, see Susan Uchitelle and Richard L. Nault, "The Social Choice Behavior of Parents Afforded Public School Options: A Case Study of Parental Decision Making in One Suburban

Community'' (Paper presented at the spring 1977 meeting of the American Educational Research Association, New York); and Richard L. Nault and Susan Uchitelle, ''School Choice in the Public Sector: An Exploration of the Consequences for Parental Behavior'' (Paper presented at the spring 1979 meeting of the American Educational Research Association, San Francisco).

2. See, for example, John E. Coons and Stephen D. Sugarman, *Education by Choice: The Case for Family Control* (Berkeley: University of California Press, 1978); and Mario Fantini, *Public Schools of Choice* (New York: Simon and Schuster, 1973).

3. See, for example, chapter 6, ''What's Wrong with Our Schools?'' in Milton Friedman and Rose Friedman, *Free to Choose* (New York: Avon Books, 1981), pp. 150–188.

4. See, for example, Mario Fantini, ''Options for Students, Parents, and Teachers: Public Schools of Choice,'' *Phi Delta Kappan* 52 (May 1971):541–543; Christopher Jencks, ''Giving Parents Money for Schooling: Education Vouchers,'' *Phi Delta Kappan* 52(September 1970):49–52; and Donald A. Erickson, ''Educational Vouchers: Nature and Funding,'' *Theory into Practice* 11 (April 1972):108–116.

5. Gary Bridge, ''Information Imperfections: The Achilles' Heel of Entitlement Plans,'' *School Review* 86 (May 1978):504–529.

6. Ibid., pp. 519, 521.

8

Salient Considerations in Program Choice: The Student Perspective

Robert B. Kottkamp and
Richard L. Nault

When presented with real choice between distinct programs, what factors influence high school students? What considerations are most salient in their program decisions? Although few public high school students are given program choice wider than traditional tracking systems and selection of elective courses, these questions are central whenever serious consideration is given to initiating schools-of-choice programs, magnet schools, or voucher plans. Indeed, several recent reports, including those by the National Commission on the Reform of Secondary Education and the Panel on Youth of the President's Science Advisory Committee, have advocated allowing secondary students more educational decisions than they are now allowed to make in modal school systems.[1] Though generally unrecognized, these questions may be important to systems presently maintaining schools that allow little student choice, for the available evidence indicates that salutary outcomes generally accrue to both schools and students from the exercise of choice.

McPartland and his colleagues, for example, studied student participation in decision making in fourteen urban high schools. Of these schools, one in particular provided students with an "unusual degree of academic choice."[2] Each quarter, students in this school made specific choices of courses and instructor. McPartland found that these students were more committed to the school, evidenced higher attitudes of responsibility, and had more personal and carefully considered reasons for attending than did students not given choices. Furthermore, students given real choice expressed higher satisfaction with both their teachers and the instruction they received than did other students. Choice also led to higher teacher-student trust and concomitantly lower hostility between these role partners. Finally, McPartland reported that students who made decisions did not generally "take the easy way out" by selecting only the courses with less stringent requirements and grading scales.

Nault studied the differential commitments of students affiliating with schools by their own choice and those affiliating through parental compulsion. Using a sample of freshmen attending six Catholic high schools, Nault found that students allowed to make their own affiliation decisions were significantly more committed to their schools on each of four dimensions: behavioral expectation of the school, extending oneself on behalf of the formal school organization, expectations in academic performance, and extracurricular participation.[3]

Kottkamp partially replicated Nault's findings in a public high school setting. Students who made their own choice among five distinct programs, as opposed to those whose parents made the choice, behaved better both inside and outside the classroom. Choice-making students also produced higher grade-point averages.[4]

These studies suggest that providing students with program choice benefits both the student and the school. But how does this benefit occur? And what factors do students consider as they make their choices? This chapter examines the factors considered salient by students in the choice process.

Possible Explanations

Several internal and external referents may influence a student making a program choice. Each of these may serve as explanatory variables in student choice-making behavior.

Students may attend to parents or to an internalized value system received from parents. Campbell, for example, makes a strong argument for parental influence: "Children tend to be like their parents. . . . It seems clear and basic that any observation about the strength and pervasiveness of peer influences, and youth culture must be *in addition to,* or supplemental to, the central fact that parents are the major shaping influences in the lives of adolescents."[5] Whereas Campbell argues that peers have only a secondary effect on adolescents, others, notably Coleman and Gordon, contend that peer culture exerts a strong influence on adolescents in school settings.[6]

Riley examined which reference group—parents or peers—adolescents typically consult when making specific kinds of decisions, and found that they are more likely to turn to parents in decisions involving moral issues, school problems, educational plans, and politics but to turn to peers in decisions concerning interpersonal relations with peers, popularity, and status.[7] The finding that adolescents tend to consult parents rather than peers about academic matters and educational plans was partially replicated in Brittain's study of parent-peer cross-pressures.[8] There is also evidence that guidance counselors exert influence on student course and track selection.[9] And it is quite possible that teachers and older siblings may serve as choice-affecting referents when students make program choices.

Internal referents may also influence program choices. Students may base their choice on their knowledge of self in relation to the most appropriate learning environment. This is the main rationale advanced by school officials in the setting where the empirical study occurred: "Each student, with his parents' consent, may choose the school-within-a-school which offers him an education environment that most accurately reflects his individual learning style.'' The assumption was that students would choose a setting in which they would learn best.

Stinchcombe's work suggests two other possible internal reference points.[10] Students may consider the articulation between available programs and their perceived future status. Another internal pressure may be the attraction of short-term hedonism, which seeks "the easy way out." On this point, however, McPartland and his colleagues report that at least for individual course selection, when given wide enough choice, students generally pick one or more demanding courses (usually those in which they are already strong) and several less demanding ones (generally those in which they are less strong) rather than all "easy" courses.

Method

Setting

Education-by-Choice High School (EBC High) offered juniors and seniors a choice among five distinct school-within-a-school programs. Students made their choice at the end of their sophomore year. All alternative programs were housed in a single physical plant; they varied along dimensions of curriculum, locus of responsibility for direction of student learning, time allocation, and norms of teacher-student interaction:

1. *Conventional School:* School the way mom and dad experienced it; general/college prep curriculum, structure, straight rows of chairs, no non-sense, teacher control of learning, consistent homework, and supervised study.
2. *Flexible School:* general/college prep curriculum; structure, but less than in Conventional; teacher control, but with more options for student input; flexible schedules; opportunities for work on community projects and for spending more time in subject areas found difficult.
3. *Individual School:* general/college prep curriculum, structured more on a junior college model (not every class meets every day), more free time for independent learning, more student responsibility for learning, stronger teacher-student relationships than in traditional school.
4. *Arts School:* fine arts curriculum, loosely structured, much student responsibility for learning, close interpersonal relationships among students and teachers.
5. *Voc-Tec School:* a sophisticated vocational-technical curriculum, structure,

teacher control of learning, opportunities to make direct transitions into the existing work structure of the community.

Sophomores about to enter EBC High chose one of the five alternatives; allowed to take elective courses in any of the five, their basic academic courses (such as English and math) were to be taken in the school of their choice. The choice process was elaborate. Sophomores were provided with attractive printed materials on the alternatives. Faculty and students from each of the alternatives came to the sophomore building to "sell" their approach to education. An alternative would remain in existence only as long as it could attract a reasonable number of students. Thus, a quasi–market economy and competition for students existed. Finally, sophomores were taken to EBC High for tours of the alternatives. With the consent of at least one parent, each student chose an alternative in which to begin the junior year.

Samples

Two samples were used in this research. The first was drawn from juniors and seniors already in the alternative program who were asked to recall their choice-making process. This sample consisted of 50 EBC High juniors and seniors selected as follows. All 1,122 EBC students were surveyed with a seven-item instrument to ascertain whether they perceived their choice to be totally their own or whether they perceived direct parental intervention in the decision. Of the 93 percent who responded, 50 percent perceived the decision as *totally* their own. Only students who perceived no direct parental intervention were used in the sample because the study sought to identify those considerations that are most salient when students are given real choice. The sample was further reduced because the primary method of data collection was intensive interviewing. Students were assigned to cells by program membership and sex within program. Five students were randomly selected from each cell, yielding a sample of 50 students.

The second sample was drawn from sophomores who had just made their choice of program and were entering EBC High in September. Eight students were randomly selected from those choosing each program. Only twenty-eight, however, were interviewed because interviews were all conducted on a single day. Several parents refused permission, several students were absent, and several failed to show up. The sample was skewed toward the more traditional options.

Data Collection

Data were collected from the first sample through intensive retrospective interviews. The interview schedule contained twenty-five open-ended questions, two of which elicited responses about choice behavior:

21. How was the decision made that you would enroll in your official EBC school? (Probe: role of parents, role of friends, other factors).
22. What were the most important reasons you wanted to go to ——————— school?

The larger interview was designed to elicit responses that could be used to construct a general strategy of accommodation to schooling. The construction of the interview allowed for two complementary methods of analysis: across subjects on the basis of the two questions dealing with choice; and construction of an individual case study for each student, permitting the placement of the choice within the larger perspective of the student's overall approach to school.

The interview for the sophomores in the second sample did not elicit the more global aspects of a student's orientation toward school; it contained questions and checklists and focused more specifically on the recent choice process. This interview was constructed with partial knowledge of responses from the older students and was designed to confirm in part the findings emerging from the first interviews.

Data Analysis

Interview data were analyzed in several ways. The longer, more open-ended interviews were both analyzed in depth to develop individual case studies and compared with other students' answers to questions dealing specifically with choice; the sophomore interviews were only compared because of their more limited nature. The analysis aimed at what Smith terms "miniature theory" and Glaser and Strauss term "substantive grounded theory."[11] The checklists were analyzed through calculation of means and rankings.

Findings

The Articulation Perspective

Stinchcombe hypothesized that rebellion among high school students could be partially explained by the absence of perceived articulation between present aspects of schooling and future status: "*We hold that high school rebellion,* and expressive alienation, *occurs when future status is not clearly related to present performance.* When a student realizes that he does not achieve status increment from improved current performance, current performance loses meaning."[12] Stinchcombe's rebellious students were trapped in a situation of perceived non-articulation. The concept of articulation is useful in the study, but the approach here is from the student's perspective. So the question becomes: What factors do students consider when given choice? The students in this setting, although making individual choices, appear to develop a common perspective arising from a common problematic situation—which school to choose?[13] The best explanation appears to be that they choose a program that best articulates with their perceived future status.

This explanation was constructed from several more specific categories emerging from the interview data. The procedure for deriving the articulation perspective involved reading the fifty broad-ranging interviews to construct an individual case study for each interview such that the choice-making behavior was put into the context of the student's larger set of goals and the general strategy he or she had developed for use in school. Once the individual case studies had been constructed it was possible to compare them for categories or specifically mentioned threads of orientation and behavior. Several categories were found to hold across a large number of interviews. The final step in constructing the perspective was to extrapolate the larger, but not explicitly stated, perspective from the commonly held categories.

The twenty-eight more specific interviews of sophomores were used to confirm the articulation perspective, especially some of its nested categories, detailed below:

1. The relationship between curricular types and anticipated career and/or future education
2. The *degree* of academic achievement desired in their school careers (usually future related)
3. The relationship between the type of learning environment provided by a school and what the student understood about his or her own "learning style" (assuming a given level of desired performance)

Curricular Type. It was clear that in most cases students had weighed the relation between the curriculum offered by the chosen school and their anticipated educational and career goals. The Voc-Tech students were the most direct about this relationship. One of them observed:

> I didn't plan on going to college, and I figure if I was going to college I would get into one of the harder schools where you learn about college things. And I've tooken a vocational class, and its easier, and you learn about what I am going to do, and if you wanted to go to a trade school I'd have enough education.

No student interviewed from Voc-Tech planned on going to college, although some did plan to attend a technical school.

The content of the core curriculum in three schools—Conventional, Flexible, and Individual—was identical, even to the use of the same textbooks. These schools attracted both students who were college bound and those who were not. The majority of students commenting specifically about the curriculum were, however, college bound.

> Definitely going to college and mainly participating in grades. . . . And I imagine I'll go for some graduate study . . . engineering, and I see that as pretty much being required. . . . (Relation of academic program and future?) They have the courses I want. I looked at some other schools . . . and they didn't have physics and calculus. . . . (Flexible)

> Well, you learn in Individual that you have to make decisions on your own and they're not going to tell you every little thing to do all the time. And that probably when you get into college . . . you have to make your decision of what kind of career you're going to get into. So I think that Individual really helps you prepare for that. (Individual)

Students choosing Arts were also college and noncollege oriented. Their comments are interesting because they recognize the link between their choice and future career.

> I'll be in some type of sales . . . in a fairly large corporation. . . . (Do you see any connection between what you are doing now and what you'll be doing in sales?) Well, that would be the plays and things like that. . . . My father, he interviews a lot of people for jobs. . . . He's always bringing people home, and I try to work myself into conversations and things like that. . . . And the plays and being nervous and all of that, I try to work around that. (So you see . . . stage presence in theater as being connected with stage presence with people?) Yeah, I think that you got to set up your own personality when you first meet a person because your first impression is always real important.

Degree of Achievement. Closely related to curricular type as a criterion of choice was the criterion of desired degree of academic achievement. For some students the choice of schools was made to maximize achievement or at least grade-point average. For example, "I thought I'd learn more in Conventional than in Flexible." Or, "I think in Flexible lots of it is classroom participation . . . more of a discussion than it is a lecture type, and I think that's about the best way that you can make the grade, you know." Other students selected a program on the basis of the minimal compliance required; for them achievement and grades were less directly linked to their perceived future. A student in Arts said, "I think it's a lot easier 'cause I don't have to worry about going to every class on time and that. And like here, you know, you can just walk in and start doing what you want to do."

One student's future was marriage and life as a housewife. (She was engaged at the time of the interview.) Her school investments were primarily social and she put her achievement goal succinctly: "I just expect to graduate." She had chosen her school according to her desired level of achievement.

Another student with the same goal chose Conventional. She was heavily involved in social affairs too, but wanted to be the first high school graduate in her family in two generations. She reasoned that choosing Conventional would force her to achieve at a level that would ensure graduation. She also deliberately chose a school that separated her from close friends who had influenced her to skip classes in the past.

Learning Environment and Learning Style. The River City school system posited that the primary mechanism students would use in making choices was the matching of their individual learning style with the most congruent of the several available learning environments, although they did not seem to have anything as specific in mind as the environmental matching model of Stern or the more specific cognitive model of Hunt and Sullivan.[14] Generally, however, the prediction seems accurate. The matching of personal learning attributes and school environments was an integral and the most explicit component of the overall articulation perspective. The awareness of matching individual style with environment was also directly related and integrated with the student's career and educational aspirations and desired level of academic achievement.

Learning style is a term not precisely defined by the school system. From the interviews, however, it is possible to deduce what meanings students gave to what the adults termed learning style. Students spoke implicitly about a continuum of responsibility for the learning enterprise. They defined one pole as "freedom," the other as "structure." Freedom meant that the student accepted the responsibility to attend class, allocate time, choose content, and complete the work. Freedom also implied physical mobility within the learning environment. This term was used mostly by students attending the individual and five arts schools. *Freedom* and *structure* with their attendant meanings, were both student terms; neither appeared in the EBC literature distributed by the school district or in the interview schedule and probes.

> I started it [Individual] in eighth grade. And by the time that I got up here I don't think I could have gone back to traditional. I would never have been able to take it—sitting still and working. . . . It's just the freedom and the ability to do things.

> I think choice separated the men from the boys in a way . . . in an exact way if you're going to use it literally. . . . I think a lot of the more mature people went there [Arts], but it helps you to realize where you're at, as far as maturity goes. . . . I think a lot of kids realize, well, I want to be in Individual School, but gosh, I don't know if I can handle that, so I'll just go back to Conventional and wait another year, maybe learn a little more. . . . That's why its important to have the choice. Its important to me that something like this keeps happening.

At the other end of the continuum, structure meant the imposition of external motivation by the adults. This included pressure to complete work, to do homework, and to attend regularly. It also meant that the student was in a "captive," nonmobile position for each fifty-five-minute period but that the teacher was constantly available for help during that time. It also implied a didactic style of pedagogy. Many students in Conventional indicated that structure was a major reason for their choice.

> . . . classes are structured and stuff, like having to attend class regularly and having home work due, like having your homework done the next day . . . is good practice for . . . college or if I do teach someday or working. I was in Individual in seventh and eighth grade and I couldn't—the deadline was at the end of school and I had trouble getting my work in because I would slack off. I need the push.

> I have to pay attention to catch it because when I read I don't catch it the first time. So I try to pick it up on the lecture. (It's easier to hear things than read them?) Right, right!

Students choosing Flexible generally saw it as an intermediate environment, somewhere between the structure of Conventional and the freedom of Individual. They also used the terms *strict* and *lenient,* which seem to be peculiar to Flexible. These terms appear to have similar meanings on the continuum already described: "I didn't want Conventional because it's too strict. . . . I didn't really want that and I didn't want Individualized because it's too lenient, and I'd rather have class structure with more leniency than Conventional, something in the middle."

Student perception of the match between how they learn and the available learning environments (with future plans and desired level of achievement taken into account) seems to be a very salient element in making a choice. Perceptions of their needs on the structure-freedom continuum seemed particularly important for students choosing among the three schools with similar curricular content. Most of these students recognized their own learning and environmental needs. Many recalled specific past situations that had taught them where on the continuum they could maximize their desired degree of learning. Arts students were also keenly aware of the person-environment matching criterion. Only the Voc-Tech students failed to mention, or apparently even consider, this dimension. For them, curricular content was the overriding concern.

Influences of Significant Others

Students did not make school choices in an interpersonal vacuum. During their deliberations they were potentially exposed to the influences of teachers, parents, friends, and others. This section examines the extent to which the influences of significant others compete with the articulation perspective to explain student program choices. The analysis draws heavily on the twenty-eight interviews with sophomores who had just made their choice. The sophomores were asked more specific questions about the influence of significant others. They also had sharper recollections of attempts by others to influence, probably because their experience was recent. Finally, they were a sample who had experienced various influences from parents, unlike the older sample, who were selected because none had experienced parental intervention.

Teachers. Teachers might influence student choice in at least three ways: EBC teachers might have such strong reputations as to attract sophomores directly; teachers and counselors might directly influence the sophomores' choice for the coming year; and teachers of freshman and sophomore students might have preferences for or biases against certain EBC schools, thus creating a decision-making atmosphere that denigrates some choices while endorsing others. Sophomore students indicated, however, that teachers influenced them in none of these ways; the juniors and seniors, with only a few exceptions, did not even mention teachers when they discussed their decisions.

None of the sophomores reported being influenced directly by a specific EBC High teacher. Few even knew about the teachers except through vague reports of older siblings. One junior in Flexible reported being partially influenced by his tennis coach, an EBC teacher he had come to know as a sophomore on the tennis team. The student was attracted to Flexible not because of sports but because he perceived the coach as "bright" and expected him to be an excellent teacher. Thus, the influence of the coach should probably be seen as an indicator of the articulation perspective. Several Arts students mentioned being influenced by EBC Arts teachers. These students, as sophomores, had participated in drama and other Arts School activities. They had been introduced to both the teachers and the whole Arts program through participation. Apparently these students were influenced more by the totality of this experience than by the specific reputations of teachers. Both sophomores and EBC students reported being motivated by how they thought teachers in a particular school might teach or how "good" they were. These influences, however, seem more logically a part of the articulation perspective than direct teacher influences. References were to groups of teachers rather than to individuals and seemed associated with learning climate considerations or notions of achievement for college preparation.

About half the sophomores reported talking with teachers or counselors about EBC choice. They spoke with counselors more than with teachers, but discussions focused mostly on specific courses rather than school selection. Juniors and seniors reported no such conversations. Sophomores who did interact with these adults reported that they received balanced information about the various alternatives. Two sophomores received prescriptions; both students selected schools other than those recommended. For most sophomores, contact with teachers was limited, and the advice received seemed balanced. Information provided by teachers was generally considered helpful. No student, however, reported choosing an EBC school because of teacher influence.

Teachers, however, can also influence students in indirect ways by shaping a climate that might impede some choices while facilitating others. Half the sophomores reported no detected teacher preference for specific schools. The other half reported sentiments in at least some teachers; some ninth- and tenth-grade teachers generally preferred EBC Individual, and teachers in the traditional program favored Conventional and Flexible. Sophomores did not, however, perceive themselves as being influenced by these sentiments; they doubted that such sentiments swayed their friends.

It is difficult to say just how limited teacher influence was. Students could not judge and the data collection procedures were not sensitive to the cumulative effect of teacher sentiments on the decisions of school-oriented students. Students choosing Arts and Individual reported ignoring the negative sentiments of some teachers whose orientation was traditional. What cannot be determined is whether students more likely to comply with teacher expectations may have failed to consider some alternatives because of disapproval they sensed from teachers. This possibility is reinforced by a generally negative perception of the Individual and Arts Schools among the conservatives in the community at large. Although nearly all students reported no effect from teacher attempts to influence them, the possibility of subtle influence remains.

Friends. The dependence of adolescents on friends for interpersonal support in school is well documented.[15] Riley, however, reports that adolescents tend to communicate predominantly with peers on matters of interpersonal relations, dress, popularity, and status but primarily with parents on matters of schoolwork, moral problems, and educational plans.[16] An effort was made to determine whether students picked schools simply because their friends were going there or whether the articulation perspective would prevail over the influence of friends.

Sophomores were asked which schools their three best friends had chosen. By comparing friend and respondent choices it was possible to tabulate the extent to which student choices differed from best friends, as indicated in table 8–1. These data may be interpreted in several ways. Over half the students selected schools chosen by at least two best friends. On the other hand, 40

Table 8–1
Percentage of Best Friends Selecting the Same EBC School as Interviewed Sophomores

All Three	Two of Three	One of Three	None	Students Unaware of Friends' Choices
20 ($N=5$)	36 ($N=9$)	36 ($N=9$)	4 ($N=1$)	4 ($N=1$)

percent broke with at least two-thirds of their friends in choosing schools. These data are ambiguous and at best suggestive. More direct queries were also made about the influence of friends.

During the sophomore interviews students were asked whether they had been influenced by others to enter a particular school and whether these influence attempts contributed to their decisions. They were also asked whether they had tried to influence others and whether those attempts were successful. Table 8–2 shows the responses to these questions.

Two-thirds of sophomores reported that friends had tried to influence them, but the majority said they were unswayed by these attempts. Successful attempts were few.

> Joan and Mary were the ones that influenced me. They're going into Conventional. Mary was the one that influenced me most because she thought that is what I needed. . . . Although Mary talked to me a lot about it, I made the decision on my own. (Conventional)

Even in this case the student feels she made the judgment on her own and that the attempts at influence took the form of arguments about what would be the best learning environment for the respondent.

When asked if they had tried to influence others, over a third of the sample reported they had not. Most of those who reported they had tried to influence friends said that they had been unsuccessful.

In contrast with the specific questions about influences of friends reported above, both sets of interviewees were also asked open-ended questions about their choice decisions. Selltiz notes that open-ended questions are used to raise issues without suggesting or providing a structure for the reply, thus allowing the respondent to answer in his or her own terms or frame of reference.[17] Piaget notes that unstructured questions also elicit indications of centrality and intensity.[18]

Prior to the more specific questions about friends, the sophomores were asked, "Could you describe to me how you decided upon the school you did?" Nine of the twenty-eight students at some point mentioned friendship influences or a desire to remain with friends. Few, however, mentioned these considerations first. In contrast, nearly all students mentioned learning environment con-

Table 8–2
Friendship Influences on Sophomore Students' Decisions

Direction of Influence Attempt	No Attempts Reported	Outcome of Influence Attempts		
		Some Influence	Unsuccessful	Could Not be Determined
On student	7	4	14	3
By student on others	10	4	9	2

siderations. In terms of centrality and intensity, the articulation perspective seems to overshadow the influence of friendship in the responses of sophomores.

An open-ended question was also posed to juniors and seniors. After students had provided spontaneous answers to this question, they were specifically probed about the influence of parents and friends. Twelve of the fifty respondents mentioned peers in their spontaneous response to the question. Of these twelve responses, five contained references to older siblings rather than to friends. Only 10 percent of juniors and seniors mentioned friendship influence in the open-ended question, compared with 32 percent of sophomores. The influence or attempted influence of friends appeared to be less important when more time had passed since the choice.

When the content of the seven spontaneous responses mentioning friendship influence is examined, the pattern is similar to the spontaneous responses of the sophomores. Only two of these students indicated that friends were the primary influence on their choice. "I think I signed up for another school, Voc-Tech or something, and then at the last minute all of my friends that I knew were getting into Flexible, so I got in Flexible too." This student transferred to Arts for her senior year. The remaining five students who spontaneously mentioned friends did so in a context of seeking what they perceived to be the learning environment best suited to them. A student in Conventional said, "I thought that I really wanted a push. I didn't want to slack off anyway. Some kids say that the better teachers are in Conventional." In these cases, references to friends were quite general; all references arose in the context of applying criteria from the articulation perspective.

Finally, all juniors and seniors were specifically probed about friendship influences. Table 8–3 shows the tabulation of responses into the constructed categories. From the distance of at least a year, these students clearly report that friendship influences were not great, since the category "some influence reported" includes all degrees of reported influence. Only two students reported friends to be the determining influence in their school choices.

The conclusion seems warranted that although many students debated the merits of the various options with friends, the majority of students appeared more attentive to the criteria contained in the articulation perspective than to the influences of friends. Given that shared orientations and values form the basis of friendship, most students picked the same schools as at least some of their friends.[19] Most responses indicated, however, that a desire to remain with friends was not their sole nor most powerful motivator. Finally, although no exact measurement is possible, among juniors and seniors there appeared to be an inverse relationship between a strong sense of future status and friendship influence. Students with clear future perspectives were not deflected by friends in choosing a school; those with a weak sense of school-future articulation were more susceptible to peer influence.

Table 8–3
Friendship Influences on Junior and Senior Students' Decisions

| | Influence Reported | | | |
School	Not in District as Sophomore or Did Not Discuss with Friends (N=6)	Friend Had No Real Influence (N=33)	Broke with Friends, Went to Another School (N=4)	Some Influence Reported (N=7)
Conventional	1	8	2	0
Flexible	1	9	0	2
Individual	0	4	0	3
Arts	2	6	2	0
Career	2	6	0	2

One caveat is necessary on the conclusion about friendship influence. The proximity of the alternative schools may have alleviated some concern about separation from friends. Students had free access to peers in other schools except during classes. Given the open campus and generally nonrestrictive climate of the school, most students could spend some time daily with almost anyone in any school. We speculate that concerns about separation from friends might become a larger factor in school choice in circumstances such as magnet school systems, in which peers are geographically separated and have no access to friends during the day.

Parents. The preferences of students are not always those of their parents. Among students who perceived that choice was totally their own, the right to choose had actually been delegated to them by their parents. The school, through its rule of required parent consent, acknowledged that the ultimate power of choice remained with the parents. Coons and Sugarman define "voice" as the degree to which a child is heard on his or her own behalf in a school choice decision.[20] Because the sophomore sample was drawn from all students entering EBC High, the interview contained questions to ascertain how large a voice they had in the selection process and whether parents deflected students from their preferred choices.

The results of questioning sophomores about voice are reported in table 8–4. Five analytic categories depict the relative perceived weight of parent influences and student voice in the choice process. The categories range from parent dictation of school to almost total student voice. In over half the cases students reported the decision as theirs, although they did consult parents. About a third of the sophomores reported that parents eliminated one or two schools but allowed them to choose freely among the remaining options. Parents most often eliminated Individual. Because no student in this category seemed inclined toward that school, however, no friction resulted. In four cases parents

Table 8–4
Extent of Sophomore Voice in Family-Choice Deliberations

	Percent	N[a]
Parents dictated choice of school.	0.0	0
Parents exerted major influence. The student was persuaded, without rancor, to follow the preferences of the parents.	12.0	3
Parents attempted to exert major influence, but the student persuaded the parents to accede to his or her wishes.	4.0	1
Parents eliminated one or two options but let the student choose among remaining options.	34.8	8
Parents discussed options with the student but left the decision largely to the student.	52.0	13

[a]Because of defective tapes, three students could not be categorized.

exerted major influence on the decision. In one of these cases the student was able to win her parents over to her choice. In three cases parents exerted major influence, and students accepted the judgments without rancor. There were no cases of absolute dictation of choice by parents.

In terms of the relative weight of student versus parent influence in school decisions, sophomore reports of the voice they exercised in school choice were roughly similar to the results of the initial survey of all EBC juniors and seniors. In that survey less than 2 percent of EBC students reported being compelled to attend an alternative against their own will. In his survey of nearly thirteen hundred freshmen entering Catholic high schools, Nault found that only 11 percent were coerced by parents to attend a school against their wills. Thus, heavy-handed influence by parents is not the norm. Rather, most parents give major voice to their offspring. When they do intervene, it is likely that they do so with the intention of producing what they perceive to be the best articulation between schooling and their own desire for their child's future.

Finally, it is likely that, at least indirectly, parents deeply affected the choices made by most students. Parents socialize their children to prefer certain environments, futures, and attitudes toward adult authority. Family socialization must, in general, have a large influence on students when they choose between alternative schools. Most parents (perhaps because they sensed that they had done their socializing well) were content to delegate the final choice of schools to their children. Most students therefore approached their junior year feeling that they had major responsibility for school choice.

Summary

A summary schematic presentation of choice-making behavior of the sophomore sample was derived from a checklist given them at the close of their interviews. They were asked to weigh eight potential influences on their choice making on a three-point scale, 3 being high. Table 8–5 shows the mean weights attributed to the eight influences. The weights are distributed into two distinct clusters. The more heavily weighted cluster contains influences consonant with aspects of the articulation perspective. The less heavily weighted cluster contains influences that might be seen as deflections from that perspective. Thus, the sophomore checklists seem to verify the perspective extrapolated from the junior and senior interviews.

Conclusion

The most general and obvious finding (so obvious as to be overlooked in many research and curricular models) is that these high school students are intentional beings. Rather than being empty vessels or clay easily molded by adults, they are active, purposeful, selective, and variously motivated persons. They take and make meanings as they interact with their school organization and the other persons in it.

What was salient, then, in the meanings that students developed when they were given authentic program choice? We conclude that the best explanation for student choice is the articulation perspective. That is, students generally worked within a matrix of concerns that included: the relationship between curricular type and anticipated career or educational goals, the degree of academic achievement desired (usually future related), and the relationship between potential learning environments and self-knowledge of "learning styles" or needs for particular environments (assuming a given level of desired performance). Simply put, students chose schools that maximized the likelihood of achieving their personal visions of the future. Those visions, of course, were quite varied.

Table 8–5
Relative Importance of Choice Factors to Sophomore Students Interviewed

Weight	Item
2.84	I thought I would learn best in the school I chose.
2.81	I liked how classes are run in the EBC school I picked.
2.71	I thought the school I chose would help me most in what I will be doing after I get out of high school.
2.52	I liked how the teachers deal with students in the EBC school I selected.
1.97	This was the school my parents thought would be best for me.
1.84	Most of my friends were going to the EBC school I chose.
1.68	I wanted to take classes with some of the teachers I knew in EBC High.
1.32	My sophomore year teachers advised me to select the school I did.

Within the articulation perspective, students chose the same school for quite different reasons and perceiving quite different futures. Some chose a school because they perceived a high articulation with college entrance and even success in graduate school. Others chose the same school because they believed that the climate would force them to complete sufficient credits to graduate. In all schools except the Voc-Tech, the resulting student bodies were indistinguishable in terms of socioeconomic status.[21] This finding seems important for those wrestling with questions of the effects of choice upon the makeup of resulting student bodies. The findings in this case, however, are probably heavily influenced by the context. EBC High was the sole public eleventh- and twelfth-grade facility in the community. No student was inconvenienced or traveled an extra distance to attend any of the various alternative programs. There were no noteworthy neighborhood differences among schools. Like the caveat offered in the discussion of friendship influences, the fact that all alternatives were contained within the same building probably affected the resulting student constituencies. Had the schools been geographically separated, the student bodies might have differed significantly.

Some students spontaneously described their school choice decision as a major life event, describing it like Robert Frost's roads that diverge in the woods. Some saw that each choice might lead to differences in future life. Others described the event as one of the major decisions they had to make in their life span. The event forced them to take stock of and responsibility for themselves in new ways. Some students, especially those choosing the less structured schools, saw the choice event as an opportunity to test their own maturity. The students who chose the less structured options were in fact taking more responsibility upon themselves. Most students did not describe school choice as a major life event, but then they were not asked to describe its significance in their lives. On the other hand, the vast majority of students were clearly not making their choices on the basis of short-term hedonism or finding the "easy way out"—although a sizable portion of the more conservative community at large apparently attributed that motivation to them.

The articulation perspective does not totally explain choice behavior. Parents and peers did exert influence on some students. The parental influence was of two types, a pervading one stemming from socialization and, in a smaller number of cases, a more specific and overt one of limiting choice. We have, however, argued that the vision a student holds of his or her personal future is strongly influenced by family socialization. That the individual's perception of the future is strongly influenced by parental socialization does not negate the articulation perspective. Rather, the perspective is a more general conception that subsumes the varied content of each individual's specific choice criteria.

Peers, too, exerted some influence although friends did not seem to deflect the vast majority of students from making choices that articulated with perceived future status. Teachers and counselors were not described as having much influence. The possibility remains, however, that they exerted subtle influence not detected by most students.

Finally, it seems useful to recall that there is general consensus and some empirical evidence that the circumstances under which an individual begins organizational membership are linked closely to the quality of initial involvement in the organization.[22] If this is so, then EBC High teachers and students began the junior year under favorable conditions. The students began their year by selecting a school in which they believed they could function most effectively, given their own visions of the future. They also exercised autonomy, which is gratifying to adolescents.[23] Both conditions seemed likely to elicit initial commitment to the programs selected.

Notes

1. National Commission on the Reform of Secondary Education, *The Reform of Secondary Education* (New York: McGraw-Hill, 1973); Panel on Youth of the President's Science Advisory Committee, *Youth: Transition to Adulthood* (Chicago: University of Chicago Press, 1974).

2. J.M. McPartland, E.L. McDill, C. Lacey, R.J. Harris, and L.B. Novey, *Student Participation in High School Decisions: A Study of Students and Teachers in Fourteen Urban High Schools* (Baltimore: ERIC Document Reproduction Service, 1971), p. 21.

3. R.L. Nault, "The School Commitments of Nonpublic School Freshmen Voluntarily and Involuntarily Affiliated with Their Schools" in *Educational Organization and Administration*, ed. Donald A. Erickson (Berkeley: McCutchan, 1977), pp. 264–295.

4. R.B. Kottkamp, "Student Choice and Denial in a Public School of Choice" (Paper presented at the meeting of the American Educational Research Association, San Francisco, April 1979).

5. E.Q. Campbell, "Adolescent Socialization," in *Handbook of Socialization Theory and Research,* ed. D.A. Goslin (Chicago: Rand McNally, 1969), p. 827.

6. J.S. Coleman, *The Adolescent Society* (New York: The Free Press of Glencoe, 1961); C.W. Gordon, *The Social System of the High School* (Glencoe, Ill.: The Free Press, 1957).

7. M.W. Riley, "Adolescents Talk to Peers and Parents," mimeographed (New Brunswick, N.J.: Rutgers University Department of Sociology, 1955).

8. C.V. Brittain, "Adolescent Choices and Parent-Peer Cross-Pressures," *American Sociological Review* 28 (1963):385–390.

9. S.A. Davis and E.J. Haller, "Determinants of Eighth-Graders' Placements in High School Tracks" (Paper presented at the meeting of the American Educational Research Association, Boston, April 1980).

10. A.L. Stinchcombe, *Rebellion in a High School* (Chicago: Quadrangle Books, 1964).

11. L.M. Smith, "Reflections on Trying to Theorize from Ethnographic Data" (Paper presented at the meeting of the American Anthropological Association, New Orleans, December 1973); B.G. Glaser and A.L. Strauss, *The Discovery of Grounded Theory: Strategies for Qualitative Research* (Chicago: Aldine, 1967).

12. Stinchcombe, *Rebellion in a High School,* pp. 5–6.

13. H.S. Becker, B. Greer, and E.C. Hughes, *Making the Grade: The Academic Side of College Life* (New York: Wiley, 1968); H.S. Becker, B. Geer, E.C. Hughes, and A.L. Strauss, *Boys in White: The Student Culture in Medical School* (Chicago: University of Chicago Press, 1961).

14. G.G. Stern, *People in Context* (New York: Wiley, 1970); D.E. Hunt and E.V. Sullivan, *Between Psychology and Education* (Hinsdale, Ill.: Dryden Press, 1974).

15. Gordon, *Social System of High School;* Coleman, *Adolescent Society;* P.A. Cusick, *Inside High School: The Student's World* (New York: Holt, Rinehart and Winston, 1973).

16. Riley, "Adolescents Talk," passim.

17. Claire Selltiz, Marie Jahoda, Morton Deutsch, and Stuart W. Cook, *Research Methods in Social Relations* (New York: Holt, Rinehart and Winston, 1959).

18. Jean Piaget, *The Moral Development of the Child* (New York: The Free Press, 1965).

19. C.N. Alexander and E.Q. Campbell, "Peer Influences on Adolescent Educational Aspirations and Attainments," *American Sociological Review* 29 (1964):568–575.

20. John E. Coons and Stephen D. Sugarman, *Education by Choice: The Case for Family Control* (Berkeley: University of California Press, 1978).

21. Every student's residence was marked on a detailed community map with a color code for the student's school. The map was then partitioned into areas representing seven different SES levels on the basis of earlier work by Havighurst. See further R.J. Havighurst, P.H. Bowman, G.F. Liddle, C.V. Matthews, and J.V. Pierce, *Growing Up in River City* (New York: Wiley, 1962). Visual estimates of areas built up since the earlier study provided a rough estimate of the SES breakdown for the total population of each alternative school. Analysis of these data indicated a broad and relatively equivalent spectrum of SES backgrounds in all schools except Voc-Tech, which contained a considerably lower average SES constituency.

22. A. Etzioni, *A Comparative Analysis of Complex Organizations* (New York: Free Press of Glencoe, 1961); R.O. Carlson, "Environmental Constraints and Organizational Consequences: The Public School and its Clients," in *The Sixty-Third Yearbook of the National Society for the Study of Education: Be-*

havioral Science and Education Administration, pt. 2, ed. D.E. Griffiths (Chicago: University of Chicago Press, 1964); pp. 262–276; C.E. Bidwell, "Students and Schools: Some Observations on Client-Serving Organizations," in *Organizations and Clients: Essays in the Sociology of Service,* ed. W.R. Rosengren and M. Lefton (Columbus, Ohio: Charles E. Merrill, 1970), pp. 37–69; McPartland, *Student Participation in Decisions;* Nault, "School Commitments of Freshmen"; Kottkamp, "Student Choice and Denial."

23. C.E. Buxton, *Adolescents in Schools* (New Haven: Yale University Press, 1973).

Private Schools: The Client Connection

William T. Garner and Jane Hannaway

Proponents of private schools claim many virtues for them. They contend that the educational programs are in accord with parental preferences, that the schools are responsive to client wants, and that parents generally have considerable influence in determining what happens in the schools. These conditions, they explain, result from the nature of the relationship between the client, whom we identify as the parent, and the school. Parents affiliate with a school through choice, not through assignment; and private schools depend for their survival largely on tuition monies from parents. Consequently, parents choose schools of whose programs and philosophies they approve, and the schools try to retain their clients by keeping them satisfied . . . or so the story goes.

In this chapter we examine the client-school relationship in private schools. The story proves to be not as simple as proposed above. The nature of the client-school relationship varies considerably from school to school, and in the following discussion we attempt to isolate some of the factors that contribute to this variability. We proceed by examining the client connection from both an economic and a political perspective, drawing heavily on the thinking of A.O. Hirschman in *Exit, Voice, and Loyalty*.[1] In both perspectives we are interested in the implications of the relationship for client control. First, we view the relation as one between consumer and producer and discuss the applicability of a consumer model of control; second, we view the parent as a political actor with influence and investigate the extent of parental participation in school matters.

Consumer Control and the Market Model

Institutions can be controlled or held accountable through a variety of mechanisms. One is the mechanism of market organization, in which the control behavior is "exit." In a market of voluntary buyers and sellers, the consumer

This chapter reports work performed by the authors under Contract No. 400-78-0030 with the National Institute of Education, U.S. Office (now Department) of Education. Another version of this paper appears in *The Private High School Today* (Washington, D.C.: U.S. Department of Education, National Institute of Education, 1981).

or purchaser is free to exit from any firm whose prices are too high or whose product's quality is unsatisfactory. The analysis of market behavior in economics proceeds from a rather strict set of assumptions about ideal markets in which "pure competition" prevails. In the case of schooling, the pure competition model would suppose that there was a very large number of schools and that parents were free to choose any school they liked. The model would assume that parents had a good understanding of what they wanted and what each school provided, leading us to expect a close match between parental preferences and school offerings. The model would also assume that parents would not pay a higher tuition (price) than necessary to purchase a particular type and quality of service, leading us to expect schools with similar offerings to have similar levels of cost. Schools that did not keep their clients satisfied would lose clientele to other schools. Likewise, schools that overcharged would lose enrollment to lower-priced schools of similar quality. Because parents exercise choice in selecting a private school for their child, and because private schools do not have the relatively assured revenue of public schools, some observers assume that private schools operate the way firms operate in a competitive market; that is, they assume that the interaction between parent and school (demand and supply) in private schooling produces a closer and more efficient match between parental desires and school offerings than it does in government-owned and -operated public schools.

The case for expanding school choices may not rest on the degree to which private schooling fits the competitive market model of economics; yet these are the arguments most commonly advanced. There has been much discussion and speculation about the limits and consequences of an educational free market; but not many data have been brought to bear on the reasonableness of the assumptions of the market model as applied to education, much less its predictions.[2]

In the following section we analyze the applicability of the free market model to education and suggest four ways in which the private school market differs from the simplifying assumptions of the model of pure competition. These differences from the market or competitive model (we use the terms interchangeably) may require adaptations of that model or even the grafting of new elements suited to the education market. We discuss in detail one of these four differences on which we have empirical evidence from the NIE Survey of Private Secondary School Heads.

The Economic Model

According to the economic model of pure competition, the exercise of choice by consumers regulates the system. The consumer is sovereign: consumer demand determines what is produced and, together with production technology, determines the relative prices at which products may be sold. Demand for a commodity is a measure of the amount that consumers are willing and able to buy. Consumers seek the products they desire at the lowest price available, and producers compete for consumers by offering the "best value" for a dollar. The result is efficient production. Firms that cannot produce efficiently, or do not produce what consumers want, fail the competitive test and die when enough consumers exit from the firm's clientele and take their business elsewhere.

The other factor determining price is supply. Supply is the measure of the amount that producers are willing and able to produce. Owners of firms and consumers are both assumed to behave so as to maximize their individual welfare. Voluntary trading in the market leads to production and consumption of market clearing quantities and prices of goods (where demand and supply intersect). Every party is as well satisfied as can be, given the initial distribution of income.

A pure economic model, however, is not completely satisfactory when applied to private educational instituions. Four factors in particular contravene a pure model: not-for-profit orientation, the nature of the commodity produced, imperfect competition, and imperfect information. These factors are not completely independent, but they are conceptually distinct.

Not-for-Profit Orientation. The economic model assumes that the behavior of firms is primarily motivated by profits; but the same assumption does not generally hold for private schools. Because it is difficult to specify the motivating forces, or preference function, for schools, their behavior under certain conditions may differ significantly from that of profitmaking firms.[3] When demand exceeds supply, for example, the profitmaking firm will normally ration its product (and increase its profits) by raising the selling price. The resulting higher-than-normal profit level would then attract new firms into the market, thus increasing the amount supplied and lowering price to a normal profit level. The not-for-profit school, however, depending on its preferences, may ration places by raising its admission standards or by forming a waiting list, not by raising prices.

The Nature of the Commodity Produced. The "output" of educational institutions is different in some respects from other types of commodities. For example, the market model assumes the production of homogeneous goods that are essentially the same regardless of who supplies them. This assumption is problematic in educational production, where there is not even agreement about what the primary product of schooling is, much less about whether any particular product is homogeneous. Some argue that education is primarily a screening mechanism by which different types of people are sorted and labeled.[4] Others argue that education produces changes in individuals; but some stress normative changes and some stress cognitive changes. One way to view the commodity marketed by educational organizations is as a set of services purchased in an all-or-nothing package by the consuming household, not as a single good or service. Some of these services are sufficiently subjective or unclear to permit two observers of the same school to reach different conclusions about what the school is offering. Even after schooling has taken place and the services have been performed, identification of the value added by whatever was done is still a problem.

Imperfect Competition. Imperfect competition arises when a consumer or producer has some degree of control over price. The perfect competition model assumes that no individual or small group can influence quantities or price. Because firms are motivated by profits it is quite reasonable for them to strive to obtain as much control over price as possible. There are basically two ways for a firm to affect its profit: through the efficiency of its production; and through raising the price of its product. The second way is effective only if there are no competitors offering the same product for a lower price. Therefore, a common strategy is for firms to attempt to distinguish themselves from competitors and to gain some control over the market by offering a slightly different product or by emphasizing different aspects of their process in marketing. The consumer is encouraged to see the firm's product not as homogeneous with that of other suppliers, but rather as different and worth paying more for.

Schools, however, are not profit maximizers, and their preference function is unclear. Therefore, they might not be as interested in control over price as firms. It is probably safe to assume, however, that managers of a private school prefer to control the allocation of the school's resources, and that their preferences for that allocation (such as the amount allocated to administration) may differ from those of the clients (parents). The way to achieve such control is similar to that used by profitmaking firms to achieve some control over price. That is, a school's control over allocations and its ability to resist parental influence are presumably greatest when there is no rival school to which the parent can exit.[5] The school can achieve this condition by finding a market niche—by offering something special (or leading buyers to think it is doing so). The ability of a school to differentiate its product in this way will be limited by the size of the market in which it is operating.

Imperfect Information. The fourth reason for deviation from the competitive model is the one to which we devote the most attention in this chapter. The pure market model makes assumptions about the informational states of actors: actors' choices are assumed to be based on complete and accurate information, available at no cost to them. Thus, in the case of schooling, the pure economic model assumes that parents have complete and accurate information about the availability and the quality of a school (what it will produce relative to other schools), and the model predicts that parents would choose the school that yields the desired results at the lowest price. The particular expected result guiding the choice is based on the preferences or tastes (and income) of the parents. It is reasonable to assume that different types of parents have different preferences, that is, that they value different types of results. Some parents may choose a school on the basis of its academic quality; others may base their decision on a school's athletic achievement, religious training, discipline structure, or innovativeness. In general, though, the model would lead us to expect that within any one school parental tastes would be similar to each other and that the services the school offers would reflect those tastes.

Imperfect information refers to situations in which consumers, for example, are not able to assess all the relevant characteristics of different products or services; that is, they do not possess complete information about what their dollar can actually buy. This condition impairs the workings of the market; it has serious implications for efficiency. Even if information about schools were considered accurate and reliable, the cost of obtaining it must be taken into account. And if there are systematic differences in the types and quality of information available or differences in the amount or type of information received (or the way information is interpreted) by particular groups, appropriate modifications of the pure model predictions would be required.

Markets can be characterized in terms of imperfect information on three levels. On the first level, obtaining information is costly and/or slow, but possible. On the second level, there is a natural assymetry in information between the producer and the consumer, such as when the doctor knows more than the patient and the patient does not know the value of what has been purchased until after the purchase has been made.[6] But it is the third level that seems to describe best the condition of imperfect information in education: neither the producer nor the consumer has much understanding about what is produced. Although education professionals (producers) know more than parents (consumers) about what goes on in school, they are usually unable to specify beforehand either the effect of their efforts or the best way to proceed with production. And even after the professionals have finished their work, they are unable to isolate what difference their efforts made. Therefore, both consumers and the producers possess only very limited relevant information about the process of education.[7]

Table 9–1 summarizes the differences we have found between the pure competition model and the private school reality.

Model Predictions and Survey Results

In this section we focus in more depth on imperfect information as one of the reasons the market for private schools might behave differently from the pre-

Table 9–1
The Pure Competition Model and the Private School Reality

Model	Reality
Profit orientation	Not for profit
Homogeneous goods, purchased separately	Bundles of different goods, some of uncertain nature
Many producers	Often few producers
Information freely available	Information costly, inaccessible, or of uncertain value

dictions of a perfect competition model. We also present some empirical results based on a national sample survey of private secondary school heads.[8] Because we do not have data on individual parent information, we cannot directly test the adequacy of that information. It is possible, however, to explore the role of information in private school markets indirectly, by hypothesizing what findings would be expected if information were freely available and comparing the actual survey findings with those expected. We have done this in three areas for which survey data are available: expenditure variations, parent and school goal congruence, and parent goal and school outcome congruence. In each of these areas, the results differ from those predicted by the hypothesis of perfect information. Taken singly, none of these tests can be considered conclusive. Together, however, we believe they support the view that information is not freely or uniformly distributed in the private school sector, which suggests that the private school market does not fit the perfect competition model.

Expenditure Dispersion. If information were perfect in the market for schooling, we would expect to see similar prices charged for similar schools, on the assumption that knowledgeable parents would not willingly pay more than the lowest available price for a given quality of schooling. As Stigler said, "Price dispersion is a manifestation—and, indeed, it is the measure—of ignorance in the market."[9] In the case of schooling, we are faced with the difficulty that it is not always possible to determine to what degree schools are similar. If no two schools are alike, then different prices for different schools would not be surprising.

Because the survey data do not contain actual tuition charges (prices), we assess dispersion indirectly by relying on expenditure per pupil. This calls for the construction of a model that should account for differences in expenditure among schools. In this model, per-pupil expenditure is considered to depend on the size of the school (to account for possible scale effects), on whether or not the school is a boarding school (boarding schools must provide residential services in addition to education services), on geographic location (different regions of the country may have different typical cost levels), on school affiliation (Catholic and independent schools may have different cost structures), on the percentage of graduates going to four-year colleges (college preparatory curricula may have different cost characteristics than other curricula), and on the percentage of school parents who have white-collar or professional occupations (both willingness and ability to pay may differ by parent occupation).

This model accounts for about half of the variation in per-pupil expenditures, which means that about half of such expenditure variation is *not* accounted for by these factors. Furthermore, the findings show that even if two schools are alike on the factors above, there is about one chance in three that their expenditures per pupil will differ by more than $1,700, a range which is large when compared to a mean expenditure of about $1,400 for the sampled schools.

As we are not certain that our model includes all the most important factors that influence school expenditures, we cannot conclude that the remaining variation in cost is due to imperfect information. Moreover, we do not know to what extent any of the sampled schools faces competition from nearby schools. Because there is substantial expenditure variation among otherwise similar schools in this model, however, we do not reject the idea that education markets are characterized by imperfect information, as our earlier arguments suggested. We proceed therefore to examine the data further for evidence of imperfect information by assessing the degree to which the goals of parents and school heads are congruent, and the match between the goals of parents and the output of the school.

Parent and School Head Goal Congruence. If information about private schools were freely available to clients and potential clients, we would expect to find that parents choose schools that have educational goals and philosophies like their own. In the survey, private school heads rated the importance of each of seven educational goals. Elsewhere in the survey, the school head also rated the same seven goals as the majority of the school's parents would. To examine the similarity of these sets of ratings, we constructed an index of parent and school head goal congruence indicating the degree of agreement on all seven goals.[10] This index, which has a standard deviation as large as its mean, shows that there is considerable disparity between parent and school head ratings. In a further breakdown, the disparity between parent and school head ratings was found to be significantly related to the proportion of parents in the school with white-collar or professional occupations: the higher the proportion of such parents, the closer the congruence between parent and school head goal ratings. We interpret these findings as another indication that information is neither perfectly nor uniformly distributed in the private school market.

Parent Goal and School Output. In a third test of the perfect information hypothesis, we examined the congruence between parent educational goal ratings—again, as reported by school head—and school output indicators. The notion of imperfect information in schooling suggests that parents will not always get what they want when selecting a school. This may result from one or a combination of the conditions discussed earlier, such as the cost of obtaining information, the uneven availability of information, or even the obscure or ambiguous nature of some of the information. On these grounds, then, we expect to find variation in the degree to which parent educational goals are matched by actual school offerings and outcomes.

To investigate these relationships, we constructed indexes of course offerings related to two educational goals: college preparation and preparation for the world of work. Also available in the survey data are the proportions of each school's graduates entering the labor force and the proportion entering four-year colleges. If information about the schools were freely available, we would expect parent educational goal rating to be strongly related to actual course offerings and to student outcomes (postgraduate college or labor force percentages).

The results of these analyses show that there is a relation between parent educational goal rating and the measures of course offerings and student outcomes. But there is an even stronger relation between parent occupation and the offerings and outcomes. That is, of two schools with identical parent goal ratings, the correspondence of school output to those ratings will be substantially higher in the school with a higher proportion of white-collar and professional parents.

These results, though not conclusive, lend support to the view that schooling information is not equally available to all consumers in private school markets; higher-status parents seem to make better-informed choices. The findings together (see table 9–2) support our broader suspicion that market mechanisms may not be fully effective as a means for the regulation of private schooling.

Another Means of Consumer Control: The Political Perspective

In the first part of this chapter we discussed the applicability of a model of control based on competition and consumer choice: a traditional economic

Table 9–2
Evidence on Imperfect Information in the Private Schooling Sector

Criterion	Evidence
Expenditure dispersion	Wide expenditure dispersion not fully accounted for by school or client characteristics
Parent/school head goal congruence	Goal congruence higher in schools with higher proportions of white collar and professional parents
Parent goal/school outcome congruence	Goals and outcomes more congruent in schools with higher proportions of white collar and professional parents

model. Here we consider another form of consumer control, one based on client participation. This mechanism, called "voice," refers to attempts by consumers to control the producing organization through internal influence, that is, through influencing policy and decision making, in order to obtain outcomes more congruent with consumer desires.[11] Voice can take many forms, among them protest, lobbying, petition, and formal representation. We examine the nature of voice by looking at the extent of formal mechanisms for consumer participation, such as parent advisory groups, and then asking how the opportunity for this type of involvement varies across schools. Specifically, we are interested in how the extent of choice, or the amount of competition facing a school, affects voice. That is, we can argue that the amount of competition affects the extent of voice *demanded by parents* as well as the extent of voice *supplied by schools*. The demand and the supply arguments, however, lead to opposite predictions, explained below. Empirical results supporting the supply view follow the discussion and suggest that schools facing greater competition supply parents with more formal channels of voice.

The Demand Argument

According to the demand argument, voice is more likely to be exercised as exit opportunities decline. Parents are more likely to attempt to exercise control within a school (demand input into policy) when the availability of other school options is limited (the school has little competition). In other words, the extent and volume of voice by parents would be inversely related to the extent and intensity of competition faced by the school.

This idea leads to a number of expectations about the extent of parent voice under various conditions, and these expectations form the first set of ideas investigated. Specifically, we focus on factors that limit the number of alternatives available to parents (limit competition) and estimate their effect on the level of parent input into a school (voice).

Assuming the presence of the market mechanism, one might ask whether control through voice is an appropriate way to approach the study of private school management. Voice seems more appropriate for studying public schools than private schools, and in general we would expect voice to play a more important role in the former. Many private schools, however, operate with only limited competition. And because the cost to the student (psychological, social, and educational) of changing schools is so high, the exit option is limited. For these reasons we would also expect voice in private schools to play an important role.

This leads us to another question. If the exit option in private schools is limited, why would managers listen to their consumers? When we try to address this question, the relationship between competition and voice in school organizations becomes more complicated than the demand argument suggests. The demand argument focuses on the conditions under which consumers are likely to demand voice, but it does not analyze the conditions that would motivate managers to *provide* channels for voice. Why would managers supply voice channels?

The Supply Argument

There are at least three reasons why we might expect school managers to provide voice channels. The first is related to competition and, in the case of schools at least, runs counter to consumer demand argument. In general, the idea is that the bases of competition are unclear among organizations (such as schools or mental health agencies) with unspecifiable outcomes and with a technology that is not well understood. In the case of private schools, given the difficulty of a parent's predicting how well a child and a school will interact, the provision for continued parental involvement may in fact be one of the appealing factors that parents weigh when making a school choice. Such channels for involvement make parents feel assured that if things are not going well, they will have a say in making changes. The extent of provisions for parent input, then, may well be one of the bases of competition among schools, leading us to expect it to increase with competition.

Second, private schools may supply channels for voice in order to stem any public expression of parental discontent. The idea is basically one of cooptation. Because of the ambiguous nature of their output, schools are highly dependent on their reputations for obtaining clients. Therefore, whereas the possibility of exit may not be particularly threatening to private school managers, the future costs associated with loss of reputation, and thus of future clientele, may be.

Another reason to expect voice to vary positively with competition, even when the probability of exit is low, is that of comparison. Given the lack of precision in the schooling technology, comparisons of what schools are doing is one way for parents to obtain information about the appropriateness of what their particular school is doing. The more comparisons that can be made, that is, the greater the number of similar schools nearby, the more information parents would have about what programs and services are available. This increased information about the range of possibilities may motivate schools to engage in harder selling effort. (Indeed, it may also increase the likelihood of attempts by parents to influence their own school.) Without such comparisons, given the ambiguity surrounding the production process in schools, parents would not know if they could be better off. As a result, we would not expect a high level of parent involvement.

There are other reasons why not-for-profit organizations may be particularly open to voice. Precisely because private schools are not profit maximizers, and because education markets are characterized by imperfect information, a school's management has the latitude to be concerned with other objectives, including a happy clientele. In a purely competitive world every firm is threatened by the actions of more efficient or innovative competitors to whom clients may exit. Thus, any behavior directed to objectives other than profit maximization could put a firm out of business. But in the case of schools, because it is unclear exactly what they are producing or how they are going about production, school managers may, on the one hand, need the detailed, complex information feedback that client voice provides and, on the other hand, have the freedom to be responsive with no discernible cost to production.

Some Caveats

The preceding arguments are based on consumer response to discontent: consumer exit and consumer voice are seen as mechanisms that can improve an organization's performance. If consumers are well satisfied, we might expect neither exit nor voice. To investigate these ideas properly requires using at least two time periods, one to measure the extent of discontent and one to measure the response. The design of this study, however, is one-period cross-sectional, and therefore we are making certain assumptions. The basic assumption is that the phenomenon being studied is in equilibrium; that is, that the conditions that lead to voice have already had their effect and that we are measuring the result in the form of institutionalized channels. This is probably not an unreasonable assumption given that during the 1970s the fortunes of educational institutions have in general fallen and public attitudes toward schools have steadily declined.

Another possible problem is that the data are based on the reports of school heads. A refined analysis of the ideas posed in this paper would require data collected at the level of the individual consumer. The school level reports, however, though perhaps not useful for precise quantitative estimates, should give us some indication of the validity of the ideas and of whether the factors discussed below are positively or negatively associated with voice.

Competition Factors

The basic idea being investigated here is whether the extent of choice available to parents (that is, the extent of competition faced by the school) is related to the extent of formal participation in school matters by parents (voice). Because we have no direct measures of competition in the survey, we rely on indirect measures commonly assumed to be related to competition. These factors are specialization, quality, expenditure per student, and population density. Greater levels of specialization and higher quality constrain competition; higher costs and greater population density are associated with more competition.

Specialization refers to product differentiation: a school offers a ''product'' different enough from those of its competitors that it is able to secure a niche in the market in which it functions with only limited competition. According to the consumer demand argument, we would expect this to increase the likelihood of voice; alternatively, from the supply side, if it were protected from competition by virtue of specialization, we would not expect schools to feel it necessary to provide voice channels. A specialization index was constructed to measure the range of programs and course offerings in each school. Specialized schools were those with the narrowest range of offerings. A school could specialize in providing services for high-achieving college-bound students or for students preparing for vocational careers.

The second factor related to competition is the quality of the school, which we measured in terms of the percentage of graduates attending four-year colleges. Exit options are particularly limited for schools at the upper end of the quality continuum.[12] The idea is that exit is discouraged because for the quality-conscious consumer there is no place to go but down, and therefore parents demand involvement to ensure high-quality production. That is the demand argument. But we can also argue that, given their position in the market, these schools may be the least responsive (supply argument).

A third factor associated with competition is expenditure per student, which we assume varies directly with tuition. The idea is that parents of students in expensive schools are generally wealthier than parents of students in inexpensive schools and could therefore be less constrained in their choice of a school. Consequently, expensive schools would be subject to more market pressure. According to the demand view, we would expect this to have a negative effect on voice, since such parents could exercise the exit option; and, according to the supply view, we would expect it to have a positive effect, since schools would seek to retain clients by staying ''in tune'' with their desires.

We might also expect competition to be greater in more densely populated areas. There would simply be more schools from which to choose. The demand view would lead us to expect a negative relation between population density and voice, whereas the supply view would predict a positive relationship.

The Arguments and the Findings

The results shown in table 9–3 reveal that there is some evidence for both the demand argument and the supply argument, although the findings that are significant all support the supply view that there is a positive relation between competition and voice.

Notice that the pattern of response for Catholic schools is different from the pattern for other nonpublic schools. This could be interpreted in two different ways. First, we could argue that Catholic schools are fearful of losing further enrollment. The enrollment in Catholic schools has been declining in recent years (although this trend may be turning). This may be due to increased tuition costs, a possible decline in religiosity, and the general reduction in the school-age population. Catholic schools, then, may be attempting to be increasingly responsive to parents to maintain enrollment. This is consistent with the supply argument. The second reason is that there is something about the school's being a religious one that reduces the effect of competition on voice; Hirschman might argue that this is loyalty. (Data at the individual client level would be necessary to distinguish clearly between these two interpretations.)

A second finding of interest is the consistent and usually significant positive relation between population density and voice. Since we assumed that there would be more schools from which to choose in urban areas, we assumed there would be more competition and therefore less voice. Our initial assumptions, however, did not take into account the recent increase in demand for private

Table 9-3
Relationship between Competition Factors and Extent of Voice

	Demand Argument	Supply Argument
All (N = 202)		
Specialization	+	⊖
Percentage of graduates attending college	+	⊖**
Per pupil expenditure	⊖	+
Population density	−	⊕***
Noncatholic (N = 37)		
Specialization	⊕	−
Percentage of graduates attending college	⊕	−
Per pupil expenditure	⊖	+
Population density	−	⊕**
Catholic (N = 165)		
Specialization	+	⊖
Percentage of graduates attending college	+	⊖
Per pupil expenditure	⊖	+
Population density	−	⊕***

The regression results on which these tables are based can be found in William T. Garner and Jane Hannaway, "Competition and Client Participation in Private Schools" (Paper presented at the annual meeting of the American Educational Research Association, San Francisco, April 10, 1979). The signs show the predicted slope for the demand argument and the supply argument. The circled sign denotes the empirical findings.

** p < .01
*** p < .001

schools in urban areas. Demand, in fact, may far outrun supply. Consequently, many schools are requiring students to enroll in earlier grades to ensure a place in the school in the upper grades. (In a competitive firm under these conditions we would expect an increase in price, but in schools it seems to lead to rationing places.) The exit option in urban areas is therefore severely limited because most places in urban private schools are taken, resulting in more voice.

Policy Implications

A general policy issue is whether increased competition among schools will affect parental involvement—that is, voice—in schools. The idea is one of consumer protection, especially given conditions of imperfect information. (This question, of course, is separate from that of whether increased competition will lead to better schooling.) Although our tests are indirect, the results suggest that in conditions of greater competition schools provide more mechanisms for parental involvement in school matters.

Control through exit and control through internal influence may go hand in hand in the case of private schools, rather than substitute for each other. This finding becomes more important when we look specifically at the effect associated with higher expenditures, which implies that wealthier parents have fewer involvement mechanisms available than do lower-income parents. The conventional wisdom is that schools are more responsive or more open to the rich than to the poor. Our findings suggest otherwise, at least with respect to formal opportunities for communication; at the same time, we find that schools with larger proportions of white-collar and professional parents are more likely to provide the services and outcomes parents want. These results should be further assessed by comparing public schools with private ones. In public schools we may find that schools are more open to the wealthier parents, and the explanation would lie in the insularity of the public school system from competitive forces; that is, teachers and principals may prefer to interact with higher- rather than lower-status people, and behave consistently with these preferences. But under competition, they have no choice. If they do not want to lose their clients, they have to be open to all of them. Follow-up studies should also investigate the use and effectiveness of formal versus informal channels of involvement to assess whether the formal channels actually retard or facilitate attempts at influence. Formal channels may be more available to lower-status parents but less effective than informal channels, and these informal channels may be more often used by higher-status parents.

Notes

1. Albert O. Hirschman, *Exit, Voice, and Loyalty* (Cambridge, Mass.: Harvard University Press, 1972).

2. John E. Coons and Stephen D. Sugarman, *Education by Choice: The Case for Family Control* (Berkeley: University of California Press, 1978); and Henry M. Levin, "The Failure of the Public Schools and the Free Market Remedy," *Urban Review* 2 (June 1968):32.

3. See William A. Niskanen, *Bureaucracy and Representative Government* (Chicago: Aldine Atherton, 1971), for a discussion of managers in not-for-profit organizations; and Jane Hannaway, "Administrative Structures: Why Do They Grow?," *Teachers College Record* 79 (February 1978):413–436.

4. Joel Spring, *The Sorting Machine* (New York: David McKay, 1976).

5. Hirschman, *Exit, Voice, and Loyalty,* p. 55.

6. For a discussion of this point see Kenneth Arrow, *The Limits of Organization* (New York: W. W. Norton & Co., 1973), p. 36.

7. See Hirschman, *Exit, Voice, and Loyalty,* p. 12 about the effects of ignorance on the part of producers and consumers in different sectors, among them education.

8. Susan Abramowitz and E. Ann Stackhouse, *The Private High School Today* (Washington, D.C.: U.S. Department of Education, National Institute of Education, 1981).

9. George Stigler, "The Economics of Information," *Journal of Political Economy* 69 (June 1961):213–225.

10 .For details of index construction see William T. Garner and Jane Hannaway, "Imperfect Information and Private School Selection" (Paper presented at American Educational Research Association Annual Meeting, San Francisco, April 10, 1979).

11. We draw heavily for this section on the thinking of Hirschman in *Exit, Voice, and Loyalty.*

12. Ibid., p. 54.

10 The Tuition Tax Credit: Uncertain Directions in Public Policy

Donald E. Frey

Although all efforts for more than a decade to enact a federal tax credit for tuition payments have failed, prospects for the passage of such legislation seemed considerably brighter after the 1980 election. Defining the tax credit for tuition paid to elementary and secondary schools is considerably easier than assessing its many implications. A tuition tax credit permits an individual to reduce the amount of federal income tax he owes by some percentage of tuition paid to nonpublic elementary or secondary schools. A maximum limit may be placed on the amount of credit that may be claimed; in the past, proposed bills have tended to set relatively low limits. Once the principle of a tuition tax credit is established in law, however, an effort to raise the limit would undoubtedly begin.[1] A tax credit is deemed refundable if parents who otherwise owed less income tax than the credit for which they qualified received the balance from the government. The credit can also be characterized in economic terms as a reduction in the net tuition paid by parents of nonpublic school pupils. The credit is technically a demand-side device, for the consumers, or demanders, of education are the nominal recipients of the subsidy. Just as the incidence of taxes, however, may shift from those upon whom they are levied to others, the incidence of a tax credit may shift, in whole or in part, from parents to the schools.

This paper analyzes some of the implications of the tuition tax credit for public policy. The first section defines several of the policy goals enunciated by proponents of the credit. The second section explores two ways in which constitutional requirements limit the freedom of Congress in dealing with church-related private schools. Following a brief discussion in the third section of the case for the credit in economic theory, the remainder of the paper suggests several of the possible consequences of a tuition tax credit. In what follows, terms like *nonpublic* and *private* are used interchangeably.

Portions of this chapter reflect the author's paper presented at a conference titled Restoring Confidence in Public Education: An Agenda for the 1980s, sponsored by the National Urban Coalition, which has granted permission to republish. The original paper, titled "Public Education, Private Education and the Tuition Tax Credit," appeared in *Restoring Confidence in Public Education: An Agenda for the 1980s—Conference Research Papers*, (Washington, D.C.: The National Urban Coalition, 1979).

135

Goals and Fears

The tuition tax credit suffers from an abundance of goals, some competing with others. In the early 1970s, President Nixon's Commission on School Finance, mindful that the Supreme Court required aid to church-run schools to be extended only for secular purposes, emphasized the need to keep nonpublic schools from closing so that public schools might be spared the necessity of absorbing displaced pupils.[2] This rationale for federal aid is now rarely used because recent enrollment figures for nonpublic schools fail to show a declining trend.[3] By 1978, the tuition tax credit (for college as well as elementary and secondary education) was being promoted heavily as a form of tax relief for the middle class, who, it was alleged, suffered particularly acutely from tuition expenses.[4]

Other proponents of the credit have emphasized rather different goals. Economic theorists have favored education subsidies for parents as a means of enhancing consumer choice.[5] If parental preferences about education are diverse, then tuition subsidies would enable parents to choose from among the diverse offerings of the private sector those that best suit their preferences. Some who are concerned for urban education use a variant of this argument when they claim that a tuition tax credit would enable low-income or minority children in large cities to afford a private alternative to the public schools— alleged to be of low quality.[6] A last group of credit proponents finds the purpose of the credit a redressing of injustice. One alleged injustice is the "double taxation" that occurs when some parents pay not only tuition for their own children, but also education taxes as well.[7] Still others claim that justice requires the government to subsidize private education for students who are forced to leave public schools perceived to be advocating values hostile to the students' values.[8]

These purposes are highly diverse and some are incompatible. If the tax credit were efficiently designed to maximize tax relief for the middle class, for example, then little aid would be available to help low-income students attend urban parochial schools. In 1978 the major tuition tax credit bills in Congress were broadly written, without the restrictions and qualifications that would have focused the credit on one or a few of these goals. Had the credit passed, therefore, it would have been an inefficient instrument in the sense that for every dollar disbursed to achieve one goal, several would have been disbursed that did not serve that goal.

Opponents of the credit fear that it may be incompatible with other federal purposes. They claim that the distribution of benefits from the credit would be regressive (that is, favoring high-income taxpayers), that local support for public schools might be eroded, that the racial integration of public schools might be hindered, and that the credit might compete for limited federal education funds.[9]

The Constitutional Bind

Because almost 90 percent of nonpublic schools in the United States are church-run institutions, any aid to nonpublic schools or their pupils has traditionally been closely examined to see that it does not violate the establishment clause of the First Amendment. The Supreme Court has developed a threefold test of constitutionality: that the purpose of the aid from the government be secular; that the primary effect of the aid be neither to advance nor hinder religion; that the aid create no excessive entanglement of state and church. I argue here that a bill designed to meet these criteria to the greatest degree possible, especially the entanglement standard, will be inherently deficient in other respects.

One alleged legal advantage of a tax credit over direct aid to nonpublic schools is that the nominal beneficiary is the parent, not the school. According to the theory, the parent becomes a buffer between the school and the government, thereby minimizing entanglement.[10] To minimize entanglement further, the major tax credit bills of 1978 avoided establishing any federal education standards that private schools would have to meet in order for their students' parents to claim the credit; that is, sponsors of tax credit bills did not want to create the possibility of federal inspectors visiting church-run schools. Thus, the direct effect of the effort to avoid entanglement of church and state was a tax credit plan envisioning federal subsidization of nonpublic education unbalanced by any accountability of the private schools to the federal government.

Perhaps in recognition of the weakness of such an arrangement, the 1978 tax credit amendment of Senator Moynihan, which is typical of most, shifted accountability to the states, defining eligible private schools as those accredited or approved by the states, or those that satisfied state attendance laws. It is difficult, however, to imagine a more ill-timed proposal. A developing trend finds state oversight of nonpublic schools being reduced through both legislative and court challenge by aggressive private-school organizations (usually representing fundamentalist Christian schools); in other states where private enrollment is likely to grow, state oversight is already weak.[11] In short, a federal tuition tax credit might direct substantial amounts of public funds to a nonpublic sector that is not accountable to the public—at least not in several states. Although the issue of accountability is most acute with respect to educational quality, the issue also involves student rights and employee bargaining rights.

A rather unusual constitutional claim is made by some who assert that public schools cannot be neutral in matters of religion. Some sectarians insist on interpreting the refusal of public schools to endorse particular religious positions as hostility to their faith. In this perspective, the possibility of neutrality or silence on issues of religion is not entertained. Failure to endorse sectarian positions is viewed as though it amounted to the endorsement of an antireligious position. Consider the following testimony at a congressional hearing: "In the last few years Christians across this land have come to believe that their children are being taught in the public schools a religion that contradicts their own religious convictions. A religion that is nontheistic but a religion nevertheless.''[12] In this view everything has a religious meaning by definition; thus, neutrality cannot exist. The public schools cannot win. The call for a tuition tax credit in such a case can be interpreted as a demand to be relieved from supporting an oppressive, hostile, nontheistic religion in the public schools.

The government cannot accept this argument, for then public policy would be dictated by the philosophic assumptions of a private group rather than by reference to the nation's own fundamental law. Whether it is possible to be neutral on matters of religion is a philosophical issue whose answer is wholly dependent on one's first principles. The only set of first principles from which the federal government has the right to derive answers are those embedded in its constitution. The First Amendment, in forbidding Congress to establish religion or to prohibit the free exercise of religion, clearly commands what is thought possible to perform, namely the maintenance of neutrality.

The Economic Philosophy of Choice

Neoclassical economic theory, which gives normative significance to consumer sovereignty, tends to favor tuition subsidies to parents as a way of extending choice. In the neoclassical model, individuals or families attain a maximum of "utility" when the constraints on their consumption patterns are relaxed. When parents are constrained by cost to send their children to a public system, the result is a severe limitation on choice and a reduction of utility. Subsidies to parents—such as the tuition tax credit—however, widen choice because the subsidy could be spent in the private sector, where a diverse set of schools is said to exist. In this model, governmental regulation of schools is not necessary, because competition is assumed to keep quality high.

While raising the maximization of consumer choice to a norm whereby government policy ought to be judged, neoclassical theory fails to provide any criteria whereby specific choices may be evaluated. From strictly within the neoclassical position, the choice of a private school because it is racially seg-regated is qualitatively no different from the choice of a private school because it has a strong curriculum in the fine arts. To establish choice maximization per se as the goal of public policy, without taking into account the content of actual choices, is to provide an incomplete criterion for measuring the success of policy. The tuition tax credit and other forms of subsidization would always be recommended by the standard of choice maximization no matter how bad the outcome by any other standard.

Although the neoclassical case assumes that parental choice is possible only in a market context, there is little reason to accept this without qualification. Public school systems are designed with a variety of mechanisms to make them responsive, ranging from election of school boards to conferences with teachers, to opportunities to transfer teachers or schools and to select courses in secondary school. A study of options actually open to students and parents within the public systems might reveal a surprising amount of choice. Conversely, the actual market, as opposed to the ideal, theoretical one, might provide very little choice in matters of education. If the only nonpublic schools in a city are maintained by a particular denomination, the choice for members of other faiths or of no faith might not seem significant. Furthermore, in low-income areas of declining cities, it is unlikely that a tuition subsidy would induce entry by new private schools that had to support themselves from tuition alone.

Finally, the choice-maximization argument does not pay enough attention to the fact that schools serve geographic areas. Unless an area has an exceptionally high population density, its student population might be large enough to support only a few schools of optimum size. Optimum size is determined by scale economies, which make average costs per pupil less in larger schools than in smaller schools, at least up to a point.[13] In order for schools to be large enough to reap the benefits of scale economies, many communities may be unable to divide their students among more than a handful of schools. This is hardly compatible with choice maximization. Instead, limited choice argues for the democratic control of public schools.

Possible Consequences of a Tuition Tax Credit

Simple Analytics[14]

A tuition tax credit lowers the effective price (tuition minus credit) that parents pay for nonpublic education for any stated rate of tuition. In the general case, a reduction in the effective price of anything will increase the amount demanded (in the aggregate if not in the case of individuals), although the increase might not be large. The responsiveness of demand to price changes is defined as elasticity, the percentage of change in enrollment desired per 1 percent decrease in effective tuition. What is important for subsequent analysis is the possibility that different classes of potential students (such as high-income, low-income, ethnics, or fundamentalists) might exhibit different elasticities of enrollment demand, so that a given tax credit might enhance enrollment among some groups far more than among others. Also, the design of the tax credit (such as nonrefundable) might result in different groups' receiving varying proportionate reductions in effective tuition, so that changes in enrollment demand would differ even if elasticities were the same.

If the nonpublic sector in education behaved like a profit-maximizing, competitive industry, a supply function would exist that would relate stated tuition levels to the number of places available in private schools. In the case of an elastic supply function, where tuition increases permit schools to expand the number of places, some aggregate predictions would be possible about the effect of a tuition tax credit. In general, the shift in enrollment demand at any stated level of tuition would result in some overall increase in private enrollment, some increase in the stated levels of tuition, and some decline in the net level of tuition (tuition minus credit).

The nonpublic sector, however, engages in behavior that is clearly not profit maximizing. Some private schools, for example, apparently continue to operate on the basis of church subsidies even when tuition income does not cover variable operating costs—the shutdown point for profit-maximizing firms. Thus, pure economic theory provides only limited insight into the actual consequences of a tuition tax credit. Some private schools, for example, might simply take the increase in enrollment demand as the occasion to become more selective in admissions rather than changing tuition or total enrollment. Undoubtedly, a variety of responses would be observed.

The Urban Alternative

Some have suggested that federal policy should enhance the ability of low-income students in large cities to leave ailing public schools for nonpublic schools, which presumably are of higher quality; the tuition tax credit would help achieve this. Despite notable exceptions, where inner-city private schools do serve a predominantly low-income and minority student population, recent enrollment data show that this is not a pattern that is generally true. Table 10–1 reveals that in central cities nonpublic schools have a student population that is about 86 percent white and only 11 percent black with 8 percent of Spanish origin; in contrast, the central city public schools are about 36 percent black, or have about three times as many minority students. Table 10–2 shows that

Table 10–1
Composition of Enrollment in Public and Private Central City Schools, by Race or Ethnic Group, 1978
(percent)

	White	Black	Spanish Origin
Public	61.1	35.8	12.1
Private	85.6	11.2	8.0

Source: Derived from U.S. Bureau of the Census, "School Enrollment—Social and Economic Characteristics of Students: October 1978," *Current Population Reports,* Series P-20, No. 346 (Washington, D.C., 1979), Table 3.

Note: The Bureau of the Census defines racial groups as white, black, and other. Due to the substitution of the ethnic group "Spanish origin," the entries do not add up to 100 percent.

about 22 percent of whites attend private schools, compared with only about 6 percent of blacks. The aggregate data of tables 10–1 and 10–2 are a strong corrective to impressions generated by the patterns in specific cities, which may deviate widely from the aggregate pattern.

Of course instituting a tax credit might induce changes in these data, so that minorities would enroll more heavily in central city private schools. It is possible, however, that the tuition tax credit would have the opposite effect, inducing relatively more whites and fewer minority students to enroll in private schools. Suppose that to reduce costs the tax credit were made nonrefundable, so that low-income students whose parents owed no federal income tax would not benefit from the credit; then only higher-income families would receive the net reduction in effective tuition. We would expect more higher-income students to enroll in private schools as the credit raised their enrollment demand but left low income demand unaffected.

Serious methodological problems are involved in the claim that nonpublic schools provide a better education than urban public schools. Even if private school pupils perform better on standardized tests than do public pupils, the crucial difference may lie in the students or their families rather than in the schools. Based on their willingness to pay tuition, one may infer that parents who enroll their students in private schools have an above-average interest in education. Thus, simple comparisons of public and private pupils may reveal nothing but the advantage of pupils whose parents take a strong interest in education, not any intrinsic superiority of nonpublic schools.[15] Paradoxically, if this is the case, the expansion of the private system would cause it to lose its advantage, for expansion would occur only by enrolling students whose parents' concern with education was less exceptionally high.

The methodological problem is intensified if we suppose that student performance reflects past instruction. Suppose also that in a mobile society a certain portion of this year's public (private) students were enrolled in a private (public) school last year or the year before that, and so on. In such a world the performance of a class of private (public) students might reflect to a substantial degree public (private) instruction received in previous years. Only in studies

Table 10–2
Percentage of Racial or Ethnic Groups Enrolled in Public and Private Central City Schools, 1978

	White	Black	Spanish Origin
Public	77.8	94.0	88.2
Private	22.2	6.0	11.8

Source: Derived from U.S. Bureau of the Census, "School Enrollment—Social and Economic Characteristics of Students: October 1978," *Current Population Reports*, Series P-20, No. 346 (Washington, D.C., 1979), Table 3.

where students were tracked over a period of time could the benefits of public and private education be fully disentangled.[16] Suppose, finally, that something about private schools was identified as definitively enhancing learning. Is the proper federal strategy to encourage abandonment of public for private schools, or to design programs that would transplant this element to the public schools?

Distribution of Benefits

Both proponents and opponents of the tuition tax credit use the distribution of the benefits in their arguments. Proponents link the tax credit to middle-class tax relief, though only by expanding their definition of the middle class far above true middle-income levels. Meanwhile, opponents claim that the credit will distribute benefits in a regressive manner. It is also possible to speak of the distribution in terms of racial or geographic categories. Specifically, critics of the credit suggest that whites and families residing in the northeastern and north central parts of the country would be favored over others. The basis of these claims, until recently, has been knowledge of the characteristics of private school students. The distribution of benefits would, however, also depend on the design of the credit and the levels of tuition paid by the various categories of students.

A new study by Martha Jacobs uses information not previously available.[17] Although this more complete study essentially confirms the claims of opponents of the tax credit, one surprise does emerge. Under a generous version of the tax credit (that is, a 50 percent credit up to a limit of $500), benefits for elementary students would flow disproportionately to the South. Although the South has the lowest rate of private attendance, the median tuition there for elementary private schools is substantially higher than in regions with more pupils. With a generous tax credit, parents in the South would obtain a much larger benefit per child than other parents, and this would more than compensate for the lower rate of private attendance in the South.

The same line of reasoning, however, produced virtually no other surprises in the Jacobs study. In general, the characteristics of the student population of nonpublic schools dominate in determining who would benefit most from a tuition tax credit. Thus, the share of benefits to whites is greater than the representation of whites in the overall U.S. student population, and the share to minorities is less. Similarly, the share to students from upper-income families is larger than the proportional representation of such students in the total student population, and lower-income students receive less than their proportional share. Table 10–3 shows the ratio of the tax credit benefits received per pupil for certain income and race groups to the average tax credit benefit per pupil for the total U.S. student population. The ratio 1.00 would indicate a group whose per-pupil benefit from the tax credit just equalled that of the average in

Table 10–3
Ratios of Benefits per Pupil, by Income and Racial Group, Relative to National Average Benefit: Two Credit Plans

	Low Income	Middle Income	High Income	White	Black
Elementary Level					
Stringent	.50	1.12	1.60	1.11	.40
Generous	.42	.96	2.20	1.06	.53
Secondary Level					
Stringent	.45	.89	1.76	1.13	.33
Generous	.36	.85	1.95	1.16	.33

Source: Derived from Martha J. Jacobs, "Tuition Tax Credits for Elementary and Secondary Education: Some New Evidence on Who Would Benefit," Technical Analysis Paper No. 7, U.S. Department of Health, Education and Welfare, Office of the Assistant Secretary for Planning and Evaluation (Washington, D.C., 1979), Tables 3 and 4.

Note: Stringent plan: 35 percent credit, $100 cap; generous plan: 50 percent credit, $500 cap. Low income = under $9,999 per year; middle income = $10,000–24,999 per year; high income = over $25,000 per year.

Figures are based on 1978 data.

the total student population. Smaller numbers indicate groups receiving less-than-average benefits, and vice versa. Table 10–3 reveals a pronounced tendency for tax credit benefits to be distributed to groups in the population that are already considered privileged. Thus, the tuition tax credit plans shown in table 10–3, which are not unrepresentative of the bills introduced in 1978, would represent a departure from previous federal education policy, which has directed aid to less privileged students.[18]

Jacobs estimates that in 1978 the plans shown in table 10–3 would have had a low cost of $448 million and a high cost of about $1.1 billion.[19] Although the lower expenditure might be small enough not to compete with other federal educational funding, the amount of $1.1 billion is almost certainly large enough to compete for scarce education funds.

Jacob's calculations were based on actual enrollment patterns. The enactment of a tax credit might well change those patterns. Although it is possible that the credit might induce an increase in the relative enrollment of low-income students in private schools, thereby automatically shifting more benefits to low-income families, the opposite effect seems at least as plausible. That is, that induced enrollment shifts in private schools might have the effect of focusing benefits even more on higher-income groups than table 10–3 suggests.

Support for Public Education

The tuition tax credit would be at least implicitly a federal policy toward public education. Given that public school budgets in many states are subject to the will of local voters, including the parents of nonpublic school pupils, any inducement for larger private enrollment would tend to reduce voter support for the public system. In a revealing quantitative study of voters in two school budget elections, Daniel Rubinfeld studied elections in Troy, Michigan in the early 1970s.[20] My own calculations suggest that Rubinfeld's results implied that the typical private school parent was 46 percentage points less likely to support the budget in the first election than a public school parent with otherwise comparable characteristics, and 52 percentage points less likely in the second.[21] By any standard this is a dramatic difference and in accord with intuition.

One should not be hasty, however, to conclude that the shift of a relatively few students from public to private schools in response to a tax credit would necessarily cause large changes in the level of support for public education as measured by per-pupil expenditures. For one thing, those parents most likely to be induced by a relatively small tax credit to transfer their children would probably be among those least satisfied with public schools in the first place; and the support in budget elections of such parents might well have been less than that of the average public school parent.

Another consideration also supports skepticism that the much lower level of support for public expenditures among private school parents would necessarily be translated via the political process into much lower actual levels of per-pupil expenditures in the public schools. Suppose voters' preferences about the most desirable level of public school expenditures are randomly distributed according to some frequency distribution, like the normal, that is dense in its central region near the mean or the median. Suppose also that the median voter's preferences determine actual levels of expenditure. Then, if the tuition tax credit were to induce a relatively few parents to switch their children to private schools, thereby changing their place in the frequency distribution, the level of public educational expenditure favored by the median voter probably would not change much. Shifting only a few voters from the high side of the distribution to the low side would result in the new median voter's location among those in the dense central part of the distribution, where large numbers of voters have similar preferences about public school expenditures. This reasoning is supported by available evidence that shows that cross-community variation in private school enrollment does not seem to be associated with very large differences in per-pupil expenditures in public schools under current conditions.[22] Lest one too readily dismiss the concern that the tuition tax credit might undermine local support for public education, note that the model just proposed implies that as successively more parents switch to private schools (for example, as the tax credit increases in subsequent years), the impact on the median voter would become progressively larger.

The question then becomes whether the tuition tax credit can be expected to have a large or small impact on private enrollment. Daniel Sullivan estimated a range of enrollment elasticities with respect to tuition for Catholic schools and found elasticities that were all closer to zero than $-.20$, which must be characterized as very low.[23] Even with a tuition tax credit of 50 percent, this range of estimates suggests an increase in nonpublic enrollment of less than 10 percent. Stated as a percent of public enrollment, the loss to public schools would be less than 2 percent. Although all this argues that a tuition tax credit is unlikely to create large amounts of switching from public to private schools, it is important to realize that past experience with the traditional Catholic schools and their consistency might be a poor guide to parental behavior in the future, when private school growth may occur in the South and have a fundamentalist Protestant flavor.

The Integration Issue

Advocates of aid to private schools sometimes cite data showing that nonpublic schools do indeed enroll minority students as a way of minimizing charges that a tuition tax credit would merely permit some students to flee the integration of public schools. Yet, as table 10–1 reveals, it is simultaneously true that the nonpublic schools, while serving numbers of minority students, have proportionately far fewer minority students than do the public schools of central cities. Given the proportions, it seems likely that large numbers of white pupils in private schools may find themselves in almost all-white schools.

The more important policy question concerns the impact of the tuition tax credit on racial integration in the public schools, for in this area there is a clear federal policy favoring integration. Should a tuition tax credit increase private enrollment, the effect is very likely to decrease further the proportion of public enrollment that is white and further complicate the integration of public schools. This result is possible even if the nonpublic schools were to increase the proportion of their own enrollment of minority students. The crucial variable is the ratio of minority to white students in the group that would be induced to move from public to private schools in response to the tax credit. Let $M_p{:}W_p$ be the ratio of minority to white students in the public schools before the tax credit; let $M_n{:}W_n$ be the ratio in the nonpublic schools; and let $M_s{:}W_s$ be the minority-to-white ratio among those who switch from public to private education. So long as $M_p{:}W_p > M_s{:}W_s$, the change must cause the proportion of minority to white students in the public schools to rise even further, complicating the task of integration. Paradoxically, this result may occur even when the addition of the switchers to the private school increases the ratio of minority to white students $(M_n{:}W_n)$ in the private schools. This would occur when $M_p{:}W_p > M_s{:}W_s > M_n{:}W_n$. It is difficult to imagine that in general the students induced to transfer would have a heavier minority representation than the public schools, although one may be optimistic and hope that the switchers would have a heavier minority representation than is already found in private schools.

Some may choose to argue that minority students constitute such an overwhelmingly large proportion of enrollment in certain cities that the effect of the tuition tax cedit on integration efforts would be negligible in those cities for all practical purposes. Yet table 10–1 reveals that when all the central city school systems of the nation are viewed together, the picture is more hopeful. In the aggregate, significant numbers of both white and minority students are enrolled in city systems and progress on integration seems feasible.

Summary

Although much remains uncertain about the design and eventual impact of a tuition tax credit, several conclusions are possible. Perhaps the most certain thing about a tax credit is that it cannot fulfill all the goals set for it by its supporters, if for no other reason than that these goals are often inconsistent. Although it is my opinion that a tuition tax credit of any design would ultimately prove to be unconstitutional, efforts by Congress to make the credit more likely to pass constitutional review have the predictable result that to avoid entanglement of state and church, the federal government must accept little or no responsibility for monitoring or holding accountable the private schools that would benefit from the federal funds provided. Furthermore, it appears unrealistic to expect the various states to fill the void. It also seems reasonably certain that a tax credit of almost any likely design would direct benefits in a regressive way. This, of course, represents a reversal of standing federal policy in education and taxation.

Somewhat more conditional conclusions are also possible. Based on past experience, we would expect private schools to continue to provide only a very limited amount of choice for low-income, urban students. It is even possible that a tuition tax credit would reduce the enrollment of low-income and minority students in nonpublic schools. Although the effect may not be large, the tuition tax credit would have a tendency to reduce local voter support for public schools; obviously, in the long run this effect may increase. Finally, a shift of enrollment to private schools might, in at least some school districts, make the integration of public schools more difficult. The credit therefore represents a significant change in the past direction of federal policy. Although it is possible to discuss the new policy in meaningful terms, there is much that remains uncertain.

Notes

1. The choice of credit percentages and maximum limits also has a bearing on what set of private school parents will benefit most from the credit. For

a tax expenditure of a given amount, schools charging high tuitions would prefer a lower percentage credit with a high limit, whereas schools charging low tuitions would prefer a high percentage credit with a low limit.

2. The President's Commission on School Finance, *Final Report: Schools, People and Money, The Need for Educational Reform* (Washington, D.C.: Government Printing Office, 1972), pp. 54–55.

3. Starting with 1971 and ending with 1978, aggregate nonpublic enrollment (K–12) was in thousands: 5,378, 5,203, 4,945, 4,867, 5,000, 4,804, 5,024, 4,978. U.S. Bureau of the Census, *Current Population Reports*, Series P-20, No. 241, 260, 272, 286, 303, 319, 333, 346 (Washington, D.C., Government Printing Office, 1971–1978).

4. See, for example, the statement of Congressman William Frenzel to the House Committee on Ways and Means, hearings dated 14–17 and 21 February 1978, published in *Tax Treatment of Tuition Expenses* (Washington, D.C.: U.S. Government Printing Office, 1978), p. 53. For a study providing grounds for skepticism that tuition payments had become a serious burden to the middle class, see Congressional Budget Office, *Federal Aid to Postsecondary Students: Tax Allowances and Alternative Subsidies* (Washington, D.C.: 1978).

5. See Milton Friedman, *Capitalism and Freedom* (Chicago: University of Chicago Press, 1962), p. 91.

6. See the statement of Thomas Vitullo-Martin to the House Committee on Ways and Means, in *Tax Treatment*, p. 243.

7. See the statement of Representative Willian Frenzel, ibid., p. 54.

8. See the statement of Robert E. Baldwin, ibid., p. 122.

9. For a typical but slightly different list of objections see the statements by Andrew Gunn and Ed Doerr, ibid., pp. 78–82.

10. See the statement of William B. Ball, ibid., p. 118.

11. The 1979 North Carolina legislature, for example, removed private schools from the necessity of meeting state requirements for teacher certification or curriculum. See *Winston-Salem Journal*, 1 March 1979. *The New York Times*, 26 January 1979, reports the success of court challenges by fundamentalist Christian schools against state regulation in Kentucky and Ohio courts. In several other southern states a tradition of significant state oversight of private schools does not exist.

12. Statement by Robert E. Baldwin to the House Committee on Ways and Means, in *Tax Treatment*, p. 122.

13. For evidence on scale economies in education see Elchanan Cohn, *The Economics of Education*, rev. ed. (Cambridge, Mass.: Ballinger, 1979), pp. 202–203.

14. For a somewhat different and more complete treatment of the economic analysis see Donald E. Frey, "Public Education, Private Education, and the Tuition Tax Credit," in *Restoring Confidence in Public Education: An Agenda for the 1980s—Conference Research Papers* (Washington, D.C.: National Urban Coalition, 1979).

15. One way to nullify the initial advantage of nonpublic pupils over

public pupils would be to compare increments in achievement over time. When this was done in New York City, the study showed that public schools produced a greater increment for middle-class students than did parochial schools, but that parochial schools produced a greater increment for low-income students. See Department of City Planning, City of New York, *Three Out of Ten: The Nonpublic Schools of New York City* (New York, 1972), chapter III. In any event, the case for the superiority of nonpublic schools does not appear overwhelming.

16. The need for longitudinal dimension is made in another context in Henry J. Aaron, *Politics and the Professors: The Great Society in Perspective* (Washington, D.C.: Brookings Institution, 1978), pp. 80–81.

17. Martha J. Jacobs, "Tuition Tax Credits for Elementary and Secondary Education: Some New Evidence on Who Would Benefit," Technical Analysis Paper No. 7, U.S. Department of Health, Education and Welfare, Office of the Assistant Secretary for Planning and Evaluation (Washington, D.C.: 1979). Also, idem, "Tuition Tax Credits for Elementary and Secondary Education," *Journal of Education Finance* 5 (Winter 1980):233–245.

18. In 1978 the federal expenditure for elementary and secondary education was about $5.6 billion, of which $3.4 billion was in the category "educationally deprived and economic opportunity." U.S. Bureau of the Census, *Statistical Abstract of the United States, 1978* (Washington, D.C.: Government Printing Office, 1978), p. 137.

19. Jacobs, "Tuition Tax Credits: Some New Evidence," p. 11.

20. Daniel L. Rubinfeld, "Voting in a Local School Election: A Micro Analysis," *Review of Economics and Statistics* 59 (February 1977):30–42.

21. Donald E. Frey, "Private Schools and Support for Public Education: Theory and Evidence," mimeographed, August 1980.

22. Ibid.

23. Daniel J. Sullivan, *Public Aid to Nonpublic Schools* (Lexington, Mass.: Lexington Books, D.C. Heath and Company, 1974), p. 44.

11

The New Campaign for Tax Credits: "Parochiaid" Misses the Point

William D. Burt

Anyone who has labored for educational choice has at one time or another encountered the word *parochiaid*, a term of derision used to lump together under one black cloud all measures that might, intentionally or not, redound to the benefit of nonpublic sectarian schools. Americans United for Separation of Church and State, the lobbying organization that has given the term general currency as part of its untiring campaign against private school aid, uses the word in such a way as to suggest that the mechanisms for providing such aid are not nearly as important as the economic result.

Although parochial aid may have been an apt description of the now defunct Moynihan-Packwood bill and other pre-1978 tuition tax credit/tuition grant proposals, and although Senator Moynihan has furnished a constant editorial commentary on the subject, the principal activity in the field of educational choice has recently shifted to the crucible of California politics, where voucher and tax credit ballot initiatives competed for signatures and voter support throughout 1979 and 1980.

Although they differed about a great many things, voucher and tax credit proponents agreed that the "economic result" of their measures—specifically, the increased market share of private schools—was not as important as the fairness of the rules governing educational choice. This concern for equity over economics left Americans United to attack a parochiaid straw man of its own making, which it did with considerable gusto, intimating that both the voucher and tax credit were nothing more than sheep's clothing on the old wolf of sectarian school subsidy.

Of the two initiatives, the voucher sprang from sources closer to the traditional private school sector. John Coons and Stephen Sugarman, who had compiled a record of litigation in support of reforming educational finance in California, developed their initiative in open consultation with the state's education leaders, both public and nonpublic, and actively sought private school support. That they did not receive substantial support can be chiefly attributed to school administrators' worries over the voucher itself, not to any lack of communication.

The California educational tax credit proposal, on the other hand, arose in the wake of Proposition 13 and initially had to overcome an absolute gulf

149

between its sponsor taxpayer groups and the private school leaders who reputedly supported such measures. Such sectarian school support as was forthcoming came from fundamentalist, often nondenominational, schools, loosely organized and acting for the most part by local initiative. Established parochial systems withheld support because of their reservations about their new allies' commitment to lower taxes and less government, and because of simple inertia. One prominent Catholic educator opined that whereas the parochial schools had learned the pitfalls of government aid, they were not prepared to accept the growth in enrollments that an educational tax credit measure would likely bring about. National Taxpayers Union (NTU), the leading sponsor of the California educational tax credit (ETC), frankly expected the parochial schools to perceive and act upon their own interest, and thus help advance what NTU believed to be in the interest of lower taxes and educational choice.

In the process of mounting the educational tax credit drive, then, NTU and its affiliated school/parents'/taxpayers' groups created a proposal and a set of arguments utterly different from those in past tuition tax credit measures. Because the nationally based taxpayers' organization is not only continuing its California efforts but also intends to transplant the ETC to other states and to the federal statutes, this new, nonparochiaid approach to educational choice deserves some scrutiny at all levels of analysis: social origins, implementation, and constitutional validity.

The New Campaign: Social Origins

Taxpayer group activity in the western United States has traditionally centered around property taxes and local school issues, and has been fragmented by strong personalities and regional differences. Two of the most experienced and best organized of the taxpayer leaders, Howard Jarvis and Paul Gann, rode California's Proposition 13 to victory in 1978, but only Gann emerged with any kind of grassroots organization, primarily in the northern part of the state. Hundreds of taxpayer groups, especially the southern California followers of Jarvis, were left directionless during the latter part of 1978 and went casting about for a Proposition 13 follow-up. The NTU, which had been drawing these groups together in a loose confederation, proposed an educational tax credit measure in early 1979. Remembering that the teachers' unions had led the fight against Proposition 13, taxpayer groups responded enthusiastically to the tax credit measure.

Taxpayer activists had become used to hearing their politics described—incorrectly, many thought—as conservative. Whether conservative, liberal, or libertarian, many supporters of the educational tax credit were at great pains to show that they had recognized the fallacies of both "permissive" and "basic" or authoritarian education. In this sense, then, perhaps the fast pace of social change, in which both liberal and conservative educational orthodoxies have been tried and failed, is what most fundamentally explains the rise of the educational tax credit. Supporters had begun to give up on government-run schools per se, and turned to alternatives.

What is wrong with the public schools depends on who is talking. Rather than recount the litany of evils here, we would gain more by rank-ordering public school faults as educational tax credit supporters typically see them.

Surprisingly, lowest on the list is the issue of cost. Except for random, sometimes sensationalized data about salaries or purchases, the details of school system cost structures seldom percolate into the membership of most groups supporting educational tax credits.

Violence in the schools is a volatile issue but one that does not directly affect the educational tax credit campaign. Most people who are concerned about violence aim to eliminate "permissive" conditions in public schools, and are not aware of any differences in private school levels of disorder. The same is true of those for whom busing is the main issue; these people tend to push for public school reform rather than for a shift away from public schools, at least insofar as political activity goes. Those who do shift to private schools in response to busing apparently do so without becoming politically active on behalf of those schools.

Awareness of long-term declines in reading and mathematical test scores is high and most educational tax credit supporters are cognizant of the superiority of nonpublic schools in producing higher test results. The public school back-to-basics policy, competency testing, and related programs are, in view of continuing declines in scholastic performance, not judged credible, and this lack of credibility contributes mightily to support for the educational tax credit.

Highest on the list is a perceived loss of control over the public schools. Educational leaders have responded to this well-known concern by attempting to increase participation, and yet one may venture that political participation is not now and never was the key to the public's sense of control over its local schools. Rather, that control arose from values shared among educators and parents, and its loss has occurred as educators have become inculcated with a social and political ethic, as well as a jargon, that is foreign to most parents. Parents and taxpayers surmise, perhaps rightly, that in a milieu of seemingly programmed ignorance and routinized violence, students are being "taught," in so many ways, obedience to might and scorn for the right. A closer analysis might explain that children are simply being denied the means to "judge for themselves," as Jefferson said, "what will secure or endanger their freedom." At any rate, the educational tax credit is viewed by its supporters as a way of regaining control over an important part of their own lives.

What, then, is the proposal that this movement has generated?

The Educational Tax Credit: What It Is and What It Does

The educational tax credit is neither a tuition tax credit nor a voucher. The educational tax credit is a broader concept designed to facilitate maximum educational choice while disentangling education from government control.

The educational tax credit provides for a 100 percent credit against federal income taxes for educational expenses actually incurred during any taxpayer's tax year.[1]

A $1,200 maximum tax credit per student may be taken in any given year. This amount will increase if necessary to account for inflation.

Students benefited may be enrolled in elementary, secondary, postsecondary, or other similar programs but must be twenty-one or younger.

Students benefited need not be related to the taxpayer.

Individual taxpayers may defray their entire federal income tax liability with educational tax credits, subject to the $1,200-per-student maximum. Corporations may also support the education of as many students who have demonstrated financial need as they wish (subject to the $1,200 ceiling per student), but may defray only up to 50 percent of their corporate tax liability with such credits.

Educational expenses may include but are not limited to tuition and/or fees. Educational expenses are broadly defined to include noninstitutional and quasi-institutional educational alternatives as well as the currently widespread institutional ones. Examples include equivalency examinations and preparation for them, structured home-study courses, and work-study programs.

At a minimum the states will be required to refrain from impairing the evenhanded application of the education tax credit by further restricting existing educational alternatives via accreditation or other public school "protective" legislation.

Implementation

The flexible design of the tax credit makes it possible for givers and beneficiaries to ally themselves in numerous ways, and how they do so will depend upon their own preferences. It is safe to assume, however, that a consensual preference exists among a great many taxpayers, both individual and corporate, to see some portion of their present federal income tax payments spent to achieve a known good (such as education), rather than pay these sums to the tax collection agencies. Because such giving costs them nothing—taking the tax credit involves no loss of other tax benefits—the incentives for financing a wide variety of educational choices are unobstructed.

Still, familiarity and long-standing practice suggest that, when it comes to educational tax credits used outside the taxpayer's own family, what might be called the "United Way" approach will at first predominate. The ETC allows a maximum credit of $1,200 per child; thus, if the taxpayer desires to give a larger amount to educational purposes and credit all of it against his tax, it would be necessary to show that the amount benefited more than one student. There are three possible ways to do this.

1. The taxpayer can give to the United Way or some other voluntary social welfare organization, and the organization can distribute the money among the requisite number of students, either directly or indirectly.
2. The taxpayer can give to a school, and the school can distribute the money among the requisite number of students, either directly or indirectly.
3. The taxpayer can give directly to personally chosen students.

Because organizations of the United Way type are already in existence and are probably capable of performing the informational tasks of distributing educational tax credit–inspired gifts in accordance with the $1,200-per-student ceiling, most giving under the credit will probably occur via such organized voluntary social welfare organizations. Other strong possibilities include local community organizations, parent-teacher organizations, and unions.

Some Fears Considered

Given that the tax credit is designed and intended to encourage the spirit and practice of mutual aid on an individual and community level, it is proper to question whether this kind of interpersonal assistance is superior to the kind of bureaucratized, impersonal welfare assistance we now have, or to alternative programs.

Some tax credit critics, notably the National Educational Association and voucher proponent Coons, have raised the specter of chattel slavery being fostered by a system that encourages individuals to give toward the education of others.[2] Although this objection has not been raised in the past in relation to tax-deductible educational contributions and no cloud has darkened the practice of giving to colleges and scholarship funds, for some reason the full tax credit inspires fears that the rich will exploit the poor by giving them money.

What is far more likely is that educational giving will take many forms, the most common of which occur within the extended family. Nonfamily educational expenditures will, as noted above, probably be routed through the same voluntary social welfare agencies that have capably raised and administered such funds in the past.

The fear of exploitation via educational giving arises from an unreasoned extrapolation of the current shortage of givers relative to potential beneficiaries. In fact, however, an educational tax credit will dramatically expand the number of givers and the total amount of money given to educational purposes, and it is reasonable to infer that this shift will work to the advantage of the recipients of aid. It is difficult to exploit a needy student when several low-cost educational alternatives compete for his or her choice.

Few today would argue as a matter of principle that all social assistance should be centralized under the authority of government; recognition of the value of so-called mediating institutions has become widespread. Still, let us see what is claimed for government: that, because its functionaries have no interest in making a profit, it can operate at a lower cost than private agencies; and, most of all, that it dispenses social assistance without invidious discrimination.

These tenets have been fairly debunked by a spate of analyses of government welfare, and the criticisms apply with special force to education.[3] Government agencies do engage in self-seeking economic behavior, and the fact that 42 percent of black seventeen-year-olds are functionally illiterate suggests that even though public educational finance may be innocent of invidious discrimination, it almost surely discriminates according to the social and political status of various constituencies.

Still, critics such as Coons insist on government-enforced guarantees of aid, and they are willing to substitute for a diverse number of givers and multiple competing approaches a single monopolistic giver of educational aid, with whom needy students must take their chances. Their apparent distrust of true diversity runs so deep that they would distribute general tax revenues to the public via vouchers rather than allow the public to allocate educational dollars independently of the tax collection system.

Whether or not vouchers can be constructed so as to avoid government intervention in educational choice has been debated at length, most recently during the course of the two California educational finance initiative campaigns. Voucher proponents have placed considerable faith in the capacity of statutory language to restrict the natural inclination of state departments of education to regulate vouchers. But this position seems naive at best; so long as the government has the opportunity to give money, there is little that can keep it from exercising control by withholding funds selectively.

Milton Friedman, an early proponent of vouchers and one who, like Coons, sympathizes with the proposition that government should act positively to assure equal access to educational aid, nevertheless supported the NTU effort to allow voluntary, decentralized giving to subsitute for government-administered educational aid.

> I strongly support the Educational Tax Credit initiative sponsored by the National Taxpayers Union. Its effect would be essentially identical with the kind of unrestricted voucher plan I have been supporting and promoting for decades. Either plan would give all families, from the very poorest to the very wealthiest, the effective freedom to choose the schools their children attend, a freedom that is now available only to those families that can afford to pay twice for schooling.[4]

Another peculiar fear is that educational tax credits will create *too* wide a choice in schooling, opening the marketplace to quacks and unusual methods of education. Insofar as this apprehension arises from the possibility of charlatans' emerging in education, it should be answered by pointing out that free and open competition should help reduce, not increase, the incidence of consumer fraud in education. To the extent that this fraud now operates within public education, there is little recourse except to political action—an imperfect response mechanism at best.

Private schools, by contrast, have frequently taken it upon themselves to provide independent verification of the services they promise to consumers. Speaking to the issue of accreditation requirements proposed to be added to the California education code, Joseph P. McElligott, Director of Governmental Relations for the California Association of Private School Organizations, said:

> The Western Association of Schools and Colleges [WASC] is the independent accrediting agency through which almost all public and private secondary schools are accredited. At the elementary level, public schools have no accreditation requirement. In the private sector, most denominational private school groups have developed their own "WASC-like" self-study and outside evaluation processes and have been employing them for over a decade. Currently, the Catholic school systems of the Archdiocese of Los Angeles and the Dioceses of Orange and San Diego have joined WASC's *elementary* accreditation system. In summary, one could conclude that private elementary education is far ahead of public elementary education when it comes to accreditation.[5]

Apparent proof of McElligott's claim was forthcoming when the state department of education staff, urging passage of restrictive legislation over private schools in 1979, based its argument on the theoretical risks of an open education market rather than presenting a platterful of fraud and malpractice cases drawn from among California's then 3,040 nonpublic schools and 451,320 nonpublic school students.[6]

The Expected Effect of the Tax Credit

The potential for large-scale shifts in enrollment from public to private schools in the wake of educational tax credits is affected by a number of interrelated variables. First, the capacity of major urban sectarian schools to absorb more enrollments is limited by their existing plant, unless public schools demonstrate an unexpected receptivity toward selling off unneeded school buildings to re-surgent private competitors.

The possible growth of quasi-institutional educational alternatives is also a major unknown, and will be affected by the degree of inflexibility found in the major parochial systems. Unaffiliated community-based or independent Christian schools represent the fastest-growing segment of the nonpublic school sector, and their expansion appears unlikely to slow in the near future, tax credit or no.[7]

Finally, the applicability of tax and spending limits to public school systems will also shape the growth of educational alternatives. It can be expected that unless restrained, public school systems will attempt to compete against nonpublic alternatives primarily by means of increased budgets, and the threat this poses not only to fiscal sanity but also to educational choice is serious enough to warrant an effort by the federal government to see that federal funds, at least, are not used to subsidize a kind of predatory competitive behavior by local public schools.[8]

A comprehensive solution for this problem is to adopt at the state level a spending limit provision similar to that enacted as part of Proposition 4, the California spending limit passed in November 1979. Proposition 4 compels local government to restrict its spending (and to pass along savings in the form of tax cuts) in accordance with population changes and the consumer price index, but schools are obliged to use enrollments, not the general population. Thus, if an inferior public school loses students to nonpublic alternatives it is required to cut its budget accordingly. Failing state action in this regard, the federal government could begin to restrict aid to local school districts along the same lines.

Financial Impact

If the ETC induced a 70 percent increase in nonpublic school enrollments, from 4.5 million currently to 7.65 million, a sizable diversion of revenue from government control would result.[9] If each of the 7.65 million claimed the full $1,200 credit, or the credit was claimed on their behalf by parents, relatives, or other donors, the effect might be as high as a $9.2 billion tax cut.

This figure is probably an upper limit, for two reasons. First, many schools do not charge as much as $1,200 per student, so their students could not claim the maximum amount. Also, parents who have less than $1,200 in federal income tax obligations might take only the credit that could be claimed on their own return and not seek additional assistance.

The effect on federal income tax revenues, however, represents only part of the social costs and benefits. With a 1977–1978 average cost per pupil of only $819 compared to $1,739 for government-run schools, nonpublic schools offer the possibility of major savings in the total cost of education.[10]

This better than two-to-one cost differential makes possible a beneficial effect even for students whose families choose public schools, for, as some students choose nonpublic alternatives, the per-student savings at public schools would outweigh the maximum per student revenue losses, leaving more money per student for those attending public school. The differentials between public and private tend to be highest where public schools are the worst—in the major urban areas where public schools now spend upward of $2,500 per pupil.

This counters assertions that educational tax credits and the free choice they engender will leave a residual core of disadvantaged children in the public schools, now supposedly impoverished in the wake of the tax credit. First, the public schools would have to be deprived of more than the tax credit's maximum amount before they were left with as little money per student as they had before. Second, the public schools' high retention rate of socially and learning-handicapped children is the result of their own policy-determined attempts to make mainstream education attractive and useful to pupils who in the past would have been grouped together in classes for retarded or delinquent students.

Without returning to ostracism for children with special needs, it is possible that some handicapped children do best in school situations that attend to their special needs. This is an educational alternative rarely provided in mainstreaming situations, and one that is over-supplied in classes that altogether separate these students from their peers. The ETC would promote the flexibility and diversity that exist in a situation of open choice, in contrast to the provision of service by a public monopoly. One would therefore not expect the parents, guardians, and others concerned about the needs of special children to ignore those needs simply because public schools will take these students in "free"; instead, one would expect nonpublic schools to exert their ingenuity in a competitive effort to provide these students with a useful education.

Looking to the needs of the public school captive market, minority leaders such as Roy Innis of CORE and black economist Thomas Sowell have given their support to tax credits for education. In Sowell's works,

[the tax credit] is most important to those who are mentioned least: the poor, the working class, and all whose children are trapped in educationally deteriorating and physically dangerous public schools. Few groups have so much at stake in the fate of this [program] as ghetto blacks. . . .

The crux of the controversy is *choice* and *power*. If parents are given a choice, public school officials will lose the monopoly power they now hold over a captive audience. The monopoly power is greatest over the poor, but it extends to all who cannot afford to simultaneously pay taxes for the public schools and tuition at a private school.[11]

Constitutionality

During the California campaign of 1979–1980, opponents of the ETC plan routinely alleged its constitutional invalidity. That campaign's record is strewn with flat assertions that all tuition tax credits ae unconstitutional, when even a cursory review of the U.S. Supreme Court's rulings reveals a complex—some would say contorted—approach.

At the very least, the Court has displayed considerable sensitivity to intention and design as well as to the economic result that so obsesses those who think in terms of "parochiaid" and measure all proposals solely by their immediate material effect upon religious schools. In the landmark *Nyquist* decision of 1973, which disallowed a New York program of tax credits and tuition grants, the justices reflected that tuition tax benefits were "a recent innovation, occasioned by the growing financial plight of [parochial schools] and designed, albeit unsuccessfully, to tailor state aid in a manner not incompatible with the recent decisions of this Court."[12] Elsewhere in *Nyquist,* however, the Court said, "It is equally well established that *not every law that confers an 'indirect,' 'remote,' or 'incidental' benefit upon religious institutions is, for that reason alone, constitutionally invalid.*"[13]

Tuition tax credit architects like Senator Daniel Patrick Moynihan have done little to dispel the perception of tax credits as a form of subsidy to nonpublic schools. Arguing typically for tuition tax credits to shore up the precarious finances of parochial schools, these proponents lend support to the Supreme Court's supposition that if the option of direct state aid were available in any substantial way, they would exploit it.[14]

Confronted with tax credit proponents' continuing straightforward challenge to the Supreme Court's *Nyquist* decision, lower courts since 1973 have taken little heed of *Nyquist's* nuances in their rush to affirm the high court's prohibition against aid to parochial schools. Proponents' truculent demands for such aid have led the courts to adopt a virtual presumption that tax credits must represent some kind of subterfuge, focusing judicial interest on the question of material benefit to the detriment of other considerations.

This is a mistake in concept and objectives that the ETC does not share. The tax credit, as will be detailed below, advances primarily the free exercise of religious and educational liberty, and only incidentally the welfare of schools.

The School Aid Cases

Nyquist was preceded by a number of significant cases that sought to apply the First Amendment to the area of state involvement in parochial education or that raised related questions. *Everson* v. *Board of Education* (1947) allowed state reimbursement of parochial students' bus transportation fares, and *Board of Education* v. *Allen* (1968) state authorities' loaning secular textbooks to parochial school children.[15] *Tilton* v. *Richardson* (1971) upheld federal grants of funds for the construction of facilities to be used for clearly secular purposes in nonpublic institutions.[16] In the words of the *Nyquist* decision, this line of cases "simply recognize[s] that sectarian schools perform secular, educational functions as well as religious functions, and that some forms of aid may be channeled to the secular without providing direct aid to the sectarian."[17] That such "secular" aid admittedly freed more of the schools' own money for sectarian purposes was held to be of little import, for "an indirect and incidental effect beneficial to religious institutions has never been thought a sufficient defect to warrant the invalidation of a state law."[18]

In the *Nyquist* case before the Supreme Court, the State of New York relied heavily also on *Walz* v. *Tax Commission* (1971), in which New York's property tax exemption for religious, charitable, and educational organizations was upheld.[19]

In applying the precedents to *Nyquist,* the Court evinced a three-part test of constitutionality that continues in force today. First, the statute in question has to reflect a legitimate secular purpose. Second, the primary effect of the statute should neither advance nor inhibit religion. Finally, the statute should avoid excessive entanglement between church and state.[20] Seeing in the *Nyquist* measure a scheme to aid the parochial schools of New York State, the Court decided that its primary effect was to advance religion, and thus held the law unconstitutional.

Three relatively recent cases reveal that a degree of inconsistency still affects the application of these tests. In 1978 a three-judge federal court upheld a 1955 Minnesota statute that allowed parents of students attending public and private schools to claim up to $700 per year as a deduction against their state income tax returns. In *Minnesota* v. *Roemer* the judicial panel concluded that this educational tax benefit was constitutional because "the statute is neutral and neither advances nor impedes religious activity, benefits the parents of children attending both public and non-public schools, has received unchallenged historical acceptance, and is analogous to the long recognized practice of tax deductible contributions to religious and charitable causes . . ."[21] Yet a late 1979 challenge of a similar statue in *Rhode Island Federation of Teachers et al.* v. *Norberg* resulted in a federal district court's ruling out the tax deduction after finding that fully 93 percent of the students currently affected attended parochial schools.

Mid-1979 saw another of the *Nyquist* statute's progeny thrown out, when the Supreme Court affirmed without opinion a lower court ruling disallowing a New Jersey tuition tax benefit measure.[22] The New Jersey law would have allowed a $1,000 tax deduction for any state taxpayer with a child in private or parochial school. A New Jersey taxpayer with an income of $20,000 and one child in school would have saved $20 in state taxes; still, the appeals court noted that "an insurmountable obstacle" to the law's validity was that it served to advance religion. The New Jersey decision left hope that a tax benefit applicable, like *Roemer,* to both public and private school families might find greater acceptability.[23]

The Test of Effects

The ETC avoids the pitfalls of tuition tax benefit measures because it is an essentially new concept. It is a tax credit that any federal taxpayer, individual or corporate, may take for educational expenses. Beneficiaries are limited to those under twenty-one but are not otherwise restricted. Educational expenses are intended to comprehend a far broader class of expenditures than tuition, in order to encourage maximum choice. Upon consideration it becomes clear that many of the customary responses to narrow tuition tax credit proposals do not apply here.

It will not do, for instance, to point out that the immediate effect of the educational tax credit would be to allow a federal income tax credit to those who already have children in sectarian schools. This is inadequate for a number of reasons. First, like the Minnesota tax deduction but for its own reasons, the ETC necessarily applies to educational expenses in public as well as nonpublic schools; examples of these include noncore curriculum or remedial class tuition, sports fees, field trip fees, laboratory fees, and so on.[24] Second, the ETC by its nature applies not only to the entire panoply of institutional educational choices, but also to the noninstitutional ones: the Calvert courses, directed study on leave from school, and home tutoring.[25] Because the growth of these alternatives is already under way and little capital is required to insure their expansion, it is simply not possible to show that the primary practical effect of the ETC is to benefit existing parochial or even expanded parochial schools.

Finally, if we assume that the coercion implicit in the existing tax and spending structure of education is so hotly defended by members of the public education establishment at least in part because its clientele are unwilling consumers, than any survey of the practical benefit of the educational tax credit must take into account a probable market shift. In questions of market shift it is customary to consider not only existing competitors (which are the product of a historical situation) but also ones potentially likely to arise as the result of the operation of the proposed policy change.

It is certainly a valid presumption that, *ceteris paribus,* a policy change of the magnitude of educational tax credits will induce dramatic changes in the demand for, and supply of, educational alternatives. Taking these into account to test the effects means seeing the measure in light of its own consequences, rather than "arguing from ignorance" that the major historical educational choices are all we can identify for purposes of assessing the practical effect of tax credits.

These circumstances make it most difficult to conclude, as did six justices in *Nyquist,* that any educational tax credit must accrue to the benefit of a single religious group.

The Entanglement Test

Particular note should also be paid to the Court's *Nyquist* language in regard to *Walz,* the 1971 case that upheld property tax exemptions for many nonprofit organizations, including religious ones. *Walz* held that "a proper respect for both the Free Exercise and the Establishment Clauses compels the State to pursue a course of 'neutrality' toward religion." Governments, said the Court, "have not always pursued such a course, and oppression has taken many forms, one of which has been the taxation of religion. Thus, if taxation was regarded as a form of 'hostility' toward religion, 'exemption' constitute[d] a reasonable and balanced attempt to guard against those dangers."[26]

The State of New York sought to analogize the statute in *Nyquist* to that in *Walz* by arguing that the New York tax credit/grant program disencumbered religious choice. The Court found this argument insufficient for two reasons.

First, special tax benefits could not be reconciled with the neutrality required by the First Amendment.[27] Because the New York law did not explicitly single out sectarian schools for tax credit eligibility, the meaning of "special" tax benefits may amount to nothing more than a reiteration of the Court's suspicion of arrangements that confer primary de facto benefit upon religion. On this interpretation, showing a merely incidental benefit to parents of sectarian school attendees might be sufficient for a tax credit measure to escape being labeled as a special tax benefit. A stricter interpretation, which would require that the tax credit be applicable to expenses in public as well as nonpublic schools, or even to nontuition educational expenses as well as tuition, is also possible and is satisfied by the provisions of the ETC.

The second point on which the *Nyquist-Walz* analogy foundered was the Court's contention that the "indirect and incidental benefit" conferred upon religion by *Walz* was "the product not of any purpose to support or subsidize, but of a fiscal relationship designed to minimize involvement and entanglement between Church and State."[28] The Court emphasized that in *Walz* "the exemption tends to complement and reinforce the desired separation insulating each from the other" (citations omitted). Furthermore, "elimination of the exemption would tend to expand the involvement of government by giving rise to tax valuation of church property, tax liens, tax foreclosures, and the direct confrontations and conflicts that follow in the train of these legal processes."[29]

Turning to the law in *Nyquist,* the justices concluded that "the granting of the tax benefits under the New York Statute, unlike the extension of an exemption, would tend to increase rather than limit the involvement between Church and State."[30] Looking beyond the possibility of such bureaucratic interventions, the Court admitted to no small apprehension about the divisive political competition that could result from instituting subsidies to religious schools. Although this objection to the *Nyquist* statute proved not controlling, having been overshadowed by the effects test, there is little doubt that entanglement was a large consideration in the justices' minds.[31]

The prospect of close government supervision of nonpublic schools was raised again when federal tuition tax credits came before Congress in 1978. In hearings before the House Ways and Means Committee constitutional attorney William B. Ball warned that government could be expected to use tax credits to gain new school accreditation powers, restricting and perhaps suffocating choice.[32] Ball recommended that any standard for school eligibility should rest upon existing statutes governing establishment and operation of schools, rather than upon new accreditation language.

Similar thinking went into the construction of the NTU's California educational tax credit initiative, when that organization proposed making tax credits applicable to educational expenses at any school able to enroll students under the 1979 state education code. Fearing that the California department of education would try to tighten accreditation standards, the NTU went so far as to prohibit further restriction of educational alternatives via the education code.[33]

Basing the eligibility of various schools' tuition and/or educational expenses upon existing state codes avoids the quagmire of new accreditation standards, but not without a cost. The codes vary from pervasive to minimal regulation; an open market in educational choices should be allowed, while increasing avenues of relief against fraud. Moreover, reliance upon multifarious existing state definitions of legitimate educational institutions handicaps equal application of a federal income tax credit for educational expenses from state to state. Therefore, in statutory form the ETC necessarily introduces a definition of educational expenses broad enough to accommodate a wide range of alternatives, while at a minimum prohibiting the states from impairing application of the ETC by increasing present accreditation restrictions or denying its use for one or another of the educational alternatives now allowed to satisfy the compulsory education laws.

In a deeper sense the ETC proposal answers the Court's concern about sectarian strife by providing a relief valve for the pent-up anger and tension that many parents already feel about their lack of educational options. In particular, the tax credit can reduce the incentive to do battle over what values are taught in the public schools.

Senator Moynihan related a conversation he had with Vice-President Walter Mondale in April 1979 while both were listening to the fractious Senate debate over legislation that would have restored prayer to the public schools by denying the Supreme Court jurisdiction over the issue:

> He and I talked a bit about the debate, and I remarked that while I was opposed to the amendment I could readily understand how Americans, a religious people, would be uncomprehending of a government that seemed to deny them what they would regard as the free exercise of religion in the schools. . . . A plural school system, with a strong church-related sector, would *avoid the kind of agonizing choice the Senate was facing that day,* the choice between seeming to thwart the religious preferences of the people and seeming to circumscribe the power of the Supreme Court to rule on whether our fundamental rights are being infringed by government. . . .[34]

Were tax credits proposed and designed to subsidize sectarian schools, or primarily these, the possibility would still exist that the strife attending the political competition for such aid would outweigh the reduction in tensions occasioned by increased educational liberty, thus tipping the balance of the entanglement issue against the measure. Educational tax credits, however, unlike the *Nyquist* statute, are not merely one element in a conceptually and fiscally unrestrained package of aid to parochial schools. Their application to the wide range of educational expenditures takes them beyond the realm of parochial school tuition to encompass every educational option, and their monetary impact is intrinsically restricted by individual tax liabilities.

The Test of Public Purpose

Up to now, we have noted that the ETC, by virtue of its emphasis on expenses rather than solely on tuition, permits inclusion of a broad class of educational choices under the credit. As important as this is, the ETC can be distinguished from tuition tax credits in a more fundamental way: like the New York tax exemptions upheld in *Walz,* it is a comprehensive, integrated program whose design fosters educational free choice and opportunity.

We have already noted that the accrual of benefits to religious education is an indirect, incidental occurrence. Indeed, we go further: the proportion of benefits spent upon education for internal family members as opposed to external ''charitable'' expenditures is unimportant as far as the educational tax credit is concerned. Nor is it greatly of interest to the tax credit's proponents, who seek, among other things, to revive the vitality and educational influence of extended families and community groups, and who are also at pains to loosen the state's virtual monopoly on education.

Because the tax credit applies to educational expenses incurred by any taxpayer (including corporate donors) without regard to the familial or social relation to the beneficiaries, in relation to the existing law the ETC can be seen as replacing the currently allowed deductions for charitable educational contributions and erasing the artificial restrictions upon who may benefit from such deductible giving.[35] This approach suggests that the distinction between charitable contributions and expenditures designed to attain personal objectives is at best a shaded one, and that in the case of expenditures made for children's education, the difference between son and nephew or between any other two beneficiaries is not so precise or important as to justify obstructing maximum educational opportunity. Unlike previous narrow tuition tax credit proposals, thr ETC is a general charitable tax credit of broad conceptual as well as factual applicability that facilitates a recognized public purpose. In this respect it closely resembles the conceptually broad tax exemptions upheld in *Walz*.

Tuition tax credit proponents have at various times tried to depict their measures as having more than narrow application, employing arguments that sometimes bordered on the disingenuous. Review has understandably concentrated on defeating those subterfuges.

Rhode Island, for example, argued that because a tuition tax benefit applied in public as well as nonpublic schools, it possessed broad application; however, with 93 percent of Rhode Island's nonpublic school students attending sectarian schools (and the statute failing to provide tax credits for more than token nontuition expenses) the federal district court harshly dismissed this reasoning as "window dressing."[36]

Similarly, New Jersey contended that its tuition tax deduction was part of a broad block of exemptions passed as a unit to benefit an entire class of taxpayers regarded as likely to have "added expenses."[37] In rejecting this defense the three-judge federal panel noted that the existence of conceptually unrelated tax benefits alongside the *Nyquist* statute had not saved the New York tuition tax benefit scheme.[38] In neither the Rhode Island nor the New Jersey case was evidence established that the benefits accruing to religious education were incidental to a broad program to aid education or to promote some other recognized public interest; rather, the states argued tangential points, and thereby lost.

What tax credits for a wide range of educational expenses can demonstrate but a narrow tuition tax credit cannot, is proof that free choice and educational opportunity, rather than the welfare of the schools, come first.

The Educational Tax Credit's Constitutionality

In sum, the ETC differs dramatically from previous narrow tuition tax credit proposals and meets all three tests for constitutionality delineated by the U.S.

Supreme Court in *Nyquist:* the test of primary effects, the test of entanglement, and the test of public purpose.

Constitutional attorney William B. Ball had this to say about the NTU California educational tax credit proposal:

> Let me state, in very short form, why I believe that the Proposal is absolutely constitutional.
>
> The Proposal does not run counter to any previous Supreme Court decision. The decision of the Court in *Committee for Public Education* v. *Nyquist,* 413 U.S. 756 (1973) is not a case in point. The statute considered in *Nyquist* contained a formula whereby the net benefit to the beneficiary was indistinguishable from a tuition grant. That feature is not present in the Proposal. Further, the "tax credit" feature struck down in *Nyquist* was only a part of a comprehensive "aid to parochial schools" statute and appeared to the Court to be an inseparable part of such a package. Finally, the *Nyquist* statute was held by six members of the Court to benefit a single religious group predominantly. That cannot remotely be said of the Proposal.
>
> Putting aside now, as indeed is proper, any objection based on *Nyquist,* we come to the heart of the matter so far as constitutionality is concerned. Quite plainly the Proposal would write into the California Constitution *a provision giving wider scope to personal liberties.* There has been a widespread propaganda that a public monopoly in education is so imperative that it must override the enjoyment of basic constitutional liberties—such as the right to know, parental choice of schools, the rights of privacy, initiative and creativity in education, religious freedom, and rights of enterprise in education. The propaganda has caused a hobbling of these rights and now brings them face to face with extinction. That is due to the rising inflation and saturating taxation. These rights are becoming paper rights. Americans should not be told: "You may exercise your basic rights only if you impoverish yourself to do so."
>
> The present state of affairs plainly imposes an unconstitutional condition on the enjoyment of fundamental liberties. The Proposal, if adopted, would get rid of that unconstitutional condition. The present situation gives public education an unconstitutional preference pointing to absolute monopoly. The Proposal, if adopted, would create a measure of equality and fairness consonant with meaningful constitutional liberty.[39]

Conclusion

Occasionally one finds that political debate is ruled by ideas that only later emerge as pseudo-concepts, nonsensical in the extreme. In so many ways we have been dealing with one: the notion of tax expenditure, wherein the total of government aid to a segment of society is taken to be the sum of all monies appropriated from the public treasury for the benefit of that private activity, *as well as* all monies which government refrained from taking out of the hands of private participants through taxation. Its false logic exposed, the notion of tax expenditure implies that government subsidizes all of us 100 percent and, as an interesting corollary, that government owns us 100 percent.

Now who would defend such a proposition? Those who have promulgated the term *parochiaid* have in effect been doing so all along. To them, a tax credit is the same as an outright grant or subsidy; it matters not that tax credits allow individuals to keep what is theirs in the first place. "Is it good for the private schools? Then we oppose it!" they say.

If there is any message emanating from the new campaign for educational tax credits, it is that the difference between a subsidy and a reduction in one's taxes does matter—that the power to tax is indeed the power to destroy individual and family sovereignty over such crucial decisions as the education of children. Such sovereignty is too precious to lose.

Notes

1. The federal educational tax credit as recently proposed by the National Taxpayers Union, and by 1980 Libertarian presidential candidate Ed Clark, is here generally described. State-level measures such as those that have circulated in California, Idaho, and elsewhere vary somewhat, but the general provisions remain similar.

2. Coons claimed repeatedly during the voucher/tax credit debates of 1979 that the tax credit would increase the dependence of the poor on the government. For a reiteration of these arguments see chapter 12 of this book.

3. See, for example, Charles D. Hobbs, *The Welfare Industry* (Washington, D.C.: Heritage Foundation, 1978).

4. Milton Friedman to John Harris Dean, Committee for Educational Tax Credits, 22 May 1980. Reprinted with permission.

5. Joseph P. McElligott to William D. Burt, National Taxpayers Union, 10 April 1979. Reprinted with permission.

6. Memorandum from Robert D. McCarthy, consultant for private schools, California Department of Education, to David Campbell, deputy superintendent of programs, 12 March 1979.

7. Catholic enrollments represented 66.0 percent, other religions 15 percent, and nonaffiliated 14.9 percent enrollment in 1976–1977. By 1978–1979 this pattern had shifted to 64.5, 16.4 and 14.8 percent, respectively. National Center for Education Statistics, *Digest of Education Statistics 1979* (Washington, D.C., 1980).

8. This is facilitated by linking aid to average daily attendance, as is now quite common.

9. Study for 1980 libertarian presidential candidate Ed Clark.

10. National Center for Education Statistics, *Digest of Statistics 1979*.

11. Thomas Sowell, "Tuition Tax Credits: A Social Revolution," *Policy Review* 6 (Spring 1978):79–83. Reprinted with permission.

12. Committee for Public Education et al. v. Nyquist, 413 U.S. 756, 93 S. Ct. 2955 (1973); id. at 2975.

13. Id. at 2965 (italics added).

14. See, for example, Daniel Patrick Moynihan, "Private Schools and the First Amendment," *National Review* 31 (3 August 1979):962.

15. 330 U.S. 1; 392 U.S. 236.

16. 403 U.S. 672.

17. 93 S. Ct. at 2967.

18. Id.

19. 397 U.S. 664.

20. Sec. 93 S. Ct. at 2965.

21. 452 F. Supp. at 1522.

22. Public Funds for Public Schools of New Jersey v. Byrne, 590 F. 2d 514 (1979).

23. Id. at 519, n. 8. Id. at 520, n. 11 further observes that "the Supreme Court has reserved the question whether 'a genuine tax deduction, such as for charitable contributions,' would satisfy the neutrality test in *Walz* [citations omitted]. *As we interpret the phrase 'genuine tax deduction,' it refers to the comprehensiveness of the tax relief granted by the challenged statute.* Because New Jersey's scheme is insufficiently comprehensive, the law questioned in this case does not create a 'genuine tax deduction' " (italics added).

24. Such fees are becoming widespread in the wake of tax revolt–inspired limitations on general revenue sources for education; this phenomenon is most advanced in California, where a family can easily spend up to $1,000 a year for fees related to courses and extracurricular activities in public school.

25. The Calvert courses are structured correspondence home study courses.

26. 93 S. Ct. at 2975.

27. Id.

28. Id.

29. Id.

30. Id.

31. See 93 S. Ct. at 2977, 2978.

32. Russell Kirk, "Taxes and Vouchers," *National Review* 30 (13 October 1978):1286.

33. California's campaign to tighten accreditation is documented in a memorandum mentioned in note 6 above. This memorandum lays out rationales for proposed legislation to regulate more thoroughly the booming California private school sector.

34. Moynihan, "Private Schools and the First Amendment," p. 962. Reprinted with permission. Copyright 1979 by National Review, 150 East 35th St., New York, NY 10016. (Italics added.)

35. Found at I.R.C. § 170 (a).

36. Rhode Island Federation of Teachers et al. v. Norberg, 479 F. Supp. 1364.

37. 443 F. Supp. 1228.

38. These consisted of exemptions for supporting dependents, having a spouse, being blind or having a blind spouse, and being sixty-five or older or having a spouse sixty-five or older.

39. William B. Ball, "One Lawyer's Opinion," *Inform* 2 (May 1980):3. Reprinted with permission of the Center for Independent Education, San Francisco (Ball's italics).

12 Educational Tax Credits versus School Vouchers: Comment on the California Tuition Tax Credit Proposal

John E. Coons and
Stephen D. Sugarman

The National Taxpayers Union (NTU) has recently sponsored an unusual educational tax limitation scheme. The proposal (appendix 12A) was circulated unsuccessfully for signatures in the form of a constitutional initiative. The California state income tax was its principal target. The proposed reform would have reduced the tax liability of corporations and individuals by awarding a tax credit for specified expenditures for elementary, secondary, and higher education. Under the NTU proposal the taxpayer would qualify for the proposed credit by paying the tuition and/or "incidental expenses" of a person attending a private school or the incidental expenses of a person attending a public school. The individual or corporation could claim tax credit for as many—and whichever—students he or it chose. The maximum credit allowable all contributing taxpayers for any one pupil would be $1,200. Corporations could use the credit to eliminate up to half their tax liability to the state. Individuals could use the credit to eliminate their entire income tax liability to the state.

The NTU device has several unique features of intrinsic interest. Moreover, it provides a useful perspective on the relative advantages of tuition tax credits and direct educational subsidies to families, sometimes called vouchers or scholarships. Plans of the latter sort would provide families not liking their assigned public school a voucher or scholarship to be used to pay for educational costs at qualifying elementary or secondary schools of their choice, public or private. Both voucher and tax credit advocates have captured public attention lately with their talk about choice and competition. The intended beneficiaries of the plans, however, differ significantly. We are unenthusiastic about the eductional tax credit plans we have seen proposed and we are especially cool to the NTU scheme. In this essay we explain why.

Tax Credits Provide Smaller Benefits to Families Than Do Vouchers

Consider first a voucher plan that would make available to participating families a scholarship worth, on average, about 90 percent of what is spent on children

169

in public schools. We have recently proposed such a plan for California (appendix 12B); in 1981 dollars the average voucher would be worth more than $2,000. Now compare tax credits. In practice, such proposals presuppose far lower benefits. Recent federal proposals by Senators Moynihan and Packwood envisioned tax credits worth at most $500 per child. Plans enacted in a few states and struck down by the courts (a matter to which we shall return) have provided benefits of under $200 per child. Even the NTU proposal under consideration here, while seeming to call for a substantially larger benefit—superficially, up to $1,200 per child—is considerably less valuable to families than our voucher proposal would be.

Moreover, a state income tax credit plan such as the NTU's inevitably will provide less adequate funding for schools of choice than will our voucher proposal. If for no other reason, this is true because the entire pool of state personal and corporate income tax is far smaller than the total now spent on public schools; the larger sum is potentially available for voucher plans, if all families participate and are given vouchers worth something near to current public spending levels.

In addition, even for the rich, the size of the $1,200 figure is misleading. Those whose state income taxes are lowered by a credit will have less to deduct for federal income tax purposes. Thus, for those who itemize federal tax deductions, part of the benefit from the state credit must be sent to the federal treasury. The tax cutters' proposal thus becomes a form of inverse revenue sharing helping out Uncle Sam.

Consider, for example, a California family with a yearly income of $40,000 and two school-age children. Today this fairly well-to-do family pays a maximum state income tax of about $2,400; it probably pays considerably less because of itemized deductions for mortgage interest, property taxes, and the like. The NTU initiative would permit such a family, by spending $1,200 or more on the education of each child, to wipe out all its state taxes. Because of the interrelation of state and federal tax laws noted above, however, the net cash benefit to the family would not be $2,400. The family in our example will probably be in the 35–40 percent marginal tax rate bracket for federal tax purposes. On the normal assumption that it itemizes deductions for *federal* purposes, its real benefit from the NTU plan would be only about $1,500, not $2,400. The difference, $900, would be redirected from California to the U.S. treasury.

An educational voucher, in contrast, is worth its full face value to both family and school. Thus, credits generally would have to be larger than vouchers in order to deliver the same dollar benefit. Given the current level and structure of state income tax plans, however, this cannot happen: in short, people pay too little state income tax to produce this effect. This brings us to the next general point.

While Vouchers Provide Equal Benefits to All, Tax Credits are Highly Regressive

We have shown that the hypothetical well-to-do California family with two children may benefit as much as $1,500 from the NTU tax credit initiative. Now consider the outcome of the credit for other families. One with $20,000 of income today will owe roughly $440 in state income taxes (and often less if it is a homeowner family that itemizes deductions). This sum, minus any increase in federal income taxes caused by the state credit—perhaps $90—represents its maximum savings under the initiative. The effect is that government would pay only $350–$440 toward the education of the children in the $20,000 family, compared with $1,500 toward the education of the children in the $40,000 family. This is plainly regressive.

The point becomes more vivid as we move down the income scale. Families with income of $10,000 and under would receive virtually no benefit from the NTU initiative. Hence, when others exercise their choice to attend private schools with the financial support of the state, these families will not have that option. Put simply, tax credits provide no increase of choice to any family that pays no state taxes. The only way for credits to begin to be equivalent to vouchers is to make them "refundable"—that is, to subsidize families whose tax liability is too low to need the credit. Politically, this is unlikely. Tax credit plans tend to be promoted by groups whose purpose is to let taxpayers control the use of their own taxes and not to redirect those dollars to empower lower income families. Moreover, even tax credit advocates would agree that making the credit refundable would transmute their idea into an unnecessarily complex voucher plan. In sum, because tax credits principally benefit high-income families and very low-income families not at all, if the objective is educational opportunity for children and autonomy for families, tax credits are a poor second choice.

The Extension of the Tax Credit to Include Educational Expenditures by Taxpayers without Children Lacks a Rationale and Will Have Negative Consequences

Unlike typical tax credit plans, the NTU scheme does not restrict the credit to those spending on their own children. We find this puzzling. What is the point of helping corporations and nonparents avoid state income taxes by spending on the children of strangers? Why is the corporation or individual given power to decide which child and which school is worthy? Do higher-income persons and corporate boards of directors have the best judgment about where the children of blue-collar workers should study? No one so argues.

If the point of the initiative were to shift authority for assignment away from the public school bureaucracy, that power surely would be given to the family, as it is in any voucher plan. It would not be bestowed on some person or corporation with little or no relationship to the child. But this is precisely what the tax credit initiative does. It is tempting to infer that the proposal is designed merely to cripple the state income tax, and that schools are incidental to its purpose.

In any event, the children who would actually benefit from support by strangers would in many cases be children of middle- and upper-middle-income families. Those who have more than one child and have exhausted their own tax liability could nevertheless benefit from someone else's tax credit. It would be quite natural for friends to assist one another; and friends will generally be of the same social class. Corporations will institutionalize this practice by setting up special tuition fringe benefit programs for their executives.

This tax credit provision creates yet another perverse incentive, for the opportunity for private bargaining would not be neglected. Jones pays Smith $600 in exchange for Smith's paying $1,200 in tuition for Jones's son. Everyone is ahead except the state treasury and public morality. Such fraud could not be policed.

If the argument for giving tax credits to corporations and nonparents is that this would stimulate private donations to educational institutions, it must be remembered that this incentive already exists in both the state and federal tax codes for those wanting to make an unrestricted gift to a tax-exempt school. Thus, today, government already "pays" for half or more of any charitable gift made to a school by most corporations and well-to-do individuals. To be sure, this incentive might be enhanced—indeed made nearly irresistible—by converting today's charitable tax deductions into tax credits. However, we think the tradition of having government reimburse part, but not all, of one's educational gift is a wise one to preserve. Painless charity is meaningless. Moreover, if government attaches extra tax benefits to gifts for education, this will surely divert gifts away from churches, hospitals, and other charities. That seems highly undesirable.

Conversely, it is not clear that the tax credit initiative will actually stimulate greater educational giving. This is because, in order to obtain the tax credit, a donor's funds have to be identified with an individual child. This earmarking, while securing the proposed credit, will probably destroy the charitable tax deductibility of the payment. If so, the tax advantage of the credit is eroded. Consider table 12–1, which sets out the financial implications of the case of X, an individual or corporation whose income today is $50,000 and who, we will assume, is in the 50 percent federal tax bracket and the 10 percent state tax bracket (which is roughly the case for a California resident).

Table 12––1 shows that if the choice comes to making an unrestricted gift and getting the charitable deduction or making a restricted gift and getting the credit, for our hypothetical taxpayer the following conditions exist:

Table 12–1

Comparison of the Consequences of Unrestricted Charitable Gift and of Earmarked Gift under NTU Initiative

	Unrestricted $1,000 Charitable Gift		Earmarked $1,000 Gift under NTU Initiative	
Tax Changes				
State taxable income	− 1000		No change	
State tax change		− 100		− 1000
Federal taxable income (assuming itemizing)				
From charitable gifts	− 1000		No change	
From lower state taxes	+ 100		+ 1000	
Net federal taxable income	− 900		+ 1000	
Federal tax change		− 450		+ 500
Net tax change (state and federal)		− 500		− 500
Revenue Flows				
To school		+ 1000		+ 1000
From/to federal government		− 450		+ 500
From state government		− 100		− 1000
From donor		− 450		− 500

1. In neither case is the gift free to the individual; it will cost about the same—one half—in each case. Thus, there is no increased stimulus to give.
2. The benefit to the school is less if the donor takes the credit, for the gift is not unrestricted.
3. Because some will prefer, at the same cost to them, to be able to earmark the gift for a particular child, the social consequences are very likely to be worse. Tax-exempt schools can usually be counted on to use their donations for scholarships for the needy or for all pupils; restricted gifts will more often go to children of the middle class. Moreover, under the NTU initiative, funds will flow to schools that are not tax exempt, which may result in a social loss.
4. The intergovernmental impact of the tax credit route is far greater. Instead of the federal government's losing $450 and the state $100, as happens with the charitable gift, the restricted gift costs the state $1,000 and brings in a $500 windfall to the federal treasury. This is hardly a contribution to "local control."

It is true that the picture changes somewhat in the case of less wealthy donors and small businesses. But again, if the purpose is to let individuals give to charity some of what they now pay into the state treasury, the NTU device is not ideal. Instead let us have an initiative that does just that. Imagine, for example, a measure that allowed persons to direct 50 percent of their state income taxes (up to $500) to tax-exempt charities of their choice. As noted above, we would prefer a provision that also required taxpayers to contribute something out of their own pockets and not just out of their taxes; but we would surely prefer this hypothetical proposal to the NTU initiative. And we would prefer a family educational subsidy to any of these tax schemes. Voucher plans, by empowering families, avoid all these pitfalls, while leaving in place the general tax incentive to private charitable giving.

The Extension of the Tax Credit to Cover "Incidental" Expenses of Public Education is Ill Conceived and Legally Risky

What are the "incidental expenses" for which the credit may be taken under the NTU initiative? Would they include the cost of transportation, the cost of lodging if the child lives at a boarding school, the cost of lunch for school children generally, the cost of after-school tutors? None of these considerations are made clear by the initiative, but they are extremely important. If this term includes the provision of a car to a Beverly Hills sophomore, one can see how useful it will be to some income groups. Let us suppose, however, that it is limited to such things as school supplies, musical instruments, fees for field trips, and other, similar school activities. Even so, the result is highly unfortunate. Rich families will get these things free by way of the credit, while welfare families will pay cash. The poor will not only pay more; they alone will pay anything.

This bizarre provision, of course, was not designed for that purpose. Its intent was to give the appearance of including public school users in the system. It was thought that this might bring the initiative within the possible exception to the establishment clause barrier suggested by Justices Powell and Burger in the 1973 cases concerning aid to parochial schools. The justices reserved judgment about "general" systems, those designed to help families using all kinds of schools, public as well as private. The "incidental expense" provision, however, is such a transparent device it is likely to have the opposite of its intended effect. It gives the entire enterprise a quality of deceit—worse, of amateur deceit.

The Extension of the Tax Credit Initiative to Higher Education Is Unwise and Ineffectual

There is, of course, much to be said for the reforms of educational finance at the postsecondary level. Currently, however, it is far fairer and more rational than the financing of schools. California higher education has a mature and balanced system of financing that can adapt to different tuition levels for the different kinds of state higher education systems; it thus provides reasonably tailored subsidies for the varying needs of students. There also exist an elaborate system of federal loans and scholarships (through the basic educational opportunity grant program) and some state scholarships for private education.

The tax credit proposed would cause serious dislocations of this system. If the payoff were sufficient, such dislocation would be justified. It appears, however, that the NTU initiative gave very little, if any, thought to the effects upon higher education. The real interest of the sponsors is to avoid the establishment clause. In our judgment the effort is vain. It will be a very simple matter for the justices to sever their treatment of higher education from the rest of the proposal.

Tax Credits and Vouchers Are Not Distinguishable in the Degree of State Regulation Involved

Tax credits often are advertised as simpler to administer and as less of an encroachment on the freedom of private schools. Proponents of tax credits claim that only the taxpayer has to deal with the government; the school gets its money without bureaucratic hassle. Vouchers, in contrast, are said to involve the school inevitably with government.

This is a simple misunderstanding. Tax credits can be less intrusive than subsidies to families; or they can be more intrusive. It all depends upon the conditions attached to the taxpayer's claim of the credit and how these conditions compare with those that limit redemption of the voucher by the school. Imagine, for example, a tax credit available for only those whose children are enrolled in racially integrated, secular, private schools that do not charge over $2,000 and that must be approved by the state superintendent of public instruction. This plan plainly would involve the bureaucracy with participating schools and would force some schools to alter their basic structure in order to participate. In contrast, a particular voucher scheme might involve no regulation of schools at all, direct or indirect. Schools could cash the vouchers as simply as, or even more simply than, supermarkets redeem food stamps. The alleged abstract advantage of either credits or vouchers in this respect is imaginary.

In practice one must evaluate the specific regulations required by the particular proposal. Both our proposal and the NTU initiative would protect participating private schools from further regulation in the areas of curriculum, hiring, and facilities. Ours would, however, impose three important additional controls on schools. They could not charge extra tuition to low-income families and could charge others only in accord with their ability to pay; they would have to admit applicants on a nondiscriminatory basis except for a limited preference for low-income families; and they would have to provide public information about themselves. Not all voucher proposals contain all these rules, or any of them. We prefer them because they give the consumer greater control over the entry process. This promotes the objective of providing poor and uninformed families the same opportunity as others. The school market is truly open to all. In contrast, the California tax credit proposal would encourage the rich, the talented, and other elites to use exclusive schools to buy isolation from others for their children. Values are a personal matter, but the issues are too important to resolve solely on whether more or less regulation is required. We too have a strong bias against regulation—except where it is necessary to maintain the freedom of the family's choice.

There is, by the way, a good reason for the antibureaucratic policymaker to prefer a voucher system to a tax credit. The voucher device opens a vast opportunity for deregulation of the public sector. Credits, by themselves, do not. Public voucher schools that would operate in the same deregulated fashion as their private competitors are readily imaginable; indeed, they are a central part of our proposal (appendix 12B). To achieve the same result with credits would require accepting the idea of U.S. public schools charging tuition. That is not readily imaginable at this time.

The Tax Credit Initiative Is Probably Unconstitutional to the Extent that It Allows Credits for Educational Expenses at Religious Schools

Inasmuch as the U.S. Supreme Court has already held one private school tax credit plan unconstitutional (in the *Nyquist* case), to avoid the same result new proposals must be different in ways that will matter to the Court. The strategy of the drafters of the NTU initiative is to expand the class of beneficiaries by extending the benefits of the plan to nonparents and to users of both higher education and the public schools. We believe that this technique would fail to sanitize the proposal. As we have said, the extension to higher education can easily be severed. As for elementary and secondary schools, the Court will see, as in *Nyquist*, that the initiative promises no change in California's existing dual educational structure—public schools on the one hand and private, mostly religious schools on the other. Therefore, the "primary effect" as in *Nyquist* will be seen to aid religious schools and their users; the side effect of benefiting nonpoor public school families and some nonparents will be perceived as just that—a side effect.

Perhaps the Court could be talked into severing religious school users from the NTU plan. The results, however, would limit benefits to secular private schools, causing many religious schools to perish from the new competition. In contrast, many constitutional scholars predict that a properly drawn voucher system will survive scrutiny with religious schools included. While people may differ on the desirability of these outcomes, they are plainly and importantly different.

The necessary and sufficient conditions of validly including religious schools consist in the extension of real choice to all elementary and secondary school familes. This requires that a plan promise the creation of large numbers of new private nonreligious schools and/or new public schools of choice; and it requires that working-class and poor families be given the leverage, through choice, to make their existing public schools more responsive to their wishes. Only then is any benefit to religious schools and their users likely to be seen as an incidental, rather than the primary effect. Although none of the tax credit initiatives has promised any of these changes, properly designed voucher systems that aid all schools and children promise all of them; and that is why the constitutional outlook for the two is very different.

The differing constitutional prospects, in the end, reflect the differing educational aims of the plans. Tax credits really aspire to provide tax relief to current private school users. Vouchers aim to extend choice to all.

Conclusion

The artificiality of schemes like the tax credit proposal should now be transparent. As relief for the taxpayer it is weak tea. As aid to education it would affect the small percentage of children enrolled in secular private schools. Its structure betrays its genesis. It was developed as a political device to exploit both dissatisfaction with public education and the taxpayers' revolt. In the end, it is to be recommended only to those who seek to sidetrack efforts at basic educational reform.

Appendix 12A
National Taxpayers Union Proposed State Constitutional Amendment Providing Tuition Tax Credits

Income Tax—Educational Expenses Credit—Initiative Constitutional Amendment.

Article XIII. Section 26.5

(a) For tax years ending on or after December 31, 1981, every taxpayer shall be entitled to an educational tax credit, to be deducted from income taxes payable to the State of California.

(b) The term "taxpayer" shall mean any individual, corporation, or other entity required to pay income taxes to the State of California.

(c) The term "income taxes" shall mean any taxes imposed pursuant to any law authorized by Article XIII, Section 26 of this Constitution, or similar taxes upon income, regardless of the authority for their enactment.

(d) The term "educational tax credit" shall mean a credit against California income taxes for authorized educational expenses incurred or paid during the taxpayer's applicable tax year, provided, however, that in case of individuals, the educational tax credit shall not exceed the amount of income tax payable, provided further, that in case of corporations or other taxable entities, the educational tax credit shall not exceed fifty percent of the income tax payable.

(e) The term "authorized educational expenses" shall mean sums paid by a taxpayer on behalf of eligible scholars for tuition and other educational fees actually charged by educational institutions in which such scholars are enrolled, and on behalf of eligible students for tuition or other educational fees actually charged by institutions of higher learning in which such students are enrolled, and for incidental expenses incurred for and in connection with attendance by the eligible scholars or students in such institutions. For tax years ending on or before December 31, 1981, authorized educational expenses may not exceed $1,200 per eligible scholar or student whether received from one or more taxpayers. This maximum amount shall be increased by ten percent of the previous year's maximum for each tax year, provided, however, that the Legislature may each year specify a smaller or larger percentage increase upon a finding by two-

179

thirds of all members elected to each of the two houses of the Legislature that such percentage increase is equal to the rate of inflation for the preceding calendar year.

(f) The term "eligible scholar" shall mean any California resident who is enrolled on a full-time basis in an educational institution.

(g) The term "educational institution" shall mean any institution, public or private, enrollment at which constitutes compliance with the Cumpulsory Education Law of the State of California. The State of California shall be prohibited from imposing any requirement(s) upon private educational institutions more restrictive than those in effect on January 1, 1980, for either the private educational institutions or their attending students to be in compliance with the Compulsory Education Law of the State.

(h) The term "eligible student" shall mean any California resident who is enrolled on a full-time basis in an institution of higher learning.

(i) The term "institution of higher learning" shall mean any public or private junior college, college, university, professional school or similar institution which requires a high school degree, or its equivalent, as a condition of admission.

(j) If any provision hereof, or the application thereof, is held invalid, such invalidity shall not affect other provisions or applications of this section which can be given effect without the invalid provision or application, and to this end the provisions of this section are severable.

Appendix 12B
Initiative for Family Choice in Education: Proposed State Constitutional Amendment for Educational Subsidies or Vouchers to Families

An Initiative for Education by Choice

The following section shall be added to Article IX of the California Constitution:

Section 17.   The people of California have adopted this section to improve the quality and efficiency of schools, to maximize the educational opportunities of all children, and to increase the authority of parents and teachers.

1.   *New Schools*

(a)   In addition to the public schools and private schools presently recognized by law, there shall be two classes of schools together known as New Schools.

(b)   New Private Schools are private schools eligible to redeem state scholarships.

(c)   New Public Schools are schools organized as public corporations eligible to redeem state scholarships.
School districts, community college and public universities may establish New Public Schools. Each shall be a public nonprofit corporation governed by rules fixed by the organizing authority at the time of incorporation. Such schools are free common schools under section 5 of this article; section 6 of this article shall not limit their formation. Except as stated in this section, New Public Schools shall operate according to the laws affecting New Private Schools.

(d)   New Schools shall be eligible to redeem state scholarships upon filing a statement indicating satisfaction of those requirements for hiring and employment, for curriculum and for facilities which applied to private schools on July 1, 1979; the Legislature may not augment such requirements. No school shall lose eligibility to redeem state scholarships except upon proof of substantial violation of this section after notice and opportunity to defend.

No New School may advocate unlawful behavior or expound the inferiority of either sex or of any race nor deliberately provide false or misleading information respecting the school. Each shall be subject to reasonable requirements of disclosure. The Legislature may set reasonable standards of competence for diplomas.

No school shall be ineligible to redeem state scholarships because it teaches moral or social values, philosophy, or religion, but religion may not be taught in public schools or New Public Schools; a curriculum may be required, but no pupil shall be compelled to profess ideological belief or actively to participate in ceremony symbolic of belief.

2. *Admission to New Schools*

(a) A New School may set enrollment and select students by criteria valid for public schools under the federal constitution other than physical handicap, national origin, and place of residence within the state.

(b) Each New School shall reserve at least twenty-five percent of each year's new admissions for timely applications from families with income lower than seventy-five percent of California families. If such applications are fewer than the places reserved, all shall be admitted and the balance of reserved places selected as in paragraph (a) of this subsection; if such applications exceed the reserved places the school may select therefrom the reserved number.

3. *Finance*

(a) Every child of school age is entitled without charge to a state scholarship redeemable by New Schools and adequate for a thorough education as defined by law. Scholarships shall be equal for every child of similar circumstance differing only by factors deemed appropriate by the Legislature; they shall reflect the educational cost attributable to physical handicap and learning disability, and, for children of low income families, the cost of reasonable transportation. Except for children enrolled in schools in which parents or other relatives have primary responsibility for instruction of their own children no scholarship shall be less than eighty percent of the average scholarship for children of similar grade level. A nonprofit New Private School shall use scholarship income solely for the education of its students. The Legislature shall provide for an appropriate division of the scholarship in the case of transfers. Nothing required or permitted by this section shall be deemed to repeal or conflict with section 8 of this article or section 5 of Article XVI.

(b)   New Schools shall accept scholarships from low income families as full payment for educational or related services. Charges to others shall be consistent with the family's ability to pay.

(c)   The average public cost per pupil enrolled in New Schools shall approximate ninety percent of that cost in public schools. Public cost here and in subsection (3)(d) shall mean every cost to state and local government of maintaining elementary and secondary education in the relevant year as determined by the Department of Finance according to law; it shall not include the costs of funding employee retirement benefits which are unfunded on June 3, 1982.

(d)   For school years 1982–1983 through 1987–1988 the total public cost of elementary and secondary education shall not exceed that of 1981–1982 adjusted for changes in average personal income and total school age population. The Controller shall authorize no payment in violation of this sub-section.

(e)   Excess space in public schools shall be available to New Schools for rental at actual cost.

4.   *Rights*

(a)   A pupil subject to compulsory education who attends a New School may continue therein unless she or he is deriving no substantial academic benefit or is responsible for serious or habitual misconduct related to school. With fair notice and procedures each school may set and enforce a code of conduct and discipline and regulate its academic dismissals. No pupil enrolled in any such school shall suffer discrimination on the basis of race, religion, gender, or national origin.

(b)   The Legislature shall assure provision of adequate information about New Schools through sources independent of any school or school authority. Non-literate parents and others with special information needs shall receive a grant redeemable for the services of independent education counsellors.

5.   *Transitional Provisions*

The Legislature shall promptly implement this section, ensuring full eligibility for scholarships of at least one-fourth of all pupils in school year 1984–1985 and a similar additional number yearly thereafter.

13 The Public Monopoly and the Seeds of Self-Destruction

E.G. West

For a long time economists have attempted to delineate those goods and services that are "natural" for governments to supply. They now reserve the term *public good* for a project that people cannot, or will not, by individual effort produce successfully for themselves. One reason is the difficulty of getting individuals to pay for it. Normally when people do not consent to pay the price for a good it is not supplied to them. This is not necessarily the case, however, with a public good. Consider, for example, the production of a television beam. Once in operation it is very difficult to stop individuals tuning in to obtain its benefits free of charge. This creates the now-familiar "free rider" dilemma, in which nobody will produce the good because nobody is willing to pay sufficiently to cover the costs. To resolve the dilemma, it is argued, the government should step in and coerce contributions for the public good via compulsory taxes.

From Lighthouses to Public Schools

Paul Samuelson, who pioneered the concept, uses the example of the lighthouse: "Its beam helps everyone in sight. A businessman could not build it for a profit since he cannot claim a price from each user. This certainly is the kind of activity that governments would naturally undertake."[1] Current research is, however, challenging the view that the problem is intractable. It is finding that those goods that can be technically defined as public goods do not necessarily have to be produced by government. Government can confine its activities to financing them—that is, to purchasing them from the market. For instance, although expensive aircraft for defense can be regarded as public goods in the technical sense just explained, we rely on the private sector, not the government, to produce them; and governments finance the purchase from tax revenues. The same is true for the lighthouse.[2]

At the other end of the scale of economic categories is the private good. In this case if the good is produced for one person its benefits are not automatically made available for all others in society. The benefits of the private good are, in other words, enjoyed exclusively by the individual who is willing to purchase them at a price. It so happens that real world governments often produce these kinds of goods in abundance; they include publicly supplied housing, water, hospitals, post offices, garbage removal, fire services, and the provision of fuel, transport, and recreation. In these cases it is feasible for governments to leave their supply to the market (since people can be induced here to make individual contributions—pay prices) and to refrain completely from spending on them; and sometimes this happens.

Economists used to argue, naively, that because a particular good or service was being supplied by government the situation could be rationalized on the grounds that only governments could provide the activity. The subsequent recognition, however, that governments are in fact supplying large quantities of private goods (which the market is equipped to handle) has forced analysts to seek other explanations, and in doing so they have enlisted the help of the newer "economics of politics." From this approach, for example, Professor Richard Musgrave concludes that the public provision of private goods can now be explained in various ways, including "political gains to be derived from the dispensing of public employment, and last but not least the power of public employee unions."[3]

Where does education belong among these economic categories? It is clear that it cannot be classified as a pure Samuelsonian public good like the lighthouse. This is because exclusion from the private benefits of education of those who are not willing to pay the price (tuition) is clearly possible. And even if education were a public good, governments could purchase it from the market (via subsidies or vouchers, for example) rather than supply it "free" themselves.

Musgrave believes that it is more realistic to consider education a "mixed good"—one combining features of both private and public good. This is the case when private consumption generates so-called external benefits. "By getting educated, [Mr.] A not only derives personal benefits but also makes it possible for others to enjoy association with more educated community." In this situation "the correct budgetary intervention . . . will not involve full budgetary provision; rather it will take the form of subsidy to private purchases."[4] The intended subsidy evidently falls short of 100 percent of the costs. So even Musgrave's analysis is not sufficient to explain the current system of public education, for it is clear that it *is fully subsidized*. Obviously we have to look further for more satisfying explanations.

The argument about externalities does not in any case imply that all external benefits should be subsidized. Consider the example of the consumption of certain kinds of food. A person who eats a given amount of fruit per month makes himself more resistant to disease and at the same time reduces the danger of transmitting disease to his neighbors. If he normally eats insufficient quantities there could well be a case for subsidizing fruit to encourage him to consume the optimal amount. The fact that fruit is not, however, universally subsidized in practice simply means that the theory of externalities is empirically not relevant in this case. Presumably most people consume enough fruit in the pursuit of their private benefit. This generates external benefits to others free of charge.

There would clearly be a sufficient argument for intervention if it were established that in the pursuit of their private benefits people were consuming only negligible quantities of fruit. The same is true of education. But the historical record of England and America shows that most people were already purchasing private education in significant quantities at the time it was made universally "free."[5] So any argument based on externalities would have called for intervention to provide free education only to a minority who were purchasing negligible quantities of it for their children.

We are then left with the third of Musgrave's hypotheses: that the motivation for government supply of education arises from political gains derived from dispensing public employment and from the (political) power of public employee unions. Musgrave's hypothesis, however, needs to be modified in one respect. The power of public employee unions could not be an explanation for initial government intervention because up to that time, by definition, there would have been no public employees. A tighter hypothesis is that labor unions in the private sector can foresee the benefits to themselves of "nationalization" because more gains are available to them when dealing with a government employer. In fact, history shows that it was associations of teachers who were the main advocates of the collectivization of education. The policy was not spontaneously demanded by the people; it had to be sold to them.[6]

Such a diagnosis obviously suggests that the costs of education will be higher under public than private auspices. And it is not just the costs of the monopoly of the labor unions that have to be accounted for; the subsequent development of the monopoly bureaucracy within the whole educational establishment also plays a considerable part.

The problem of public monopoly is the major focus of this chapter, and I shall return to it soon; let us recall meanwhile the earlier issues of theory. First, we must reiterate that even in those cases in which services qualify technically as public goods it does not necessarily follow that they have to be publicly supplied, as distinct from publicly financed. Education (which is certainly not a pure public good) may likewise be made available with the help of direct subsidies to private schools based on enrollment, through voucher systems, or through tuition tax credit schemes. The case for free or subsidized education should therefore not be confused with the case for public schools.

The Belief that Public Schools Desegregate

Despite the logic in this reasoning many would still argue for the alternative of "free" public schools on the grounds that their quality of education differs inherently from, and in some senses is considered superior to, that provided by the private school. For instance, it is often argued that the public school is more unifying than the private one in its effect on the social structure. Unfortunately for such advocates, it so happens that segregation by income and ethnic grouping characterizes a large part of the public school system. In the suburban areas of New York, for instance, there is no more than a 2 percent minority enrollment in public schools, and the proportion of low-income children attending is also minuscule. At the same time, a recent survey found that forty-four private schools in New York City that are members of the National Association of Independent Schools had a minority enrollment of twice the national average. And in half of the western states there are more members of minority groups in private schools than in public schools.[7] As for segregation according to income, the fact is that all income groups use private schools. The family incomes of private school students, moreover, are remarkably similar to the income distribution of the entire U.S. population.[8]

The tendency to segregation by income seems inherent in the public system. Seventy-nine percent of the wealthiest families in the United States enroll their children in public schools, thereby benefiting from public subsidies covering 100 percent of the costs. Their subsidies, meanwhile, are typically larger than those received by poor families.[9] In 1977, for example, in one New York metropolitan area the highest-spending public school district spent $8,600 per child, compared with $3,115 per pupil spent in New York City public schools. The property taxes that all public school parents have to pay to support such expensive public schools are tax deductible. One interpretation of this is that the federal government, in effect, pays one half or more of the tuition for the "free and public" schooling of wealthy families.[10]

The high cost of suburban public schools restricts their clientele to the local population of high-income families via strict zoning laws. It is clear that those who emphasize equality should prefer an equal-valued voucher scheme to the present public school system. This indeed is the conclusion of the 1981 "Coleman Report" on U.S. education, which argues:

> The evidence indicates that facilitating the use of private schools through policies of the sort described above [tax credits and vouchers] would not increase segregation along racial or economic lines but would decrease it. . . . Such policies would bring more blacks, Hispanics, and students from lower income backgrounds into the private schools, thus reducing the between-sector segregation, and these students would be moving from a sector of high racial segregation to a sector of low racial segregation, as well as from a sector slightly higher in economic segregation to one slightly lower.[11]

Despite all this testimony the myth persists that the public system achieves a much greater degree of desegregation than does the private sector. Such pseudo-facts are likely to take a long time to eradicate.[12] In view of these entrenched beliefs, we shall assume a conviction that public schooling is, on balance, likely to achieve a greater degree of desegregation than is a private system of schooling. We shall also assume a consensus that segregation provides inferior education for some minorities and that it is socially undesirable. Such agreement, however, does *not* imply that people will always select public school systems. The main reason they will not involves the monopoly costs of public education.

The Costs of the Public School Monopoly: The Crucial Item

Many participants in the debate believe that they have settled the issue once and for all if people accept the alleged superior qualities of public schools— such as the tendency to promote social cohesion. The error in this reasoning is the assumption that the qualities mentioned are absolutes and will be provided at any cost. Generally, however, the demand for superior quality services is not a constant; rather, it expands or contracts according to the price charged—as the price increases less of it will be demanded, and beyond some range of price the demand will shrink to zero. In the context of education this means that, despite the widespread belief that public schooling has some superior qualities, these qualities will be deemed not worth the cost as the monopoly element in public supply gathers strength.

Suppose, at one extreme, that a public system could unambiguously achieve equality of opportunity, equity, and social integration better than any alternative scheme. Suppose, however, that financing such a system would take half the national income; it is impossible to believe that this system would be adopted under such circumstances. In reply it could be argued that it would be in the self-interest of the monopoly itself to prevent costs rising to such exorbitant levels as to force the public schools out of existence. According to my argument, however, *there are no incentives within the public system itself to prevent excessive monopolization from bestowing a crucial self-inflicted wound.* The tendency appears to be one of inherent self-destruction.

Consider in more detail the full nature of the monopoly, whose source can be divided into two parts: monopoly bureaucracy and unionized labor monopoly.

The Bureaucracy Monopoly

I have discussed elsewhere a more sophisticated and technical application of the economic theory of bureaucracy to education.[13] In broad outline the theory is based on the premise that bureaucrats are prompted mainly by their own self-interest rather than by the public interest; the same theory produces the following refutable predictions:

1. There will be a tendency toward continual expansion of the public education bureau's monopoly (''bureaucratic imperialism'').
2. Alliances will emerge between the bureau and the factor supplies (such as labor) it employs.
3. The bureau will want to offer a *total* output in exchange for a total budget. This gives it the same bargaining power as a full-price discriminating monopolist offering a choice between all or nothing.

My focus here will be primarily on the first two of these predictions. Consider first the process of bureaucratic growth. In the private market a sign of monopolization is the gradual merger or consolidation of participating suppliers until one dominant firm emerges. The essence of this market structure is the restriction on entry. Entry is less possible when one dominant firm is able, at short notice, to ''police'' any part of its market against the threat of newcomers.

In education the parallel phenomenon has appeared in the geographic expansion of the size of the school district. A conspicuous feature of the earliest form of the U.S. public school system was its decentralized political structure. States left the control of schools to the local community, and parental participation in the political process afforded some effective competition. The influence of parents became more remote, however, as the size of school districts increased and their number shrank. In 1945 there were 101,000 school districts in the United States; by 1976 the number had dropped to 16,300—a reduction of nearly 84 percent in thirty years. In parts of Canada the same phenomenon has appeared more dramatically. In Ontario, for example, the number of school boards fell from 1,673 in 1965 to 175 in 1978. This growth of monopoly power is far greater than that imaginable in a purely private system.

Administrators call the process of school district mergers consolidation, which has appeared because of their influence and control over the agenda. Administrators usually join professional educators in providing justifying arguments that consolidation into large administrative areas is necessary to reap important economies of scale in education. In fact, studies have shown that economies of scale are *not* realized by school districts beyond a relatively small size.[14]

Several empirical studies suggest that an increase in the salaries of administrators and teachers will raise total educational expenditures because inelastic demand shrinks at a lower rate than price increases. Insofar as the size of the school district expands and the monopoly power of bureaucracies increases, administrators and their factor supplies are able to raise the price of their services. In the education industry, such salary increases will mean fewer teachers and higher student/teacher ratios. The result will be an increase in the average expenditure per pupil in average daily attendance. Staaf found that such expenditure did increase significantly with the size of the school district. The average per-pupil expenditure in districts with 40,000 or more students was nearly a third higher than the expenditure in districts with 3,000–7,000 enrollees.[15]

The output achievement of the educational process meanwhile does not enter into teacher salary agreements. Teachers in public schools are rewarded typically on the basis not of educational output, but on the number of years in service (experience) and on their educational degrees or diplomas. Of about twenty American studies all but two demonstrate that the educational attainments of teachers are not related to student achievement. Most of the studies also show that student achievement is not clearly related to teacher experience.[16]

The first prediction of the economics of bureaucracy—that it will constantly exert pressure to enlarge its monopoly—can therefore be seen to invite parental discontent and ultimate taxpayer rebellion. Where there are large numbers of boards (districts) and where a parent is in an educational jurisdiction with, say, 100 voters, he at least has one chance in a hundred of being the middle or controlling voter. And if "voice" is ineffective, "exit" is always possible, for there will be a large number of neighborhood school boards and districts. After consolidation, however, both voice and exit are considerably weakened. When an educational jurisdiction is increased from 100 voters to 10,000, the individual has only 1 percent of his former chance of an effective voice. Meanwhile, exit is much more difficult because he has to travel a greater distance to find another jurisdiction.

With the increase in monopoly power enjoyed by the educational bureau comes a sharing of the monopoly rents with the teachers. This can take the form of a reduction in accountability. It becomes much more difficult for citizens, taxpayers, and parents to monitor teachers. School inspectors have in many places been replaced by what are called program consultants, who enter a classroom only at the invitation of teachers. In some areas, too, the role of examinations has been reduced drastically, with the result that the relative standard of efficiency between schools is more difficult to measure.

Evidence for the second prediction of the economic bureaucracy—that it generates an alliance between the bureau and those it employs (the teachers)—was already suggested above; it is also shown in the simultaneous opposition by teachers and administrators to proposals for vouchers and tax credits that, by stimulating competition, could seriously challenge the carefully accumulated monopoly position of the joint interests of the common alliance in the educational establishment. The American Association of School Administrators, The Council of Chief State School Officers, and the National Association of State Boards of Education were all formally opposed to the 1978 federally proposed tax credit for education. The president of the United Federation of Teachers simultaneously expressed the same opposition. In Canada, union opposition to vouchers has been formally recorded in the case of the British Columbia Teachers' Federation, which struggled hard to prevent the passage of the Independent Schools Support Act—the Act that provides direct fiscal aid to independent schools for the first time in the province's history.

The Labor Monopoly

The second form of increasing monopoly costs comes through the ability of unionized teachers to secure higher wages in the public sector. Systematic evidence supports the proposition that collective bargaining leads to cost escalation. More precisely, incidence of unionization and "aggressive" bargaining is higher in the public than in the private sector of education.

One study by Victor in 1978 concluded that teachers' unions in the public schools succeeded in raising salaries from 5 to 20 percent.[17] This, however, is an underestimate, for there are additional items in negotiation that are not costed out. A recent study for the National Institute of Education traced the extension of collective bargaining by public school teachers in a sample of 151 school districts. Among its findings was the observation that teacher contracts became significantly stronger with the size of the union membership.[18] Of course membership potential is much bigger in the public than in the private sector.

The real cost of education can rise for one of two reasons, or for both. First, there can be a large increase in teacher salaries for a given (constant) supply of education. Second, there can be a reduced supply of education for a given (constant) wage bill. Some evidence of the latter kind of increased costs is available. Research reported from a sample taken by Pascal suggests that teachers reduce output by such methods as negotiating downward the length of the school day and the size of classes.[19] Table 13–1 shows that even by 1975 these items (and others) had become quite significant. In addition, conventional studies of the costs of teacher employment usually omit negotiated increases in

Table 13–1

Trends in Attainment of Some Key Noncompensation Provisions in Teacher Collective Bargaining, 1975

Item	Percent of Sample
Maximum class size specified	34
Duration of school day specified	58
Teacher can exclude disruptive student	46

Source: Anthony H. Pascal, "The Hidden Costs of Collective Bargaining in Local Government," *Taxing and Spending* 3 (Spring 1980): 36. Reprinted with permission.

fringe benefit packages such as pensions, vacations, insurance, together with the increased employment costs of negotiated subjects such as entry requirements, assignment and promotion rules, paraprofessionals, and professional development.

A new tendency in the U.S. labor field is likely to aggravate still further the escalating labor costs, especially in future years. This is the development of regulatory obligations to employ teacher-union services via agency shops in the negotiation of the terms of employment. This tendency has been encouraged by the recent deliberation of the Supreme Court in the *Abood* case.[20]

Agency shops are distinguished from union shops in that, although they compel their employees to pay a service charge as a contribution to the union's collective bargaining expenses, they do not require membership in the union. The Supreme Court in *Abood* v. *Detroit Board of Education* examined the constitutionality of the agency shop clauses in the public employment sector.[21] It held that public employees may be compelled to pay union service charges for legitimate collective bargaining activities. The subject of the case was a constitutional challenge by 600 Michigan public school teachers who claimed that the state-legislated agency shop deprived them of their right to freedom of association as guaranteed by the U.S. Constitution's First and Fourteenth Amendments.

It cannot be denied that where there are a large number of employees there are significant negotiation costs in determining salaries. But at least five institutional methods are available for handling them.

1. Employers could make individual contracts with each separate employee.
2. Groups of workers could employ competing collective agents; the latter would negotiate on behalf of the workers directly with the employer.
3. Employees could use the services of competing unions.
4. A closed shop could be established; in this case all employers agree to negotiate through one union of which all employees must be members.
5. The fifth method, the one favored by the *Abood* decision, is the agency shop: not all employees need be members of the union, but all are obliged to pay agencies sums limited to the costs of negotiation.

Those who support agency shops argue that they are the only way to keep negotiation costs low. The rationale offered is that agency shops discipline all beneficiaries of negotiated labor contracts and thus preclude "free-riding employees" from enjoying such wage increases without contributing to the costs. There are grave weaknesses in this reasoning and in the *Abood* judgement, but there is no space to describe them here.[22] Suffice it to say that one important cost is overlooked. In coercing all teachers to negotiate through one agency, the agency shop acquires powers of discipline that are normally comparatively difficult to exert in a competitive system. The agency, in other words, is enabled to undertake bargaining that is more aggressive than normal.

Although the institution of the agency shop is not yet widespread throughout most states, the Supreme Court has not removed any uncertainty that might previously have been an impediment to the growth of agency shops. I concede, however, that my main concern is to propose hypotheses that need future testing with empirical evidence.

I am not arguing that public sector collective bargaining per se is unambiguously undesirable. Indeed, workers' free access to unions of their choice is consistent with ordinary rights of freedom of association. But where there is relatively free entry one can normally expect several unions to operate in different school districts and sometimes simultaneously in the same district. This situation gives workers some positive choice. The scenario under the agency shop, in contrast, is not one of competition among unions but one of monopoly. With competing unions, the agents (the union organizers) can earn no more than normal profits for services rendered. With the agency shop only one union is selected and the spur of competition removed.

Another serious consequence of exclusive representation in the public (as distinct from the private) sector is that it has the effect of redistributing political power in a democracy as it affects decisions on the content of education. The scope of bargaining in teacher negotiation is expanding daily. As we have seen from table 13–1, the duration of the school day, class size, and student discipline have already reached the union bargaining table.[23] The same is now true of curriculum policy.[24] In consequence, the supplier of education—the teacher—is beginning to exert greater influence on the content of education (and its cost) than is the average member of the electorate.

Available Measures of Relative Costs

This analysis of the monopolization of public education suggests that the costs of schooling per unit of output will be considerably higher than in the private sector. Available evidence supports this suggestion. According to the National Center for Education Statistics the average current expenditure per pupil in private schools in the 1977/78 school year was $819.[25] In public schools it was $1,736—more than double that in the private school. Such a discrepancy is quite consistent with the explanation of the monopoly cost differences examined above. All kinds of arguments have been advanced to explain it away. But even in total, the arguments are not impressive.[26]

Induced Taxpayer Revolts

The mounting costs of public education necessarily demand increased taxes, which in turn provoke the kind of taxpayer revolts that have now become so common in the United States. By the 1970s taxpayers in several areas were beginning to refuse to vote for educational bond issues, and several large urban educational systems were facing the prospect of bankruptcy and default. Municipalities and schools in New York and Chicago, for example, ran out of credit. Cleveland was forced to close its schools for weeks at a time to live within its newly constrained financial limits.

The most conspicuous general tax revolt, of course, occurred in California in 1978. No one would argue, in retrospect, that Proposition 13 was an unambiguous success in that state. Mistakes of strategy no doubt occurred. But more relevant is the impetus the movement gave to taxpayer groups all over the country. Initiatives are now crowding onto the scene in astonishing numbers. There were perhaps as many as 500 on the November 1980 ballots, and many are no doubt benefiting now from the initial mistakes in California. Voters are attempting, in these initiatives, to limit not only the property tax but also the growth of state expenditures. And increasingly there are attempts to control the use of public funds in areas ranging from nuclear power plants to street lighting. One of the areas inevitably affected by this zeal to control public funds is education.

Those who have subsequently analyzed the phenomenon of Proposition 13 have concluded that the move to cut taxes was prompted mainly by a concern over government waste and inefficiency. According to a 1978 nationwide post-election survey conducted by the University of Michigan's Center for Political Study, people who showed the lowest trust in government were significantly more disposed to favor a Proposition 13 type of measure in their state and to support a one-third cut in taxes. This relationship held true for all ideological and partisan groups. The eventual public support shown for proposed voucher and tax credit schemes surely stems partly from the same frustration with the high costs of government. A tuition voucher or tax credit scheme that based its value on the less costly private school financial requirements could be expected to yield substantial gains to taxpayers after a given percentage of public school users had transferred to private schools.[27]

This leads us finally to speculate on the probable ultimate success of specific current schemes. The most important current initiatives are the education voucher scheme associated with Professors Coons and Sugarman in California and a tax credit scheme that is being sponsored by the National Taxpayers Union. The latter is located in the District of Columbia, where an initiative was being planned for the November 1981 election.

Current Educational Manifestations of the Revolt

The Coons-Sugarman Voucher

The Coons-Sugarman voucher unfortunately conflicts with the need to base it on least costly (most efficient) institution. Given that private schools typically appear to be delivering education at almost half the cost of public schools, efficiency would require the value of the voucher to be about 50 percent of the per capita expenditures in public schools. Coons and Sugarman, however, stipulate that their voucher is to be valued at 90 percent of public school costs.

This inconsistency is perplexing in view of the call for more competition in Coons and Sugarman's recent book. Using the analogy of food supply, they argue that "to prefer the distribution of food through agents of a public monopoly such as the local post office . . . is to us incomprehensible." They object to the way public schools are protected from private competition: "Public schools today are rarely permitted to die of unpopularity. . . . Of course public schools could actually become competitive with one another. For this to happen without private competition, however, the public school must somehow be made to risk the loss of its fiscal support if families do not choose it."[28] Coons and Sugarman obviously agree that the public system is a monopoly. This means that its costs are too high. Yet valuing their proposed voucher at 90 percent of the public school costs per student builds in and perpetuates the wasteful levels of spending that the new competition is supposed to remove.

The District of Columbia Tuition Tax Credit

The tax credit proposal in the District of Columbia has the much more appropriate value of $1,200 per student. Given that the current expenditure per pupil in the District's public schools is about $3,000, the proposed tax credit is less than half this figure. The major problem with the scheme is that because its beneficiaries will pay less tax to the state government they will have less to deduct at the federal level. This results in a leakage of the value of the credit to the federal government or to the benefit of state taxpayers elsewhere if the total federal budget is kept constant. It seems possible that this problem could be resolved in the near future, however, through some accommodation at the federal level. This is especially so in view of the fact that in his address to Congress on 19 February 1981 President Reagan announced his administration's general interest in the tuition tax credit scheme.

Conclusion

Economists usually attempt to avoid forcing their own (normative) prescriptions and to confine their attention to scientific (positive) predictions about probable future economic events. In this spirit my analysis reveals the public system to be on the verge of losing a significant amount of funding through organized taxpayer resistance to the unprecedented growth in the scope of the public school monopoly. All this is occurring despite the persistence of unsubstantiated beliefs that public schools are superior in providing equality of opportunity and social cohesion. Voters seem to be prepared to sacrifice these seeming benefits because of the excessive costs of continuing with the status quo. Because public educators seem unable to curtail their appetite for further monopoly gain, they are exceeding limits that could lead to their destruction.

Notes

1. Paul Samuelson, *Economics*, 8th ed. (New York: McGraw-Hill, 1970), p. 151.

2. Ronald Coase has demonstrated that, historically, the "public good" of the lighthouse was financed, not by the general taxpayer, but by that portion of the population that enjoyed most of its benefits. R.H. Coase, "The Lighthouse in Economics," *Journal of Law and Education* 17 (October 1974):375–376.

3. Richard A. Musgrave, "Why Public Employment?" (Discussion Paper 801, Harvard Institute of Economic Research, November 1980).

4. Richard A. Musgrave and Peggy B. Musgrave, *Public Finance in Theory and Practice* (New York: McGraw-Hill, 1980), p. 78.

5. E.G. West, "The Political Economy of American Public School Legislation," *Journal of Law and Economics* 10 (October 1967):101–128; and idem, *Education and the Industrial Revolution* (London: Batsford, 1975).

6. West, "Political Economy of School Legislation," p. 115.

7. National Center for Education Statistics, *Statistics of Nonpublic Elementary and Secondary Schools 1970–71* (Washington, D.C., 1972), p. 16. See also National Center for Education Statistics, *Condition of Education 1977* (Washington, D.C., 1978), p. 76.

8. U.S. Bureau of the Census, *Statistical Abstract of the United States* (Washington, D.C.: Government Printing Office, 1975).

9. National Center for Education Statistics, *Condition of Education 1977*.

10. U.S., Congress, Senate Finance Committee, *Tuition Tax Credit: Hearing on Bill S2 142*, (testimony by Thomas Vitullo-Martin), 8 January 1978.

11. James Coleman, Thomas Hoffer, and Sally Kilgore, "Summary of Major Findings of Public and Private Schools" (Report to the National Center for Education Statistics under Contract No. 300-78-0208, National Opinion Research Center, 1981).

12. The alleged need for desegregation is built on the twin assumptions that segregation causes inferior schooling for minority groups and that segregation inhibits a socially integrated society. The first of these assumptions has recently been dismissed as mythical by Thomas Sowell, "Heresies on Race and Education," *Taxing and Spending* 3 (Spring 1980):5–18

13. E.G. West, "The Prospects for Education Vouchers: An Economic Analysis," in *Papers on State Controlled Education Processors,* ed. Robert B. Everheart (San Francisco: Pacific Institute, forthcoming).

14. Robert J. Staaf, "The Public School System in Transition: Consolidation and Parental Choice," in *Budgets and Bureaucrats,* ed. Thomas E. Borcherding (Durham, N.C.: Duke University Press, 1977), p. 130.

15. Ibid.

16. Ibid., pp. 152–155.

17. R.B. Victor, *The Economic Effects of Teacher Unions: An Appraisal* (Santa Monica, Calif.: Rand Corporation, 1978).

18. L. McDonnell and A.H. Pascal, *Organized Teachers in American Schools* (Santa Monica, Calif.: Rand Corporation, 1979).

19. Anthony H. Pascal, "The Hidden Costs of Collective Bargaining in Local Government," *Taxing and Spending* 3 (Spring 1980):31–39.

20. Robert J. Staaf and Edwin G. West, "Agency Shops under Public Sector: An Economic Analysis," *University of Miami Law Review* 33 (March 1979):645–665.

21. Abood v. Detroit Board of Education, 431 U.S. 209 (1976).

22. For a sustained critique see E.G. West and R. Staaf, "Paying for Compulsory Union Services: The Entanglement Consequences of Agency Shops in the Public Sector," *Wake Forest Law Review,* forthcoming.

23. See also Harry H. Wellington and Ralph K. Winter Jr., *The Union and the Cities* (Washington, D.C.: Brookings Institution, 1972), p. 138.

24. See Pascal, "Hidden Costs of Collective Bargaining," p. 36.

25. U.S. Department of Health, Education and Welfare, Education Division, *National Center for Education Statistics Bulletin* (23 October 1979).

26. The reasons are given in E.G. West, *Tax Credits for Education* (Washington, D.C.: Heritage Foundation, 1981).

27. Ibid.

28. John E. Coons and Stephen D. Sugarman, *Education by Choice: The Case for Family Control* (Berkeley: University of California Press, 1978), pp. 156–157.

14 Family Choice and Education: Privatizing a Public Good

Donald Fisher

In response to what most economic analysts label as a major recession, politicians in most Western industrialized nations are returning to neoclassical, monetarist policies. Keynesian intervention by the state, it is said, seems to have little or no effect on stagflation and the rising tide of unemployment; therefore, we are advised to put our faith in the "invisible hand" of the market.

The relation between socioeconomic trends and education in turn shapes a perception that education is in crisis. Critics accuse educational systems of failing to do even an adequate job of preparing students for their adult roles in the labor market. We are bombarded by accounts of declining standards and increasing costs despite decreasing enrollments. The demand that schools be accountable has resulted in the widespread movement back to something labeled "the basics." Concerned parents seem to have missed the fact that educational systems have no control over the opportunity structure in the labor market. That governments have given additional credence to the fallacy that there is a controlling connection between the two—that is, between education and the opportunity structure in the labor market—has simply served to convince parents that educational systems (schools) are to blame. The suggestion that we should in education adopt a free market model that gives consumers the ruling voice is the next step in the process of scapegoating education. The exercise of family choice will neatly transfer the blame for unemployment or illiteracy from the schools to parents. The standards by which education is held accountable would move from legally established norms and public process to private preference. Put simply, it is a massive con game whose victims are those parents who internalize the erroneous belief that making the right educational choice for their children will assure the latter's success. Whereas the earlier versions of family choice, like the various voucher schemes, emerged from the optimism of the 1960s, today's mood of budgetary retrenchment focuses on the private sector as the source of all cures. As the economy has moved into recession so we have moved from a liberal reform policy (vouchers) to a neoconservative one (privatizing).[1] The policy of family choice in education parallels the move toward monetarist policies at the national level.

There is a wide range of family choice proposals, from the modern day free-marketers like Milton Friedman and E.G. West, who want government out of everything, to those like John Coons and Stephen Sugarman, who are realistic enough to accept the social necessity of having more than merely a "constable in the market-place," to use Carlyle's phrase.[2] Rather than describing the proposals, I intend to examine the underlying assumptions and then to discuss the foreseeable educational, social, and economic outcomes.

Assumptions

Five general assumptions underlie the proposals to privatize education. First, that the institution of education is isolated from the other social institutions in our society: education is perceived to be separate. Second, that education is an "economic good": in contrast to "free goods," which exit in superfluity, education is defined as subject to scarcity like diamonds or oil. Third, that freedom of choice is a positive attribute of any society: market mechanisms are considered to be a necessary condition of a free society; the individual or the household is the unit of analysis. Fourth, that society is composed of rational optimizers: individuals are rational, self-interested choosers; in any rational transaction the quid received is greater then the quo foregone in terms of individual self-interest; competition and accountability are the key social processes. Fifth, that if individuals or households rationally pursue goals under conditions of perfect competition, the result will be collective rational choices. Essentially, free market competition, its proponents say, leads to societal benefits. Consumer sovereignty is perceived to be the best test of any social system. This final assumption has some corollaries: that advisers will be able to connect means (an educational situation) to ends (satisfied customers); that consumers will adopt a monitoring role; and that schools will be able to change relatively quickly in order to supply the educational situations that are in demand.

A critical examination of these assumptions soon leads to the conclusion that they are grounded more in faith than in reality. First, to isolate education from other social forces ignores the obviously close relationships that exist among schooling, the economy, the state, and families. Schooling is neither separate nor neutral. Second, whereas education is in one sense an economic good, in that it is capital and labor intensive, it does not suffer from scarcity in the same way as diamonds or oil. Both the quantity and quality of education are socially controlled. Education is by definition a social product rather than a finite resource. Fiscal policy is at one and the same time social policy.[3]

Third, although I am not against the principle of choice, I do believe that in areas where the public good is likely to be affected, society should embed socially desirable principles in the institution, rather than expect them to emerge from a mass of individual choices.[4] The product of greater choice presumably is greater satisfaction. Yet satisfaction, in and of itself, has no necessary educational reference.[5] Finally, freedom of choice is too confined by the distribution of wealth in our society.

Fourth, although rational self-interest plays a part in the choices that all individuals make, individuals also make choices that take into account other people's needs and interests. Indeed, for individuals who value the collective good, the operative principle for decision-making is that each person receives according to the needs of the larger society rather than according to individual needs.[6] Further, some economists define education as a case of nonrival consumption; that is, one person's consumption in no way reduces the benefits available to another. These economists argue that we should not apply the exclusion principle to cases of nonrival competition. This principle applies to situations in which consumption is strictly dependent upon having paid a price for a service or commodity and in which that payment grants exclusive control over the consumption of the service or commodity.[7] So it seems that it is inappropriate to place education on the open market, a conclusion supported by a study by Nelson and Krashinsky.[8] Their careful research on day care provision showed that private day care facilities run for profit is an unsatisfactory way of organizing the activity. Day care and education in general are essentially collective consumption goods.

Fifth, although rational decisions at the individual level may lead to rational outcomes at the collective level, there is no reason to view these outcomes positively. A free market punishes failure just as readily as it rewards success: mass unemployment may well be a rational outcome of monetarist policies, but it is still socially unacceptable. Economists like Paul Samuelson recognize that competitive markets cannot produce a good efficiently when an individual's consumption of that good leads to no subtraction from any other individual's consumption of it.[9] In other words, if the goal is to produce collective good through education, then the educational process has to be a collective, public enterprise.

Although a free market may lead to increased satisfaction, this would not change the systematic inequality that is built into educational systems. The already high correlation between achievement scores and social class background would persist and increase.[10] Furthermore, given the corollaries, it is false to assume that advisers would be able to tell parents that one or another educational situation would produce the results the parents desire. Quotations on "educational futures" would have the same validity as the advice offered by the friendly stockbroker at a party. It is difficult for parents to monitor education partly because of time but also because they lack knowledge. Even assuming that parents could be effective monitors, how would they respond to what they perceived to be a negative educational situation? Exit as an option hardly seems appropriate.[11] Parents are unlikely to change their child's school without serious thought. Schools are not like supermarkets. Instead, geographic constraints, friendship patterns, and uncertainty about results elsewhere are more likely to produce a "wait and see" attitude. Finally, it must be clear that schools cannot change the educational situations they provide in the way that an advertising executive might decide to change the packaging of a shampoo. Such rapid change is not only difficult but also inappropriate.

Educational, Social, and Economic Outcomes

Educational

We are told that privatizing education will lead to greater accountability and a more diverse, flexible, efficient system and that this trend would improve the quality of the educational experience and increase the possibility of equal provision for all. The general prediction concerning quality is based on the notion that because parents are responsible for choosing their child's education, they will in turn be more committed, more involved, and more responsible for the outcomes. Parents will be more satisfied with the schools and students will be more committed because it is more likely that they will have been included in the decision-making process.

Of course the option of choice is important. That this option could lead to more commitment, involvement, responsibility, and increased efficiency in the market sense is undeniable. Yet I object strongly to the idea that this system would lead to more equality of provision. Privatizing education will lead to more *inequality*. Although heightened awareness about educational options and student involvement in the choice among these options are things we should strive for, there is no reason to link these outcomes with privatized schooling. Privatizing education can produce only satisfied customers. The pursuit of self-interest without regard for others will exacerbate the present inequalities in provision. Competition will harden the lines that separate rich from poor.

Social

The proponents of privatized schooling foresee that we would experience more equality of opportunity, decentralized control, and therefore less bureaucratic monopoly, more consensus, and greater racial and ethnic integration. Although privatized education does inevitably mean decentralization, this is not necessarily a good thing.

We can through the ballot box at least attempt to instill egalitarianism in our public institutions. Without governmental control education is subject to the inequitable distribution of resources observable in the rest of society. Traditionally, the state has intervened to protect the weakest members of society from the ravages of the open market. To remove education from the public sector is to deny the fact that our society is economically and socially divided. There is a clear distribution of power. We do not all exercise the same amount of control over our lives. Education would become fragmented into a series of smaller bureaucracies that would reflect the sectional interests of both buyers and sellers. Furthermore, it is possible that, as in the United Kingdom, new teacher organizations would be organized on the basis of gender and that different school types would emerge. It is my contention that privatized education will lead to less consensus, less opportunity, and increased racial and ethnic segregation.

Economic

There is no reason to suppose that the ills of the private sector would not be transferred to education if we accept privatized schooling. Accumulation, concentration, and vertical integration with respect to educational services would be the predictable outcomes. Indeed, we can already observe these processes if we examine the ownership of the major publishing companies and the producers of educational equipment. Just as we have seen the franchising of day care (kiddie-care) and performance contracting in schools in the United States, so we could anticipate a corporate takeover of schools. IBM, Xerox, or Exxon schools could well be the long-term outcome of privatized education. Apart from the direct profits accrued from fees and sales, these companies would presumably have an interest in training their future workers.

Conclusion

The attack on public education is misplaced. Although constructive criticism of public education is important, I am strongly committed to improving what is one of our best social endeavors. Education produces social benefits that cannot be dissected into individual and/or private benefits. Diversity, involvement, commitment, and quality are all available in the public school system. I am, frankly, frightened by the conservative move to privatize a public good. The neoconservatives place an enormous social burden on education and educators. The movement is a reflection of the contradiction between an economic system that produces inequality and a democratic ideology that strives to create equality. The tendency is to seek individualistic solutions to what are essentially collective and structural problems. Indeed, there is an internal contradiction because we are attempting, through an emphasis on individualistic policies, to solve societal problems that emerge and are created by the ethic of liberal individualism. If our aim is to create an egalitarian society that cares for the weak and the poor, then we must change the material conditions of people's lives. Choice or even equality of opportunity does nothing to change the inequality in the distribution of goods, resources, power, or influence in our society. It simply defers satisfaction and the problem to the next generation.[12]

Nobody chooses to be poor. Nobody chooses to be illiterate. Privatizing education would serve the interests of the establishment in our society. The middle class, who are the most vocal about accountability and who have the most to lose in the current economic recession, would be bought off. Essentially, a privilege previously available only to the rich would be extended to include them. Instead, I suggest that governments should exercise their power to require parents to remain within the public school system. Indeed, Hirschman makes the plausible argument that the major problem with public education is that the rich can exit. If the rich had to remain, they would exercise their power to bring about reforms.[13]

My immediate fear is that the majority will be convinced that it is reasonable to spend public money to pay for private benefit. All the evidence gives substance to this fear. In British Columbia the provincial government is now providing approximately $500 per qualifying pupil to private schools. In California the battle to introduce a state voucher system seems increasingly assured of success. Indeed, the Reagan administration appears to be firmly committed to a tax credit plan for education.[14]

Scapegoating, expressed in the adage that the proper person to blame is the victim, appears to be an imminent reality. The victims of privatization will not be the rich or powerful, but the rest of us: parents, students, and teachers.

Notes

1. For a discussion of neoconservatism see Peter Steinfels, *The Neo-Conservatives: The Men who are Changing American Politics* (New York: Simon and Schuster, 1979).

2. See Milton Friedman, *Capitalism and Freedom* (Chicago: University of Chicago Press, 1962), and "The Voucher Idea,"*New York Times Magazine,* September 23, 1977; and E.G. West, *Education and the State,* 2nd ed. (London: Institute of Economic Affairs, 1970); *Education and the Industrial Revolution* (London: Batsford, 1975); "British Columbia's New Aid Scheme for Independent Schools: An Economic Assessment of Precedents and Prospects" (Report submitted as part of the study, Consequences of Funding Independent Schools in British Columbia, 1979); John E. Coons and Stephen D. Sugarman, *Education by Choice: The Case for Family Control* (Berkeley: University of California Press, 1978).

3. See Richard M. Titmuss, "Public Services and Public Responsibility," in Richard M. Titmuss, *Social Policy: An Introduction,* ed. Brian Abel-Smith and Kay Titmuss (New York: Pantheon Books, 1974), pp. 121–131.

4. See R.H. Tawney, *Equality,* 4th ed. (London: Allen and Unwin, 1952), p. 47.

5. For a discussion see Robert Wenkert, "The Free-Market Model in Educational Reform," in *School Reforms of the 1970s,* Proceedings of the Third Annual Conference of the Sociology of Education Association, School of Education, University of California, 1975), p. 100.

6. See Titmuss, "Public Services and Public Responsibility," p. 141.

7. For a discussion of this argument see Charles Benson, *The Economics of Public Education,* 3d ed. (Boston: Houghton Mifflin Co., 1978) pp. 123–126.

8. Richard R. Nelson and Michael Krashinsky, "Public Contract and Economic Organization of Day Care in Young Children," *Public Policy* 22, no. 1 (Winter 1974), pp. 53–75.

9. See Paul A. Samuelson, "The Pure Theory of Public Expenditure," *Review of Economics and Statistics* 36 (November 1954): 387.

10. See Christopher J. Hurn, *The Limits and Possibilities of Schooling* (Boston: Allyn and Bacon, 1978), pp. 108–186.

11. See Albert O. Hirschman, *Exit, Voice, and Loyalty: Response to Decline in Firms, Organizations and States* (Cambridge, Mass.: Harvard University Press, 1970).

12. See Richard H. DeLone, *Small Futures: Children, Inequality, and the Limits of Liberal Reform* (New York: Harcourt Brace Jovanovich, 1979), p. 73.

13. See Hirschman, *Exit, Voice, and Loyalty,* p. 51.

14. See the interview with Secretary of Education, T.H. Bell, *The New York Times,* 3 February 1981.

About the Contributors

Stephen Arons, director of legal studies at the University of Massachusetts, Amherst, has made major contributions to our understanding of the separation of school and state and the interpretation of the First Amendment through his analysis "The Separation of School and State: Pierce Reconsidered" in the *Harvard Educational Review* (February 1976). Professor Arons spent a year investigating cases of conflict between parents and state authorities over the education of children and is currently completing a book, *Public Orthodoxy, Private Dissent.*

William Bentley Ball, partner in the legal firm of Ball & Skelly in Harrisburg, Pennsylvania, received the J.D. from the College of Law, University of Notre Dame. A distinguished constitutional lawyer and lecturer on constitutional-law issues, he has appeared in numerous educational litigations, several of which have produced landmark decisions; these include four leading decisions on parental rights: *Wisconsin* v. *Yoder, Vermont* v. *LaBarge, Ohio* v. *Whisner,* and *Rudasill* v. *Kentucky Board of Education.*

William D. Burt, member of the Libertarian National Committee is the former west coast director of the National Taxpayers Union and official proponent of the 1979 California educational tax-credit initiative. He is the author of *Local Problems: Libertarian Solutions* (1977), a book demonstrating libertarian answers to community problems, including education.

John E. Coons, professor of law at the University of California at Berkeley, received the J.D. from Northwestern University. He coauthored *Private Wealth and Public Education* (1970) with W. Clune and S. Sugarman. The book was a major spur to the revolution in school finance culminating in the landmark *Serrano* decision in California. Subsequently, in collaboration with S. Sugarman, he focused on family choice in education with *Family Choice in Education: A Model for State Voucher Systems* (1971) and *Education by Choice: The Case for Family Control* (1978). A member of the National Advisory Panel on Financing of Elementary and Secondary Education, Professor Coons is a proponent of the California Initiative for Family Choice in Education. His latest book is *Sovereigns of Childhood* (1980) with R. Mnookin and S. Sugarman.

Donald Fisher, assistant professor of educational foundations at the University of British Columbia, obtained the Ph.D. from the University of California at Berkeley in 1977. Currently he is continuing his research on the impact of American philanthropic foundations on the development of British university education, and is also examining the relationship between the economic changes in North America and the current crisis in education.

Donald E. Frey, associate professor of economics at Wake Forest University, received the Ph.D. in economics from Princeton University. From 1977–1978 he was a staff associate in employment policy at the Brookings Institution. His articles have appeared in the *Economics of Education Review, Eastern Economic Journal,* and the *Journal of Human Resources.* His interests are labor and urban economics and the economics of education.

William T. Garner, associate professor of education at the University of San Francisco, received the Ph.D. in educational administration from the University of Chicago. Interested in the economics of education and particularly in the links between school resources and educational outcomes, Professor Garner, in collaboration with Professor Hannaway, has recently been investigating the relationships between parents and the schools they choose for their children to attend. His articles have appeared in the *American Economic Review, School Review, Planning and Changing,* and *Educational Technology.*

Cornel Hamm, associate professor of education at Simon Fraser University, is a philosopher and educational critic. He received the Ph.D. from the University of London. He is interested in questions of moral education, rights in education, and the justification for compulsory schooling. Professor Hamm's articles have appeared in the *Journal of Educational Thought, Educational Theory, Moral Education Forum,* and *School Review.* He recently contributed to and coedited *The Domain of Moral Education* (1979) with Tasos Kazepides and Don Cochrane.

Jane Hannaway, assistant professor in the Woodrow Wilson School at Princeton University, received the Ph.D. from Stanford University. Her research has focused on the behavior and interaction patterns of managers and on the relationships between external funding and administrative structures. Recently, in collaboration with Professor Garner, she has examined the organization and management of private and public secondary schools. Her articles have appeared in *Teachers College Record* and the *Administrator's Notebook.*

Robert B. Kottkamp, assistant professor of educational administration in the Graduate School of Education, Rutgers University, received the Ph.D. from Washington University, St. Louis in 1979. His research interests include the study of the choice-making behavior of students.

Marvin Lazerson, professor of education at the University of British Columbia, received the Ph.D. in history from Harvard University. An educational historian and policy analyst, Professor Lazerson has published extensively on many facets of educational policy. His articles have appeared in the *History of Education Quarterly, Harvard Educational Review, School Review, Interchange,* and *Reviews in American History.* He is the author of *Origins of the Urban School: Public Education in Massachusetts, 1870–1915* (1971), and *American Education and Vocationalism: A Documentary History, 1870–1970* (1974) with Norton Grubb.

Richard L. Nault, assistant professor in the Graduate Institute of Education, Washington University, St. Louis, received the Ph.D. in educational administration from the University of Chicago. His research has focused on nonpublic school education and particularly on modes of school affiliation and student commitment and on the school choice behavior of parents and students. His articles have appeared in the *Administrator's Notebook, High School Journal, Notre Dame Journal of Education, National Elementary Principal,* and *Momentum: Journal of the National Catholic Educational Association.*

Joel Spring, professor of education at the University of Cincinnati, received the Ph.D. from the University of Wisconsin. A revisionist historian, Professor Spring has written extensively on the development of schooling. He has written numerous papers and chapters and is the author of *Education and the Rise of the Corporate State* (1972), *Primer of Libertarian Education* (1975), *The Sorting Machine: National Education Policy since 1945* (1976), *American Education: Social and Political Aspects* (1978), and *Educating the Worker-Citizen* (1980).

Stephen D. Sugarman, professor of law in the School of Law, University of California at Berkeley, is a coauthor of *Private Wealth and Public Education* (1970) with J. Coons and W. Clune, *Family Choice in Education: A Model for State Voucher Systems* (1971) and *Education by Choice: The Case for Family Control* (1978) with J. Coons. He is also an active proponent of the California Initiative for Family Choice in Education and is coauthor of *Sovereigns of Childhood* (1980) with J. Coons and R. Mnookin.

Elmer J. Thiessen, instructor in philosophy at Medicine Hat College in Alberta, received the Ph.D. in philosophy from the University of Waterloo in 1980. Interested in the philosophical analysis of the relation between religion and education, Dr. Thiessen has published in *Salt: Journal of Religious Studies and Moral Education Council.*

Susan Uchitelle, supervisor of instruction in the Missouri State Department of Elementary and Secondary Education, received the Ph.D. in education from

Washington University, St. Louis, in 1977. From 1978–1979 Dr. Uchitelle was Clearinghouse Coordinator for the Center for the Study of Law in Education, Washington University. Her research interests focus on the school choice behavior of parents, and her articles have appeared in *Education Record* and the *American School Board Journal*.

E.G. West, professor of economics at Carleton University, received the Ph.D. in economics from London University and was a research Fellow at the University of Chicago in 1966. During the 1975–1976 academic year he was visiting professor at Virginia Polytechnic Institute and State University, Blacksburg. Professor West is the author of *Education and the State* (1965), *Adam Smith: The Man and His Works* (1969), *Education and Industrial Revolution* (1975), and *Nonpublic School Aid* (1975) and is a frequent contributor to journals in economics, law, and education.

J. Donald Wilson, professor of history of education at the University of British Columbia, received the Ph.D. from the University of Western Ontario. An educational historian, Professor Wilson has published extensively on many aspects of Canadian education and has coedited five volumes that contribute importantly to our understanding of Canadian education: *Canadian Education: A History* (1970); *The Best of Times/The Worst of Times: Issues in Contemporary Canadian Education* (1972); *Precepts, Policy and Process: Perspectives on Contemporary Canadian Education* (1977); *Schooling and Society in Twentieth Century British Columbia* (1980); and *Canadian Education in the 1980s* (forthcoming).

About the Editor

Michael E. Manley-Casimir, associate professor in the Faculty of Education at Simon Fraser University, received the Ph.D. from the University of Chicago. A student of educational policy, he is particularly interested in the intersection of law and education. His articles on student rights, the use of discretion in school discipline, school governance as discretionary justice, and the school as a constitutional bureaucracy, have appeared in such journals as the *Administrator's Notebook, Journal of Research and Development in Education, Interchange,* and *School Review.* Professor Manley-Casimir is editor of *The Development of Moral Reasoning* (1980) with Donald B. Cochrane. He has previously edited the *Administrator's Notebook,* the "Law and Justice in Education" issue of *School Review,* and the review section of the *Canadian Journal of Education.*